MONUMENTS OF
DELHI
Lasting Splendour of the Great Mughals and Others

Jama Masjid

MONUMENTS OF
DELHI
Lasting Splendour of the Great Mughals and Others

Compiled By
MAULVI ZAFAR HASAN

Edited by
J.A. PAGE, et al.

Introduction By
R.C. AGRAWAL

VOLUME I
SHAHJAHANABAD

Aryan Books International
New Delhi

Monuments of Delhi

First Published 1916
Third Reprint with New Introduction and Photographs: 2026

ISBN: 978-81-7305-111-1 (Vol. I)
978-81-7305-114-3 (Set)

Published by
Aryan Books International
Pooja Apartments, 4B, Ansari Road, New Delhi-110 002 (India)
Tel.: 23255799, 41099562
E-mail: aryanbooks@gmail.com
www.aryanbooks.com

Designed and Printed in India by
ABI Prints & Publishing Co., New Delhi

INTRODUCTION

Section I: Delhi's Strategic Importance

"If the World is the body, Delhi is its soul,"
said the celebrated poet Mirza Ghalib.

Delhi has a long history going back to protohistoric period. The location of the city attracted Indian rulers of all kinds from ancient times because of its strategic and commercial value. The city of Delhi has thus seen the rise and fall of many kingdoms. A city which has witnessed so many events has many a tales to tell in the shape of monuments.

The antiquity of Delhi and neighbouring areas located on the contours of the Aravallis dates back to the Pleistocene times. The discovery of early stone age tools on the bank of palaeochannels of Yamuna have substantiated that man lived in and around Delhi and attained the present position in the evolutionary sequence of mankind.

The earliest reference to a settlement at Delhi is found in the Mahabharata. King Dhratarashta of Hastinapur gave the tracts around Delhi to Pandavas to set-up their Kingdom. This part of Delhi was known as Khandavaprastha. Yudhisthir, the Pandava prince, cleared the forest known as Khandavavan and established the capital city, Indraprastha, in Delhi. Indeed it was a formidable city so grand that it made Kauravas the enemies of Pandavas. From that period Delhi witnessed the rise and fall of many dynasties and Empires.

Section II: Delhi's Monuments

Delhi in Ancient Times

The evidence of earliest habitation around Delhi come mainly from the excavated site of Purana Qila, Asokan Rock Edict site of Srinivaspuri, Lalkot and Mehrauli area. In the excavations at Purana Qila, brick structures, potteries, coins, terracottas, beads of semi-precious stones and many other remains of Mauryan phase and belonging to Sunga, Kushana, Gupta, Post Gupta, Rajput and Sultanate Periods were found. The structural remains found in the excavation were primarily made of burnt bricks, mud bricks and of stones. In few cases post-holes were also encountered. The ring wells and remains of the drains also indicated a proper drainage system. The discovery of these remains established that Delhi was a cultural centre right from the earliest times.

Delhi During Rajput Rule

In the eleventh century A.D., Anangpal, a Tomar Rajput King established his capital at Delhi and his successors during their rule built the walled city of Lal Kot which is still a living city-Mehrauli. The famous Chauhan King Prithvi Raj, laid the foundation of Rai Pithora with defensive wall of 8 km circumference. The city of Kila Rai Pithora had 28 gates.

During the era of Tomars and Chauhans magnificent temples were built in Delhi. It is believed that twenty seven Hindu and Jain temples complex existed at the site of Quwwat-ul-Islam Mosque and Qutab Minar. The inscription affixed on the inner lintel of eastern gate-way of Qutab Mosque also testifies that the great mosque was built by Qutab-ud-din by using the materials of twenty seven temples.

Delhi Under Islamic Rule

With the arrival of Mohammedans, the Hindu rule terminated. Lal Kot was sacked and a township with impressive palaces and fortifications was re-built on its ruins. Qutab-ud-din, the slave commander of Mohammad Ghori became the ruler of Delhi in 1191 AD and thus laid the foundation of Delhi Sultanate and for next 600 years Mohammedan dynasties rule prevailed. The construction of Qutab Minar was started by Aibak and continued by Iltutmish and his successor. It became the most dominating symbol and a landmark of Delhi. Iltutmish also built a large tomb for his eldest son Nasir-ud-din, known as Sultan Ghari tomb. Five years later (1235-1236 AD), Iltutmish built his own tomb. It depicts geometrical, arabesque pattern and Saracenic tradition. It is considered one of the richest example of last flicker of Hindu Art built in Mohammedan tradition.

The successor of Iltutmish were weak and unable to control the affairs of the State. Iltutmish illuminated his daughter Razia Sultan as his successor. The elevation of the woman to the status of Sultan was severely resented by the nobles and the aristocracy, and she was put to death in disguise.

The monuments constructed during this phase of Sultanate rule laid the foundation of Indo-Islamic Architecture in India.

Delhi Under Khiljis Rule

The Slave rulers were succeeded by the Khiljis on the political scene of Delhi by the end of 13th century. The Khiljis were, in fact, a Turkish tribe and settled in Afghanistan, where they acquired Afghani manners and customs. When they came to India they were not acknowledged or accepted as a Turkish people and this led to the hostility between the Afghan and the aristocracy.

Principal Gate of Lal Qila

Cross-roads, Chandni Chowk, Delhi

Alauddin Khilji, the powerful ruler of the dynasty laid the foundation of his capital Siri in 1303 AD. He also commissioned a minar (Victory Tower) exceeding the Qutab Minar but the same could not be completed.

Alauddin Khilji also excavated a reservoir known as Hauz Khas to meet the requirement of Siri township. He also constructed a semi circular gateway with horseshoe shaped arch with lotus motifs. This gateway is popularly known as Alai-Darwaja and has been considered, in the history of Islamic Architcture, a representative of a true arch.

The characteristic features of Khilji architecture are red sandstone, marble, recessed arches under squinches and decorative mouldings. Khiljis thus developed their own style.

Delhi Under Tughlaks

Khiljis were succeeded in the second part of fourteenth century by the Tughlaks. Tughlaks established their own township, popularly known Tughlakabad. Mohammed Bin Tughlak after ruling for seven years shifted the capital to Daulatabad, Devgiri, in Aurangabad Distt. of Deccan. Daulatabad had water scarcity and the people suffered severely. After he realised his mistake, he shifted the capital again to Delhi in 1334. To reduce the suffering of his subjects, he built a new township and named it Jahanpanah.

Several buildings were constructed during Tughlak's period. Tughlaks developed their own style of architecture. The representative examples of which are Tughlakabad Fort, Bari Manzil, Khirkee Mosque and Firoz Shah Kotla having rounded bastions and tapering walls. The end of Tughlak dynasty was brought by invasion of Timur Leng in 1398. He plundered Delhi mercilessly.

Delhi Under Sayyids

The last Tughlak ruler, Mahmud Tughlak's death brought about the usual confusion. The Governor of Punjab, Khizr Khan made use of this opportunity and founded the Sayyid dynasty.

Khizr Khan was succeeded by his son, Mu'izzu'd Din Mubarak Shah. He founded a new city called Mubarakabad along the River Yamuna. No trace of this city remains.

The Sayyids made use of two designs in their tombs-the octagonal and square. The latter is distinguished by a string course, series of panels of sunk niches above and below the string course. It gives an appearance of two or three storeys to the tomb. The middle portion of each side of these tombs form a vertical rectangle within which the main arch is located. The side of the rectangle are provided with *guldastas*. The two sides of the entrance have small arches which are open or closed with a latticed screen. The other arches on the upper storeys are false. The octagonal tombs spread in the horizontal plane while square one soar in the vertical plane.

Mubarak Shah's tomb is octagonal and can be seen in Kotla Mubarakpur.

The last ruler of this dynasty was Muhammad Shah. His death in 1444 marks the end of this dynasty.

Delhi Under Lodis

The next dynasty, the Lodis, have left some tombs. The tomb of Sikandar Lodi (1489-1517) is remarkable. It is bordered by four walls which enclose a garden in the midst of which the tomb is built. It has also a walled mosque.

The Bara Gumbad Mosque in the Lodi Garden, built in 1484, has five bays and is surmounted by three domes. It is richly ornamented with foliage designs, coloured tiles and inscriptions.

With the Lodis the Afghan rulers departed from India and the Mughals began their entry. The battle of Panipat (1526) is a parting of ways in Indian History, for this battle ushers in the Mughals whose very name stands for opulance and luxury.

Delhi Under The Mughals

The first Mughal emperor Babur died within four years (1530) after conquering north India. He could not consolidate his gains. A small brick built mosque with three arched openings at Palam is all that remains of his reign at Delhi.

Humayun, who succeeded him was driven out of India by the Afghan Sher Shah Suri in 1540.

The Sur Interlude

The Sur dynasty lasted for fifteen years (1555). At Delhi Sher Shah built the citadel of Purana Qila which marks the site of Indraprastha. It is located on the right bank of the River Yamuna. He also built the Qal'a-i-Kuhna Masjid, better known as Sher Shah's Mosque within the citadel. It has five openings facing the river. The middle arched opening is framed within decorative bands of inscriptions and geometrical designs, with thin side pilasters. The niches on the western wall are also richly decorated. The *Mihrabs* are impressive, one arch enclosing a smaller arch. Oriel windows and a narrow gallery on the second storey are its impressive features.

The Sher Mandal, located close to the mosque, is also attributed to Sher Shah. It is a two storeyed octagonal tower built of red sand stone and marble lining.

His son Islam Shah (1545-54) has left two structures, the Salim Garh Fort near Red Fort and also an octagonal tomb known as Isa Khan's tomb near Humayaun's tomb as reminders of his reign.

Humayun returned in 1555 and regained his crown after defeating Sikandar Shah Sur, the last Sur luler.

Humayun

Humayun regained his throne in July 1555, and died in January 1556, so no structural remains of his exist. But his short reign witnessed the completion of Jamali Kamali Masjid.

His first wife, Banu Begum also known as Haji Begum, built his tomb. This heralds the arrival of garden tombs with its water channels and fountains - a typical Persian paradise garden with four main *parterres*. This mausoleum, begun in 1565 is a double storeyed red sand stone building standing over a terrace in the middle of a garden.

Akbar (1556-1606)

Akbar preferred Agra and confined his building activities to the town. However his foster mother Mahan Anga built the Khairu'l Manazil mosque in front of Purana Qila. Her son, Ataga Khan lies buried in Nizamuddin. His tomb is a red sandstone one in imitation of Humayun's tomb on a smaller scale, but with more ornamentation.

Jehangir (1605-27)

Jehangir's love was for Lahore and Kabul. He was also interested in building roads, kos minars, sarais and bridges. He has left no remains in Delhi.

The tomb known as Khan-i-Khana on Mathura Road belongs to his reign. It houses the mortal remains of Mirza Abdur Rahim Khan-i-Khanan. He was the son of Bairam Khan and served both Akbar and Jehangir. He wrote Hindi cuplets under the name of Rahim.

His tomb is similar in design to Humayun's tomb. It is a red sand stone building relieved by buff sand stone and marble. Unfortunately the marble lining is now gone. It was stripped off for use in Safdarjung's tomb.

Shah Jahan (1628-58)

The polished luxury and opulance of Shah Jahan marked his reign.

He transferrd his capital from Agra to Delhi and laid the foundations of Shajahanabad, enclosed by a rubble wall, bastions, gates, etc., at regular intervals. His palace, Red Fort or Lal Qila, located on the right bank of Yamuna, was completed in 1648. In 1650 he completed the Jama Masjid.

His daughter Raushan Ara laid out her garden tomb in 1650. His elder daughter Jahan Ara built a small uncovered structure walled with latticed marble screen. The insciption on her grave reads: Let naught cover my grave save the green grass; for grass well suffices as a covering for the grave of the lowly?

Aurangzeb (1658-1707)

Aurangzeb was a study in contrast to Shah Jahan. He was a puritan and an orthodox adherent of the Sunni sect of Islam. The first half of his reign was spent in the North and the second half in far off Deccan.

He built in 1659-60 the Pearl Mosque (Moti Masjid) in the Red Fort at Delhi for his own use. The Moti Masjid is built entirely of marble. It has three domes.

His daughter Zinatu'n Nisa Begum built the Zinatu'l Masjid in Darya Ganj. Though smaller in size, it resembles Shah Jahan's Jama Masjid with its red sand stone facing, white marble domes with black marble flutings and tall minarets.

Later Mughals (1707-1857)

This period marks the disintegration of the Mughal empire. Practically all construction activity ceased. The decline is clearly illustrated by the last garden tomb built in India by Shajiau'd Daula for his father Mirza Muqim Abu'l Mansur Khan, entitled Safderjung in 1754. It follows the Humayun's tomb, the first trendsetter, in its design. In the midst of a large garden divided into squares with pools and fountains along its path ways, the tomb stands majestically. The garden is enclosed on all sides by walls.

A building of a different type is Jantar Mantar built by Jai Singh II of Amber. It is an astronomical observatory housing masonry instruments.

Early British Period

Early British monuments belong to the Mutiny period (1857). The buildings associated with the Mutiny are: the Magazine Gates near Delhi General Post Office, the Mutiny Memorial and the Flag staff tower on the Delhi Ridge.

The most notable building of this period is the Metcalfe House built by Sir Thomas Metcalfe in 1835.

Section III: The Present Book

The present work is a compilation of monuments on the basis of their location by the archaeological officers posted in Delhi. Maulvi Zafar Hasan, Asstt. Superintending Archaeologist of Archaeological Survey of India surveyed the monuments in the beginning of second decade of the present century. The survey report of Maulvi Sahib doesnot provide any illustrations but sufficient information about the monuments, their history, architecture and events associated with them.

The present work includes more than 1200 monuments and covers the well known as well as the least known. It follows a set pattern. First the name of the monument, its location, present ownership, its extent or areas, and the works of reference tracing the history of the monument.

This is the only book that gives the list of monuments extant at the beginning of the century. The need for reprinting this work was felt for quite some time and it must go to the credit of M/s. Aryan Books International who have come forward to place these volumes before the scholars. Today when many of these monuments are facing the threat of extinction, reprinting of this book will serve a national cause.

R.C. Agrawal
Director (Monuments)
Archaeological Survey of India
New Delhi.

PREFACE

THE monuments listed hereafter are those included within the walls of Shahjahanabad, the city of Delhi built by Shah Jahan between the years 1638 and 1649 A.D. The map illustrates the area dealt with, and its monuments have been listed by *muhallas*, the Fort buildings forming a separate group. They have, for sake of reference, been numbered serially, starting with those in the Fort, the next group being those south of the Chandni Chauk, while the last group are those situated north of that thoroughfare. The most important will be found furnished with names, numbers and symbols on the map, those next in importance being indicated by symbols and numbers, while the least important are designated by numbers only. The exact date of many of the monuments is, of course, a matter of conjecture, but wherever there is no inscription on them to date them, they have been dated if possible by the reign of the contemporary Emperor (a list of the Emperors of Delhi with dates will be found hereafter), and where this too is doubtful, their date has been gauged by the style of architecture in which they are built, or by local tradition. Thus it will be seen that many of them are classed as "late Mughal," which may be taken as comprising the period between the end of Aurangzeb's reign (1707), and the Mutiny of 1857, and marked by but few buildings of any architectural excellence.

Muhammadan architecture in Delhi may be classed into the following eight divisions, named after the various reigning dynasties, and each of which had its own style of architecture, each style being more fully developed than its predecessor. The architecture at Delhi may be considered to have been the parent style from which the Jaunpur, Bijapur, Mandu, and Malwa styles are offshoots, and it is thus that at Delhi, within a radius of some 70 square miles Indo-Muhammadan architecture can be studied, almost in its entirety:—

The divisions of Indo-Muhammadan Architecture.

	A. D.
1. Ghazni	1001—1191
2. Turki	1191—1290
3. Khalji	1290—1320
4. Tughlaq	1320—1451
5. Afghan	1451—1555
6. Early Mughal	1555—1628
7. Middle „	1628—1707
8. Late „	1707—1857

Of the buildings of the Ghazni period there are none known in India today, and the inroads of Shihabu-d-din Ghori seem to have left no permanent landmark in architectural history as regards India itself. The *minars*, however, that are said to remain at Ghazni are considered by most authorities to be the prototype of the great *minar* of Qutbu-d-din Aibak, some 11 miles south of Delhi, and are therefore of the greatest importance.

Of the Turki buildings, the Qutb Minar, the neighbouring mosque, and the tombs of Altamsh (1) and Sultan Ghari (2) are examples with which most will be familiar.

---

(1) At the Qutb.

(2) At Mahipalpur.

The more refined work of the Khalji dynasty is seen in the Alai Darwaza at the Qutb, the work of the only great Khalji Sultan, Alau-d-din Muhammad II, while some idea of his ambitious architectural schemes may be obtained from his projected extensions to the Qutb mosque.

The first of the Tughlaq dynasty, Ghiyasu-d-din, raised his city of Delhi, Tughlaqabad, in four years. It, with the neighbouring tomb, is perhaps the most characteristic example of this particular style, while the later Tughlaq work is illustrated by the citadel of Firozabad, and the Kalan, Khirki, and Begampuri mosques.

Examples of Afghan work are seen in the Lodi tombs at Khairpur, the Moth-ki-Masjid, and the fortress of Purana Qila (Indrapat) with the mosque it contains.

The period of Early Mughal architecture may be confined to the reigns of Akbar and Jahangir. Its best work is seen at Agra and Fathpur Sikri, the only important examples at Delhi being the tombs of Humayun and Tagah (Atgah) Khan, and the tomb of "the Barber" in the garden of the former building.

The Middle Mughal style may be said to include all the work of that "most magnificent of monarchs," Shah Jahan, the Delhi Fort and its palaces, and the Jami and Fathpuri Masjids being the chief local examples. The work of Aurangzeb may be included in the same category and is illustrated by the Moti Masjid in the Fort and the Zinatu-l-Masajid.

Of the Late Mughal style the principal buildings are the tomb of Safdar Jang, which has been called "the last flicker in the lamp of architecture at Delhi," the three Sonehri Masjids and the Moti Masjid at Mehrauli.

All monuments up to the date of the Mutiny have been included in the list.

The bibliographical references are not as complete as might have been wished, owing to want of time, but it is hoped that those that are given will serve to throw light on the more important points in connection with the history and the architecture of these buildings. References regarding the historical characters connected with the monuments have not been given, except in certain cases where the characters referred to are of some especial or hitherto unknown interest. Local traditions have been added where they are of especial value, but these must be accepted with reserve. The information regarding the ownership of the buildings has been procured from the most reliable sources available, but the Government of India can accept no responsibility for its accuracy. In the case of temples the persons given under the heading "owners" (paragraph *c*.), are almost invariably those responsible for the management of the temple, and not owners of it in the strict sense of the word, nearly all the temples having been erected for the public benefit. Information regarding images has been given in some detail and will throw light on the study of the forms of Hindu worship in the new capital.

The reader is invited to study the pictures of the more important monuments of Delhi in the Fort Museum. They will be found both interesting and instructive.

The remaining monuments in the province, outside Shahjahanabad, are now being listed and will be published separately in due course.

The list of some 260 monuments at Delhi, prepared by Dr. Vogel in 1902 and published with the Annual Report of that officer, has been of the greatest assistance in the preparation of this volume, as have the lists of Delhi monuments given in the *Revised list of Objects of Archæological Interest in the Punjab* by C. J. Rodgers (Lahore, Ball and Company 1885 (?)), in *Delhi Past and Present* by Fanshawe, and in Volume IV, *Archæological Survey of India Report* (1871-72).

For information regarding the cost of repairs spent on individual archæological buildings, and the nature of such repairs, reference may be made to the Annual Progress Reports of the Superintendent, Muhammadan and British Monuments, Northern Circle. The attention of the reader who may desire something dealing with the history of Delhi in a lighter vein is drawn to *When Kings Rode to Delhi* by Festing (Blackwood), *India Through the Ages* by F. A. Steel (Routledge), *From the land of Princes*, Festing (Smith Elder & Co.), *A winter tour in India*, Sir R. Temple (Chatto and Windus), and *Globe trotters in India*, McMillan (Sonnenschein). *The Chronology of India* (Duff) although it does not deal with buildings gives a concise account of events at Delhi between 1193 and 1530 A. D., as well as a list of the Emperors. The *Delhi Gazetteer* (Lahore, C. and M. Press, 1913) contains a good brief account of the history and chief places of interest.

The work of listing these Delhi monuments has proved a far greater one than was at first anticipated, and, in consequence, I requested the Government of India to give me the assistance of a special officer who could devote his entire time to the work under my supervision. For this purpose, Maulvi Zafar Hasan was appointed and the work on the monuments listed hereafter is his, with the exception of the Hindu buildings, which, though few in number and of less importance than those met with in other large cities, for Delhi has for many years ceased to be a "Hindu" city, have nevertheless been carefully and scholarly listed by Pandit Y. R. Gupte, B.A., of the Lahore Archæological office.

To myself has fallen the comparatively easy lot of preparing the matter collected for the press, adding the bibliographical references collected from European historians and travellers, and such information as is connected with the architecture of the buildings.

The list covers a somewhat larger field than those prepared by Mr. Rodgers and Dr. Vogel, and, without wishing to draw comparisons, it may not be out of place to quote the latter officer's report for the year ending March 1902, in which, referring to his Delhi list, he states that whereas Mr. Rodgers' list gives only 106 buildings in the Delhi District, the new list (Dr. Vogel's) comprises 269 monuments systematically arranged. The present volume, dealing with Shahjahanabad alone, refers to some 410 monuments.(1) The heads under which information is given have also been increased in number. Many of the buildings are, of course, comparatively unimportant at present, but in time to come

(1) Over 300 monuments have been listed to date outside Shahjahanabad, September 1914.)

may be of considerable interest. It has been necessary in compiling this material, besides turning over the pages of famous historians or authorities on Indian History and Architecture, to scan, all but too quickly, the pages of many a diary written by some traveller or soldier, or even amateur 'raconteurs' of the gentler sex, perhaps not so skilled in the use of the pen, but who perhaps unwittingly, have thrown light on some point forgotten or omitted by their more learned "confrères." Certain information has, therefore, been included, especially under the head of bibliographical references, which the reader of to-day may think beside the point or of insufficient interest to warrant inclusion, in the hope that it may, in years to come, justify itself.

It is hoped that the material found hereafter will lend an added interest to one of the most fascinating cities of the world and be of use, not only to the officials of every class who have to deal with the buildings themselves, but to those interested in India and its history, be they residents or annual visitors. The information covers a wide field and mistakes there must be. Corrigenda and Addenda will therefore be gratefully welcomed, an interleaved copy being ready to receive them.

A debt of gratitude is due to the Hon'ble Mr. W. M. Hailey, the Chief Commissioner of Delhi, for his ready help and sympathy throughout the work, and to Major Beadon, the Deputy Commissioner, for information regarding the ownership of various monuments. The assistance of Mr. Wilson of the Municipality in the preparation of the Map is also gratefully acknowledged.

GORDON SANDERSON,

Superintendent,

Muhammadan and British Monuments,

Northern Circle, Agra.

LIST OF THE

EMPERORS OF DELHI.

Name of Ruler.	Accession.	Death.
TURKS.		
1. Muhammad I ibn-i-Sam	1193	1206
2. Qutb-ud-din Aibak	1206	1210
3. Aram Shah	1210	1210
4. Shamsh-ud-din Altamsh	1210	1235
5. Rukn-ud-din Firoz I	1235	...
6. Raziya	1236	...
7. Muizz-ud-din Bahram	1239	...
8. Ala-ud-din Masud	1241	...
9. Nasir-ud-din Mahmud I	1246	1265
10. Ghiyas-ud-din Balban	1265	1287
11. Muizz-ud-din Kaiqubad	1287	1290
12. Shams-ud-din Kaimurs	1290	...
KHALJIS.		
13. Jalal-ud-din Firoz II	1290	1295
14. Rukn-ud-din Ibrahim I	1295	...
15. Ala-ud-din Muhammad II	1295	1315
16. Shihab-ud-din Umar	1315	...
17. Qutb-ud-din Mubarik I	1316	1320
18. Nasir-ud-din Khusru	1320	1320
TUGHLAQS.		
19. Ghiyas-ud-din Tughlaq I	1320	1324
20. Muhammad III ibn-i-Tughlaq	1324	1351
21. Firoz III	1351	1388
22. Tughlaq Shah II	1388	1388
23. Abubakr	1388	...
24. Muhammad IV ibn-i-Firoz	1389	1392
25. Sikandar I	1392	1392
26. Mahmud II	1392	1412
27. Daulat Khan Lodi	1412	...
SAYYIDS.		
28. Khizr Khan	1414	1421
29. Mubarak II	1421	1433
30. Muhammad V ibn-i-Farid	1433	1443
31. Alam Shah	1443	...
LODIS.		
32. Bahlol	1451	1488
33. Sikandar II	1488	1517
34. Ibrahim II	1517	1526

LIST OF THE EMPERORS OF DELHI—*contd.*

Name of Ruler.	Accession.	Death.
MUGHALS.		
35. Babar	1526	1530
36. Humayun (deposed 1539)	1530	...
SURIS.		
37. Sher Shah	1539	1545
38. Islam Shah	1545	1552
39. Muhammad Adil	1552	1553
40. Ibrahim III	1553	1554
41. Sikandar III	1554	...
MUGHALS.		
Humayun (returns)	1555	1556
42. Akbar	1556	1605
43. Jahangir	1605	1627
44. Shah Jahan (deposed 1658)	1628	1666
45. Aurangzeb	1658	1707
46. Shah Alam Bahadur Shah	1707	1712
47. Jahandar Shah	1712	1713
48. Farrukh Siyar	1713	1719
49. Rafi-ud-darajat	1719	1719
50. Rafi-ud-daulah	1719	1719
51. Muhammad Shah	1719	1748
52. Ahmad Shah	1748	...
53. Alamgir II	1754	1759
54. Shah Alam II	1759	1806
55. Akbar Shah II	1806	1837
56. Bahadur Shah II	1837	...

LIST OF AUTHORITIES CITED.

Annual . . . . . . *Archæological Survey of India, Director-General's Annual Reports*, 1902-1911, Government Press, Calcutta.

Archer . . . . . . *Tours in Upper India and in parts of the Himalaya Mountains*, Archer. London, Richard Bentley, 1833.

A. S. I. . . . . . . *Archæological Survey of India Reports.* (Cunningham.) Government Press, Calcutta.

As. Res. . . . . . . *Asiatic Researches.* London, 1807.

Auckland . . . . . *Journal of a Tour in Upper India with the Camp of the Earl of Auckland.* C. J. French. Station Press, Simla, 1872.

Bahadur Shah II . . . . *Proceedings of trial of Muhammad Bahadur Shah II, Titular King of Delhi, 27th Jan. 1858 and following days.* Calcutta, Government Press, 1895.

Banister Fletcher . . . . *History of Architecture*, Banister Fletcher. London, Batsford. 1905.

Baxter . . . . *A winter in India*, Baxter. London, Cassell, Pelter, Galpin & Co., 1882.

Bernier . . . . . . *Travels in Mogul Empire A D. 1656-1668 by Francois Bernier*, Archibald Constable; London, Constable & Co., 1901.

Carotti . . . . . . *History of Art*, Carotti, transl. Zoete. London, Duckworth & Co., 1909.

Carr Stephen . . . . . *Archæology of Delhi*, Carr Stephen. Civil and Military Gazette and Station Press, Simla, and Thacker, Spink & Co., Calcutta. 1876.

Catalogue . . . . . *Delhi Museum Catalogue*, 1913 ed. Calcutta. Government Press, 1913.

Cavenagh . . . . . . *Reminiscences of an Indian Official*, Cavenagh. London, Allen, 1884.

Cities . . . . *Cities of India*, Forrest. London, Consabtle, 1903.

Cole . . . . First, second and third *Reports of the Curator of Ancient Monuments in India*, 1881-82, 1882-83, 1883-84. Government Press, Calcutta and Simla.

Crane . . . . *India Impressions*, W. Crane. London, Methuen, 1907.

Crooke . . . . *Things Indian*, Crooke. London, Murray, 1906.

Cooper . . . . *Handbook to Delhi*, Cooper. Lahore. 1863.

C. S. Range . . . . . *Calcutta to the Snowy Range*, by an Old Indian. London, Tinsley. 1866.

Daniell . . . . *Daniell's Oriental Scenery.* London, 1812.

Elliot . . . . *Elliot's History of India.* London, 1867-77.

Elphinstone . . . . . *History of India*, Mountstuart Elphinstone. London, John Murray, 1905.

Fall of Moghul Empire . . . *The Fall of the Moghul Empire of Hindustan*, H. G. Keene. London, Allen & Co., 1887.

Fanshawe . . . . . . *Delhi, Past and Present*, H. C. Fanshawe. London. John Murray, 1902.

LIST OF AUTHORITIES CITED—*contd.*

FERGUSSON . . . . . . *History of Indian and Eastern Architecture, by the late James Fergusson,* revised and edited by Burgess and Spiers. London, John Murray, 1910.

GARDENS . . . . . . *Gardens of the Great Mughals,* C. M. Villiers Stuart. London, Black, 1913.

HARDINGE . . . . . . *Recollections of India.* Hon'ble C. S. Hardinge. London, McLean, 1847.

HAVELL . . . . . . *Indian Architecture,* E. B. Havell. London, John Murray, 1913.

HEARN . . . . . . *The Seven Cities of Delhi,* Gordon Risley Hearn. London, Thacker & Co., 1906.

HEBER . . . . . . *Narrative of a journey through the Upper Provinces of India from Calcutta, 1824-1825, to Bombay (with notes upon Ceylon),* Reginald Heber. London. John Murray, 1828.

HISTORICAL . . . . . . *Historical and descriptive account of British India.* Edinburgh, 1832.

HODGES . . . . . . *Travels in India during years 1780, 1781, 1782 1783,* by W. Hodges, R.A. London, Edwards, 1793.

HOFFMEISTER . . . . . . *Travels in Ceylon and Continental India,* Hoffmeister. Edinburgh, Kennedy, 1848.

IMPRESSIONS . . . . . . *Impressions of Indian Travel,* Oscar Browning, London, Hodder and Stonghton, 1903.

IND. ANT. . . . . . . *Indian Antiquary.* Bombay.

J. A. S. D. . . . . . . *Journal of the Archæological Society of Delhi,* 1850.

J. R. A. S. . . . . . . *Journal of the Royal Asiatic Society,* published by the Society, Albemarle St. London, W.

KEENE . . . . . . *Keene's Hand-book for visitors to Delhi;* rewritten by E. A. Duncan. Calcutta, Thacker, Spink & Co., 1906.

KITTOE . . . . . . *Illustrations of Indian Architecture,* Markham Kittoe. Calcutta, Thacker, Spink, 1838.

LOW . . . . . . *A vision of India,* Low. London, Smith Elder & Co., 1906.

MANUCCI . . . . . . *Storia do Mogor,* or *Mogal India,* 1658-1708, *by Niccolao Manucci, Venetian,* with translation and notes by W. Irvine. London, John Murray, 1908.

MATHESON . . . . . . *England to Delhi.* Matheson. London, Longmans, 1870.

MEMOIRS . . . . . . *Memoirs of Delhi and Fyzabad,* Hoey. Allahabad, 1888.

MINTURA . . . . . . *New York to Delhi,* R. B. Mintura. London, Longmans Brown, Green and Longmans, 1858.

MUNDY . . . . . . *Journal of a tour in Upper India,* General Mundy. London, John Murray, 1858.

ORIENTAL ANNUAL . . . . . *The Oriental Annual,* Bacon. London, Charles Tilt, 1835, 1838 and 1840.

ORLICH . . . . . . *Travels in India, including Sinde and the Punjab by Captain Leopold Von Orlich,* translated by H. Evans-Lloyd. London, Longman, Brown, Green, and Longmans, 1845.

PENNELL . . . . . . *Things seen in Northern India,* Pennell. London, Seely Service and Co., 1912.

POOLE . . . . . . *Mediæval India under Muhammadan rule,* S. L. Poole. London, Unwin, 1906.

PRINSEP . . . . . . *Imperial India,* V. C. Prinsep. London, Chapman and Hall. 1876 (?).

ROBERTS . . . . . . *Scenes and Characteristics of Hindostan,* Emma Roberts. London, Allen & Co., 1837.

RODGERS . . . . . . *Revised list of objects of archæological interest in the Punjab,* Rodgers. Lahore, 1885-90.

ROYAL VISIT . . . . . . *Royal visit to India,* 1911-12, Fortescue. London, McMillan, 1912.

RUSSELL . . . . . . *My diary in India in the years 1858-59,* W. H. Russell. London, Routledge, 1860.

SALADIN . . . . . . *Manual d'art Musulman, I. Architecture,* H. Saladin. Paris, Picard et fils, 1907.

SLEEMAN . . . . . . *Rambles and Recollections of an Indian official,* by Lieutenant-Colonel Sleeman. London, Hatchard & Son, 1844.

TAVERNIER . . . . . . *Travels in India by Jean Baptiste Tavernier Baron of Aubonne,* with translation and notes by V. D. Ball. London, Macmillan & Co., 1889.

THEVENOT . . . . . . *Travels in the Levant,* M. de Thevenot. London, 1678. Part III.

TOUR . . . . . . *A tour through the Upper Provinces of Hindostan, 1804-1814,* by A. D. London, C. & J. Rivington, 1823.

TURKS IN INDIA . . . . . . *The Turks in India,* Keene. London, Allen, 1879.

WILSON . . . . . . *Rambles in Northern India, F. H. Wilson.* London, 1876. (The statements made in this book must be accepted with reserve.)

INDIAN HISTORIANS.

AB-I-HAYAT . . . . . . *Ab-i-Hayat,* Muhammad Husain, Azad. Lahore. 1887.

AIN . . . . . . *Ain-i-Akbari,* by Abul Fazl. English translation by Blochmann and Jarret. Calcutta, 1873-94.

AKBAR NAMAH . . . . . . *Akbar Namah,* Abul Fazl, Bibl. Ind. 1877-86.

ALAMGIR . . . . . . *Alamgir Namah,* Muhammad Kazim. Bibl. Ind. 1868.

ASAR . . . . . . *Asar-us-Sanadid,* Sayyid Ahmad Khan. Delhi ed. (1847) Cawnpore ed. (1904).

AZKAR . . . . . . *Azkar-i-Abrar,* Fazl Ahmad. Agra, 1908.

BADSHAH NAMAH . . . . . . *Badshah Namah,* Abd-ul-Hamid Lahori. Bibl. Ind. 1867-68.

FARISHTA . . . . . . *Tarikh-i-Farista,* Muhammad Qasim. Lucknow, 1905.

INDIAN HISTORIANS—*contd.*

HADIQA	*Hadiqatu-l-Aqalim*, Murtaza Husain. Lucknow, 1879.
IMADU-S-SAADAT	*Imadu-s-Saadat*, Ghulam Ali Khan. Lucknow, 1897.
IQBAL NAMAH	*Iqbal Namah-i Jahangir-i*, Motamad Khan. Bibl. Ind. 1865.
KHAZANAH	*Khazanah-i-Amirah*, Ghulam Ali Bilgrami. Cawnpore, 1900.
KHAZINA	*Khazinatu-l-Asfiya*, Ghulam Sarwar. Cawnpore, 1802.
LATIF	*History of the Punjab*, Syad Mahomed Latif. Calcutta Central Press Company, Limited, 1891.
MAASIR	*Maasir-ul-umara*, Nawwab Samsam-ud-daulah Shah Nawaz Khan. Bibl. Ind. 1888-91.
MAASIR-I-ALAMGIRI	*Maasir-i-Alamgiri*, Muhammad Saqi Mustaid Khan. Bibl. Ind. 1871.
MAZARAT	*Mazarat-i-Auliya-i-Delhi*, Muhammad Alam Shah. Delhi, 1330 A. H. (1912 A.D.)
MIFTAH	*Miftah-ul-Tawarikh*, Beale. Cawnpore, 1867.
MIRAT	*Mirat-i-Alam*, Bakhtawar Khan. Mss. in possession of Maulvi Mahmud-ul-Husan Khan of Tonk.
MUNTAKHAB-UL-LUBAB . . .	*Muntakhab-ul-Lubab*, Khafi Khan, Bibl. Ind. 1869-74.
MUNTAKHAB-UT-TAWARIKH . . .	*Muntakhab-ut-Tawarikh*, Abdul Qadir al Badayuni. Bibl. Ind. 1868-69.
SAFINA	*Safinatu-l-Auliya*, Dara Shikoh. Cawnpore, 1900.
SALIH	*Amal-i-Salih*, Muhammad Hamid Lahori. Mss. in Public Library. Lahore.
SHAMS SIRAJ AFIF	*Tarikh-i-Firoz Shahi*, Shams Siraj Afif. Bibl. Ind. 1891.
SIYAR	*Siyar-ul-Mutaakhirin*, Ghulam Husain. Lucknow.
TABAQAT-I-AKBARI	*Tabaqut i-Akbari*, Maulana Nizamud-din Ahmad. Lucknow, 1875.
TABAQAT-I-NASIRI	*Tabaqat-i-Nasiri*, Abu Omar Minhaj-ud-din Osman. Bibl. Ind. 1864.
TARIKH-I-MUZAFFARI	*Tarikh-i-Muzaffari*, Muhammad Ali Khan Ansari. Mss. in Government Library, Allahabad.
WAQAYA	*Waqaya-i-Nimat Khan Ali*, Lucknow. 1893.
YADGAR	*Yadgar-i-Delhi*, Maulvi Sayyid Ahmad. Delhi, 1905.
ZAFAR NAMAH-I SHAHJAHAN . .	*Zafar Namah-i Shah Jahan*, Muhammad Zakaullah Khan. Delhi, 1897.
ZAFAR NAMAH	*Zafar Namah*, Maulana Sharfuddin Ali of Yazd. Bibl. Ind. 1887-88.
ZIYA-I BARNI	*Tarikh-i-Froz Shahi*, Ziya-ud-din known as Ziya-i-Barni. Bibl. Ind. 1862.

LIST OF MONUMENTS.

REFERENCE.

No. = Number of monument, Shahjahanabad, Delhi.

a = Name of monument.

b = Situation.

c = Owners.

d = Class.

The following classification of monuments has been laid down by the Government of India and they are so classified in the margins of the different lists of Antiquarian remains issued by the Archæological Department, as well as in the various Progress reports :—

I.—Those monuments which from their present condition or historical or archæological value ought to be maintained in permanent good repair.

II.—Those monuments which it is now only possible or desirable to save from further decay by such minor measures as the eradication of vegetation the exclusion of water from the walls, and the like.

III.—Those monuments which, from their advanced stage of decay or comparative unimportance, it is impossible or unnecessary to preserve.

The monuments in classes I and II are further subdivided thus—

I (*a*) and II (*a*)—Monuments in the possession or charge of Government, or in respect of which Government must undertake the cost of all measures of conservation.

I (*b*) and II (*b*)—Monuments in the possession or charge of private bodies or individuals.

No comment is necessary upon class I, but in class II it will often be found necessary to carry out sufficient initial repairs over and above those specified, to put a building in such a state that those minor measures will afterwards suffice to keep it in a tolerably fair condition.

Because a building is put into class III, on account of its very dilapidated condition, it does not follow that there should be any unseemly haste in converting it into road metal. It may still be a monument of interest as long as it keeps together.

e = Date.

f = Inscriptions.

g = Condition.

h = Whether Protected by Act VII of 1904 (Ancient Monuments Preservation Act). "Unnecessary" signifies that Protection by this Act is unnecessary.

j = Notes on and description, etc.

k = Bibliographical references.

l = Numbers of photo negatives of the building in the office of the Superintendent, Muhammadan and British Monuments, Northern Circle, Agra.

FORT.

[NOTE.—*After the Diwan-i-Am the buildings on the East wall have been taken from South to North, i.e., beginning with the Asad Burj at the South-east corner and ending with the Shah Bur at the North-east corner.*]

Number of the Monument (Shahjahanabad Group).

No. 1. (*a*) Lal Qila or Lal Haveli, Delhi Fort.

(*b*) North-east corner of Shahjahanabad on the bank of the Jamna.

(*c*) The fenced-in area is in charge of Archæological Department. (Walls and certain buildings specified hereafter in possession of Military.)

(*d*) Walls I *b*. (For gates and interior buildings see hereafter.)

(*e*) Begun 12th Zilhajjah 1048 A.H. (16th April 1639 A.D.), completed 24th Rabi I 1058 A.H. (18th April 1648 A.D.).

(*f*) On the bridges (see paragraph *f*, page 9), on the Khuwabgah (see paragraph *f*, pp. 15-16), the Musamman Burj (see paragraph *f*, pp. 17, 18), and the Diwan-i-Khas (see paragraph *f*, p. 19).

(*g*) The buildings within the Archæological Area, *i.e.*, the Naubat Khana, the Diwan-i-Am, the Mumtaz Mahal, the Rang Mahal, Khuwabgah, Baithak, Musamman Burj, Diwan-i-Khas, Hammam, Moti Masjid, Hira Mahal, Zafar Mahal, Bhadon and Sawan Pavilions, and the Shah Burj may be said to be in excellent condition, together with their surrounding gardens, tanks, water channels and causeways. Outside this area, the appearance and condition of the Chhatta Chauk, the Lahore and Delhi gates, the Asad Burj, the pavilion immediately north-west of the Shah Burj, and the internal face of the main outer wall on the north-west and south sides, would be greatly improved by the removal of minor modern additions and by general minor repairs. The fine water gate near the Asad Burj as well as the Khizri gate below the Musamman Burj might be opened up with advantage for the use of visitors. The remainder of the fort enclosure could be laid out, without difficulty, in the same manner as has been done in the case of the immediate neighbourhood of the principal palace buildings, shrubberies being planted to represent the old buildings and arcades, with grass lawns to show the positions of the old courts. These improvements would, of course, depend on the evacuation and removal of most of the Military buildings.

(*h*) The following buildings in the Fort with all their surrounding gardens, paths, terraces, and watercourses, are Protected Monuments :—

Naubat Khana.	Diwan-i-Khas.
Diwan-i-Am.	Moti Masjid.
Mumtaz Mahal.	Hammam.
Rang Mahal.	Sawan.
Tasbih Khana, Khuwabgah and Baithak.	Bhadon.
Musamman Burj.	Shah Burj.

(*j*) Owing, it is said, to insufficiency of accommodation in the Fort at Agra, and to the many ravines and narrow streets of the city making it unsuitable and dangerous for his great ceremonial processions, Shah Jahan resolved to transfer his capital to Delhi and, with the help of Hindu astrologers and Muhammadan *hakims*, chose a site just south of Salimgarh. According to the *Shahjahan-Namah* and the *Mirat-i-Aftab Numa*, backed by the inscriptions on the Khuwabgah, its foundation was laid on the 12th Zilhajjah 1048 A.H. in the 11th year of the reign, and the city was named Shahjahanabad after the Emperor. Saiyyid Ahmad Khan (*Asaru-s-Sanadid*, Delhi, ed. 1847, chapter II, pages 2—3) says that among some other old papers a horoscope of the Fort came into his possession, and that in it the date of the foundation was given as the night of Friday the 9th Muharram of the year 1049 A. H. (12th May 1639 A.D.) Lal Qila was completed in the 20th year of the reign, Shah Jahan being in Kabul at the time. Makramat Khan who was then in charge of the building operations, requested the Emperor to come to Delhi, and see the fortress and his new palace. On receipt of the news Shah Jahan left Kabul at once, and on arrival at Delhi, entered the Fort through the gate facing the river, presumably the Khizri gate (see p. 7) and held, on the 24th[1] Rabi II 1058, his first *darbar* in the Diwan-i-Am.

The Fort, faced externally with red sandstone, is an irregular octagon with its two long sides on the east (river side) and west (city side), and the six smaller ones on the north and the south. It measures some 3,000 feet in length and 1,800 feet in breadth, the wall towards the river being some 60 feet in height (according to *Asar*, Cawnpore, ed. 1847, only 12 yards), the palace buildings standing on a level with the top of it; on the land side the walls tower to a height of 110 feet, of which 75 feet are above the level of the ground and the ditch. The walls are some 45 feet in thickness at the base and 30 feet in thickness at the level of the embattled parapets; the ditch is 75 feet in width and 30 feet deep.[2]

The *ustads*, Hamid and Ahmad, the well-known 'master-builders' of Shah Jahan (see No. 325), were employed on the construction of the Fort. Saiyyid Ahmad Khan, by reason of the *pietra dura* representation of Orpheus, on the back wall of the recess behind the 'baldachino' in the Diwan-i-Am, has assumed that some Italian architect was connected with the planning of the palace, but it would seem probable that European talent was bestowed on this particular type ornamentation only and not on the general design and arrangement, which is purely oriental. The first 'Superintendent of Works' was Izzat Khan, who was responsible for the preparation of the foundations in five months and two days, and the collection of building material. A start was also made on the walls at certain points. Izzat Khan was then transferred to Thatta as Governor and succeeded by Allahwardi Khan. The latter raised the entire circumference of the walls to a height of 12 yards in 2 years, 1 month and 14 days. He, in turn, was given a Governorship, and the duty of supervision was finally entrusted to Makramat Khan who completed the work. The Fort is said to have cost 100 *lacs* of rupees, half of which was spent on the walls and the other half on the buildings within. Other authorities give 50 *lacs* as the total cost. This latter amount may possibly have been spent on the

[1] According to *Badshah Namah* (Volume II, page 710), 21st Rabi II.

[2] Those interested in Muhammadan Military architecture may refer to the chapter on Fort, strongholds and sieges, in *The Army of the Indian Mughals*, Irvine. Luzac, 1904.

Lal Qila as seen across the Yamuna river

Lal Qila

buildings, as it is corroborated by the inscription on the northern arch of the Khuwabgah.

(*k*) ***Annual***, 1902-03, 26-28; 1903-04, 5-6, 21-22; 1904-05, 1, 3, 17, 18; 1905-06, 1, 3, 29-31, 33-42; 1906-07, 2, 6; 1907-08, 2, 3; 1908-09, 1, 2.

Archer, 1, 104, 110, *et seq.*

A. S. I. I, 132, 224 *et seq.*; IV, 69; also gives a list of the principal monuments of Delhi.

As. Res., IV, 417 *et seq.*; X (1811), 540, 545.

Auckland, 10 *et seq.*, 95.

Banister Fletcher, 656.

Baxter, 27-8.

Bernier, 241 *et seq.*

C. S. Range, 245, 250.

Carr Stephen, 216-250 (contains plan of the Fort).

Catalogue, 39 *et seq.*, J. 9, J. 35, J. 42, J. 53, K. 3, K. 5.

Cities, 142.

Cole, 1st Report, XXIV-VI, CXCVI-IX.

Cooper, 4 *et seq.*, 43 *et seq.*, 51 (Cities of Delhi), 123. *Cooper* also contains a list of monuments.

Crane, 149.

Elphinstone, 700-727.

Fall of Moghul Empire, 10, 12, 15, 17, 43, 47, 91, 185, 189.

Fanshawe, 20-43, 183, 303. *Fanshawe* gives a list of the principal monuments of Delhi, also a plan of the Fort.

Fergusson, II, 199, 309-12 (contains plan of the Fort).

Gardens, 117, 118 (Plan).

Guides to Delhi:

Three days at Delhi, Major Newell; *Municipal Directory* contains list of monuments; *Murray's Handbook to India* (contains plan of the Fort); *Seven Aspects of Delhi*, Munshi Jwala Sahai; *Harcourt's Guide to Delhi*, Meerut, 1870; *Beresford's Guide to Delhi*; *Picturesque India*, W. S. Caine.

Hardinge, Part I. The Palace of the King. (Plate.)

Havell, 209.

Hearn, 7-15, 142-162, 293 (contains plan of the Fort).

Heber, II, 297-305.

Historical, I, 310; II, 220, 227.

Hodges, 118.

Hoffmeister, 282, 283.

Impressions, 165.

Keene, 119-137.

Low, 163 *et seq.*

Manucci, I, 183 *et seq.*, 329-32; II, 445-6, 463.

Matheson, 364.

Memoirs, 19.

Mintura, 220.

Mundy, 38 *et seq.*

Oriental Annual (1835), 100 *et seq.*; (1838), 208, (Plate), 161 *et seq.*; (1835), 70, 76 (Imperial Palace); (1840), 25 *et seq.*, 34 *et seq.*

Orlich, II, 4, 22 *et seq.*
Pennell, 141.
Poole, 338-41, 367-76.
Prinsep, 24 *et seq.*
Roberts, II, 214-16, 223-224.
Royal visit, 173-4.
Saladin, 576.
Sleeman, II, 274-278.
Tavernier, I, 96-103.
Thevenot, III, 41.
Tour, 150 *et seq.*, 170.
Turks in India, 139.
Wilson, 41 *et seq.*

For a general history of the Fort Delhi see the *Guide to the Historical Buildings and Gardens* (Calcutta, Superintendent, Government Printing, 1914) (contains plans).

The following works of which copies were unavailable for reference at the time of preparation of this list may also be consulted : *Journal of Archæological Society of Delhi* (1850), *Essays on Indian Antiquities*, James Prinsep, F.R.S., ed. E. Thomas (1858).

Ab-i-Hayat, 67, 454.
Alamgir, 85, 351-382, 937.
Asar (1904), chapter II, 28-54.
Badshah Namah, I, 224. (Shah Jahan's interest in Architecture II, 320.)
Khazanah, 104.
Maasir, I, 207-215 ; II, 863-865 ; III, 462-463, 466.
Miftah, 252-253.
Mirat, Fol. 350.
Muntakhab-ul-Lubah, 680-681.
Salih, Fols. 575, 576, 578, 579, 580, 582, 585, 590-593.
Siyar, I, 277.
Tarikh-i-Muzaffari, Fols. 115, 116.
Zafar Namah-i-Shah Jahan, VII, 399-400.

(*l*) General Views only, 1343, 1344, 1345, 2332, 2495, 2496, 2505.

No. 2. (*a*) Lahore gate (also known as the Victoria Gate).

(*b*) In the centre of the West wall of the fort, facing the Chandni Chauk.

(*c*) Archæological Department.

(*d*) (Outside) I*a* ; inside I*b* (repaired by and in charge of Military Works).

(*e*) 1048—1058 A. H. (1639—1648 A.D.).

(*f*) None.

(*g*) See No. 1, paragraph *g*, p. 1.

(*h*) The gateway should be declared a 'Protected Monument' when it is evacuated by the Military.

(*j*) The most important and most frequented gate of the Fort. It consists of three storeys, the upper rooms of which now afford accommodation to the officers of the Fort, the lower ones serving as guard rooms. The actual entrance measures 41 feet in height by 24 feet in width, and is flanked by half octagon turrets crowned by open pavilions; the centre of the façade above the gate is emphasised by a row of dwarf coupled *chhatris*, each roofed by a small marble dome, a treatment commonly seen used for gateways in the architecture of this period. The row of dwarf *chhatris* is terminated at either end by a slender minaret, crowned with a small lantern. Prior to the Mutiny of 1857, the upper rooms were occupied by the "Commandant of the palace guard," an appointment created in 1811, when the favourite son of Akbar II made a demonstration against the life of Mr. Seton, then resident of Delhi. In 1857 the gate was the scene of the murder of Mr. Fraser, Captain Douglas, the Rev. Mr. Jennings, the Chaplain, his daughter and Miss Clifford, a young lady staying with them, and Mr. Hutchinson.

(*k*) *Annual* (1905-06), 1.
Bernier, 248.
Catalogue, 40 *et seq.*, J. 31-3, J. 44.
Carr Stephen, 218.
Crane, 149.
C. S. Range, 251.
Fall of Moghul Empire, 160.
Fanshawe, 21, 22, 26.
Fergusson, II, 309.
Hearn, 144.
Keene, 18, 20, 122.
Manucci, I, 184 ; IV, 434.
Oriental Annual (1835), 100.
Roberts, II, 223.
Sleeman, II, 274.
Von Orlich, II, 22, 25 (residence of Captain Angelo).
Asar (1904), chap. II, 31.

(*l*) 1181, 1187, 1349, 1366, 2326, 2330, 2331, 2498.

No. 3. (*a*) Delhi Gate (also known as the Alexandra Gate).
(*b*) In the south wall near the south-west corner of the fort.
(*c*) Elephant statues and exterior of gate in charge of Archæological Department, interior repaired by and in charge of Military Works.
(*d*) (Elephant Statues) I*a*, (Gate) I*b*.
(*e*) 1048-1058 A.H. (1639-1648 A.D.).
(*f*) None.
(*g*) See No. 1, para. g, p. 1.
(*h*) The gateway should be declared a 'Protected Monument' when it is evacuated by the Military.
(*j*) The gate is so called as it faces the sites of the older cities, and is similar in design to the Lahore Gate, previously described, but is rendered more interesting by the presence of the two stone elephants standing at either side of the entrance arch. These were erected in 1903 by Lord Curzon to fill the place of the original ones. There are many theories put forward as to the history of the original elephants and their riders, and those that

derive them originally from Gwalior and Agra Fort have been proved to be without foundation. Another of these theories is that their riders were the celebrated Rajput heroes, Jaimal and Patta, but it seems more probable that the figures were only those of ordinary *mahawats* (mahout) and that the animals were ordinary fighting elephants. The strict religious views of Aurangzeb would not tolerate the presence of these statues so their demolition was ordered, and nothing was heard of them till 1863, when some 125 fragments of the original statues were found buried in the Fort. Three years later an elephant statue was reconstructed from these fragments and set up in the Queen's Gardens. In 1892 the statue was removed to a site on the Chandni Chauk and ten years later to another position in front of the Institute.

The present statues were erected in 1903, but it was not found possible to reuse the original fragments, now placed in the verandah of Museum, owing to the mutilation they had undergone. The work was entrusted to Mr. R. W. Mackenzie, an artist with experience of Indian Art, and the statues were carried out from his models by Indian workmen. It is inconceivable how any doubt could ever have existed as to the original positions of the statues. Bernier clearly places them at the Delhi Gate and his account is corroborated by M. de Thevenot, who saw them a few years later. The misconception seems to have arisen largely from the *Asaru-s-Sanadid*, the later edition of which, published long after the author's death, places them at the Naubat Khana. In the first edition they are placed before the Delhi Gate. Carr Stephen (*Archæology of Delhi*) places them before the Naubat Khana and Keene (*Guide to Delhi*) before the Lahore Gate, the former authority being of the opinion that Bernier's descriptions of the gates are so faulty that they are correct with respect to neither. Bernier, however, after describing the statues, clearly states that "after passing through the gate at which they stand there is long and spacious street, provided with a central canal," which is also referred to by M. de Thevenot. The only street of this kind in the Fort, as is proved by the old plans, was that running due north and south from the square in front of the Naubat Khana. Bernier's description of the Lahore Gate is rendered more explicit by his reference to the "roofed street" (the Chatta Chauk, see p. 9) leading therefrom, and bordered on either side by shops. It may be added that the excavation in connection with the erection of the present statues disclosed further overwhelming evidence in the nature of the original foundations.

(*k*) *Annual* (1905-06) 34-42 (note on elephant statues).
A. S. I. (1862-65) I, 25. 225 *et seq.*; IV, 446 ; XXXII, 296, 375.
As. Res. IV, 446.
Baxter, 28.
Bernier, 256-257.
Carr Stephen, 219.
Catalogue, 40 *et seq.* J. 16, J. 40.
Cole (1st report), CCII, CCIV.
C. S. Range, 251.
Delhi Museum Catalogue (1909). 58 (note on elephant statues).
Fanshawe, 23, 41-43.
Fergusson, II, 310.
Hearn, 144.
Hodges, 118.

J. R. A. S., April 1910, 490; XXXII, 296, 375.
Keene, 18, 148.
Manucci, I, 184.
Oriental Annual (1835), 100.
Pennell, 147.
Thevenot, III, 42.
Von Orlich, II, 22.
Asar (1904), chap. II, 31; (1847), chap. II, 6.
Maasir-i-Alamgiri, 77.
Salih, Fol. 584.
Waqaya, 44.

(*l*) 1182, 1367, 2201.

No. 4. (*a*) Gate (no special name).

(*b*) In the centre of north wall of Fort and opposite Salimgarh.

(*c*) Military.

(*d*) II*b*.

(*e*) Modern.

(*f*) None.

(*g*) Excellent.

(*h*) Unnecessary.

(*j*) At a short distance to the north of this gate there was formerly an old bridge leading into Salimgarh and built by Jahangir in the year 1031 A.H. (1622 A.D.). The bridge, the marble inscription from which is now in the Museum, *Catalogue* Nos. C. 18, was removed to make way for the new Railway bridge. The bridge in front of the gate under reference is also modern. It is interesting as being that over which the King-Emperor first entered Delhi in the State Entry of the Coronation Durbar of 1911.

No. 5. (*a*) Postern or wicket (*khirki*).

(*b*) On the north-eastern wall, close to the Salimgarh Gate.

(*c*) Military.

(*d*) II*b*.

(*e*) 1048-1058 A.H. (1639—1648 A.D.).

(*f*) None.

(*g*) Good.

(*h*) Should be declared a "Protected Monument."

(*j*) The gate is faced with red sandstone and crowned by a row of "flame battlements."

(*k*) *Carr Stephen*, 218.
Keene, 121.

(*l*) S. 24.

No. 6. (*a*) Khizri Gate or 'Water Gate'

(*b*) Under the Musamman Burj.
(*c*) Archæological Department (with Military rights).
(*d*) (Inner portion) I*b*; (outside) I*a*.
(*e*) 1048-1058 A.H. (1639-1648 A.D.).
(*f*) None.
(*g*) Good, but modern additions might be removed with advantage.
(*h*) The gate should be declared a "Protected Monument" when it is no longer required by the Military.
(*j*) A flight of steps leads to this gate, which opens on the river bed. The lower portion of the Musamman Burj forms a kind of portico to the actual gateway and three of its five sides are pierced by openings. The angles of the base of the *burj* are emphasised by false minarets, linked by a circular moulding, crowned by cresting. This is the gate which Captain Douglas desired might be thrown open on the morning of 11th May 1857, in order that he might go down and speak with the mutineers.

No. 7. (*a*) Water Gate.
(*b*) Close to Asad Burj, at the south-east corner of the fort.
(*c*) Military.
(*d*) I*b*.
(*e*) 1048-1058 A.H. (1639-1648 A.D.).
(*f*) None.
(*g*) See 1, para. *g*.
(*h*) The gateway should be declared a "Protected Monument" when no longer required by the Military.
(*j*) The gate is provided with a barbican, probably the work of Aurangzeb.
(*k*) *Keene*, 121.
(*l*) S. 23.

No. 8. (*a*) Barbicans.
(*b*) In front of the Lahore and Delhi gates.
(*c*) Military.
(*d*) I*b*.
(*e*) Built during the reign of Aurangzeb (1658-1707 A.D.).
(*f*) None.
(*g*) Good. The battlements have been removed and the tops of the walls covered with earth for purposes of defence.
(*h*) The barbicans should be declared "Protected Monuments" when no longer required by the Military.
(*j*) Built by Aurangzeb as an extra protection for the gates. The barbican in front of the Lahore Gate is entered on the north side by a gateway, 40 feet in height by 24 feet in width. The façade of the gateway rises some 8 feet above the height of the walls which abut against it, and is surmounted by a parapet with "flame battlements" like the remainder of the Fort walls. The walls of the barbican are some 40 feet in height,

the north and south corners of west wall being terminated by projecting bastions, crowned by pavilions. The barbican of the Delhi Gate is entered from the west side, its south wall being treated in the same manner as the west wall of the Lahore Gate. It is recorded that Shah Jahan wrote to his son from prison at Agra and said to him of these barbicans, "You have made the Fort a bride and set a veil before her face." The glacis was constructed after the Mutiny.

(*k*) *Carr Stephen*, 218-219.
Fanshawe, 20, 22, 41.
Hearn, 144.
Heber, II, 297.
Keene, 122.
Asar (1847), chap. II, 7; (1904), chap. II, 30.

No. 9, (*a*) Bridges.
(*b*) In front of barbicans before the Lahore and Delhi gates.
(*c*) Military.
(*d*) II*b*.
(*e*) 1226 A.H. (1811 A.D.).
(*f*) On the arches :—

هوالغني

سنه ٥ جلوس والا سنه ١٢٢٦ هجري سنه ١٨١١ عيسوي در عهد شاه جمجاه محمد اكبر بادشاه غازي صاحب قران ثاني باهتمام دلاورالدوله رابرت ماقفرسن بهادر دلير جنگ پل فيض منزل تعمير يافت

Translation.

"He is Rich!"

"In the fifth year from the exalted accession, the year 1226 Hijra, the year 1811 A. D. during the reign of a King, dignified like Jamshaid, Muhammad Akbar, the King, the champion of the faith, the second lord of conjunction of two beneficent planets, under the superintendence of Dilawar-ud-Daulah Robert Macpherson, Bahadur, Diler Jang, this graceful bridge was erected."

(*g*) Good.
(*h*) The bridges should be declared "Protected Monuments."
(*j*) These have taken the place of the original drawbridges of wood and were built for Muhammad Akbar II by "Dilawar-ud-Daulah Robert Macpherson, Bahadur, Diler Jang."[1]
(*k*) *Carr Stephen*, 218.
Hearn, 144.
Asar (1904), chap. II, 30.

No. 10. (*a*) *Chhatta Chauk* or "Vaulted Arcade."

[1] Entered H. E. I. Co.'s service as a cadet in 1794; became Lieutenant. 25th April 1797; Captain, 27th February 1805; Major, 22nd January 1817, and died at Delhi, 6th January 1828. Son of Andrew Macpherson and born in 1774 in the Parish of Thingupie, Invernesshire, N.B.

(*b*) On the east side of the Lahore Gate.

(*c*) Military (repaired with advice of Archæological Department).

(*d*) II*b*.

(*e*) 1048-1058 A. H. (1639-1648 A. D.).

(*f*) None.

(*g*) See No. I, para. *g*.

(*h*) Should be declared a "Protected Monument" when no longer required by the Military.

(*j*) The vaulted arcade is some 230 feet in length and 27 feet in width. On either side of it there are 32 arched rooms for use as shops. In the centre of the arcade there is an octagonal court about 30 feet in diameter with an open roof for the admission of light and air. Fergusson is of the opinion that it is the "noblest entrance known to belong to any existing palace." Traces of the old painted plaster decoration may be seen on the walls of the central open portion.

(*k*) *Archer*, I, 110.
Carr Stephen, 219.
Fanshawe, 22, 26.
Fergusson, II, 309.
Hearn, 145.
Heber, II, 297.
Hoffmeister, 283.
Keene, 123.
Manucci, I, 184 (*bazars*).
Roberts, II, 223.
Von Orlich, II. 23.
Asar (1904), chap. II, 30-1.
Salih, Fol. 584.

(*l*) 2502, 2512, 2523.

No. 11. (*a*) Naubat or Naqqar Khana (Drum-house).

(*b*) Opposite the east end of the "Vaulted Arcade" leading from the Lahore Gate.

(*c*) Archæological Department.

(*d*) I*a*.

(*e*) 1048-1058 A. H. (1639-1648 A. D.).

(*f*) None.

(*g*) Excellent.

(*h*) "Protected Monument."

(*j*) The Naubat Khana served as the main entrance to the court of the Diwan-i-Am. Between it and the east end of the vaulted arcade previously mentioned, and leading from the Lahore Gate, there was, in former days, a court some 200 feet in length by 140 feet in breadth, surrounded by arcaded apartments, which served as quarters for the *Umaras* when on duty on the Emperor's guard. At the south-west corner of this square stood certain public buildings wherein the Emperor's *Nazir* transacted business, while its central feature was a tank fed by the canal which ran north and south down the centre of the arcaded streets, the quarters of the lesser

Umaras and officials, and leading respectively to the royal gardens and the Delhi Gate.

The Naubat Khana is said to have been fronted by a stone railing, all traces of which, together with the square and its surrounding arcades, have disappeared. Their foundations will, however, be probably found under the surface of the modern roads.

The Naubat Khana measures some 107 feet 6 inches in length, 68 feet 2 inches in breadth, and 49 feet 4 inches in height. The gateway is 29 feet in height and 16 feet in width, while on either side of it are double storeyed rooms. Over the gateway and the side rooms is the music gallery, an open hall with five open arched bays which form a third storey to the structure. Stairs, at the north and south ends of the building, give access to the upper floors. The building was also known as the 'Hathia Pol' (Elephant Gate), not because the original elephant statues (see p. 5) originally stood there, as some writers have supposed, but more probably because it was at this point that all save Princes of the blood-royal dismounted from their elephants before they could pass into the courtyard of the Diwan-i-Am.

The most serious charge against Mr. Francis Hawkins, who was removed from his appointment of resident at Delhi, was that he had violated the sanctity of the Royal palace by riding under the gateway of the Naubat Khana. The Emperors Jahandar Shah (1712-1713 A. D.), and Farrukh-siyar (1713-1719 A. D.) are said to have been murdered in the Naubat Khana, the latter after having been first blinded. The two lower rooms are now occupied by the Caretaker of the Palace.

(*k*) *Annual* (1908-09), 1; (1909-10), 1.
Bernier, 259-260 (grand gateway).
Carr Stephen, 220-223.
Catalogue, 39 *et seq*., J. 13, J. 14, J. 27.
Cities, 144.
Cole, 1st Report, CXCIX.
Delhi Museum Catalogue (1909 ed.), IV.
Fanshawe, 26-28.
Fergusson, II, 310.
Hearn, 145-146.
Heber, II, 297 (dirty gateway).
Hoffmeister, 283.
Keene, 124.
Saladin, 576.
Tavernier, I, 98 (large gate).
Von Orlich, II, 23 (eastern portal).
Asar (1904), chap. II, 31; (1847), 10.

(*l*) 1361, 1362, 2204, 2216, 2217, 2499, 2558.

No. 12. (*a*) Diwan-i-Am.
(*b*) To the east of the Naubat Khana.
(*c*) Archæological Department.
(*d*) I*a*.
(*e*) 1048-1058 A. H. (1639—1648 A. D.).
(*f*) None.

(*g*) Excellent.

(*h*) "Protected Monument."

(*j*) The original court of the Diwan-i-Am, some 550 feet long by 300 feet in width, was entered, as has been stated above, through the Naubat Khana, and was formerly surrounded by arcaded apartments used by chiefs and *Umaras* on duty. To the north of the great hall was a gateway leading to another smaller court, the "ante-court," if one may use the term, to the larger of the two courtyards before the Diwan-i-Khas. The decline of the Mughal Empire saw the south end of this magnificent building disfigured by unsightly erections used as the houses for the King's sons and built in the bastard European style of architecture which became common in India at this time. The hall, now robbed of its former gilding and stucco, is built throughout of red sandstone, and measures 80 feet in length and 40 feet in breadth. It stands on a 4 feet plinth, the roof parapet being some 30 feet above the level of the latter. The north-west and south-west corners of the roof are emphasised by small *chhatris* while a deep *chhajja* sets off the lines of the façade on the north, south, and west. The inside of the hall consists of 3 aisles, each of seven bays, each of the latter being formed of four columns supporting the engrailed arches which carry the roof. In the centre of the east wall is a recess some 21 feet in width and faced with the most exquisite designs in *pietra dura* work, representing trees, flowers, and birds. The original work is said to have been that of Austin de Bordeaux[1] who was permitted to represent himself as Orpheus in one of the upper central panels. The inlaid panels had been greatly damaged in the days of the last Emperors of Delhi, and after the Mutiny further portions were removed and taken to England. They were brought back at the instance of Lord Curzon in 1902, and restored by an Italian craftsman a few years later in their old positions, missing stones being replaced by new ones with the help of old drawings showing the recess in its original condition. (For a detailed account of the mosaics see *A. S. I. Annual 1902-03*, 26-27, 1906-07, 2-6.) In front of the recess stands a marble 'baldachino' or canopy, likewise adorned with inlay and covered by a curved dome of the 'Bengali' type, which began to be introduced into Mughal Architecture about this time. In front of this again stands a marble dais, 3 feet in height, 7 feet in length and 4 feet in width, said to have been used by the *Wazirs* of the Emperor when presenting petitions.

The Diwan-i-Am and its courtyard was marked off officially into several divisions for the *darbars* of the Emperor. The most sacred spot within the precincts was the recess, already mentioned, with its baldachino, and known as the *Nashiman-i-Zill-i-Ilahi* (the seat of the Shadow of God). Below the throne was an enclosure, measuring 40 feet by 30 feet, and surrounded with a plated railing; the remainder of the hall served as yet another division and was railed in with marble, while the courtyard outside was divided into two portions by a red sandstone railing which separated the minor officials from the general throng. It is almost unnecessary to add that the divisions nearest to the throne were those occupied by the highest rank of courtiers. The red sandstone railing was repaired by Bahadur Shah II in 1253 A.H. (1837-8 A. D.).

[1] For an account of Austin de Bordeaux see *J. R. A. S.*, October 1910, p. 1343, by W. Irvine.

It should be added that the lawns in front of the Diwan-i-Am are intended to represent the original courtyard, and the shrubberies at the sides and ends, the former colonnades. The shrubbery on the south side is unavoidably placed somewhat to the north of its correct alignment, owing to the existence of the military road at this point.

(*k*) *Annual* (1902-03) 176, (1904-05) 17, (1905-06) 2, (1906-07) (Mosaics) 2, 16; (1909-10) 1.

A. S. I., IV, 70.

As. Res., IV, 427.

Auckland, 10.

Bernier, 259, (Am Khas), 260-265, 268-272, 274-275.

Carr Stephen, 223-227.

Catalogue, 39 *et seq.*, J. 12, J. 25, J. 26, J. 54.

Cities, 145.

Cole (1st report) XXIV, CXCIX; (2nd report) CXII; (3rd report) 21, CXXXIX.

Cooper, 43.

Crane, 149.

Fall of Moghul Empire, 11, 175 (*Am Khas*.)

Fanshawe, 28-33.

Fergusson II, 311.

Gardens, 79.

Hearn, 146-9.

Heber, II, 297, 304.

Hoffmeister, 283.

Keene, 125-129.

Oriental Annual (1835), 100.

Pennell, 142.

Prinsep, 25.

Saladin, 576.

Sleeman, II, 274.

Tavernier, I, 98-101.

Thevenot, III, 42.

Von Orlich, II, 23.

Asar (1904), chap. II, 31-4.

Salih, Fols. 583-584.

(*l*) 925, 936, 939, 940, 1173, 1174, 1175, 1176, 1177, 1178, 1183, 1184, 1188, 1363, 1364, 2398, 2401, 2468, 2504, 2508, 2559; (Mosaics) 1368, 1529, 1530, 1531, 2202, 2203.

No. 13. (*a*) Asad Burj (Lion Tower).

(*b*) South-east corner of the Fort.

(*c*) Military.

(*d*) II*b*.

(*e*) 1048-1058 A.H. (1639-1648 A.D.)

(*f*) None.

(*g*) Fair, but modern additions require to be removed and petty repairs effected.

(*h*) Should be declared a "Protected Monument" on evacuation by the Military.

(*j*) The Burj was much damaged in 1803, when Delhi was successfully defended by Ochterlony against Harnath Chela. It was repaired by Akbar II, and the detail of *chhatris* is unmistakably late Mughal in feeling.

(*k*) *Carr Stephen*, p. 237.
Fergusson, II, p. 311.
Hearn, p. 161.
Keene, p. 137.
Asar (1904), chap. II, 38.

No. 14. (*a*) Mumtaz Mahal (now the Delhi Museum of Archæology).

(*b*) South of Rang Mahal.

(*c*) Archæological Department.

(*d*) I*a*.

(*e*) 1048-1058 A.H. (1639-1648 A.D.).

(*f*) None.

(*g*) Good.

(*h*) "Protected Monument."

(*j*) The building measures 88 feet north and south by 81 feet 10 inches east and west and was formerly an important apartment of the Seraglio. After the Mutiny used as a prison and till a few years ago as a Sergeants' Mess. The gilded *chhatris*, formerly existing on the corners of its roof have disappeared,[1] and the buildings as it now stands, is the result of considerable repair in 1911. The *chhajja* was also reconstructed. The lower portion of the walls and piers are of marble, and traces of some of the old painted and glass decoration, with which the building was formerly adorned, have been exposed. It is now used as the Delhi Museum of Archæology.

(*k*) *Annual* (1905-1906), 30; (1908-9), 1.
Fanshawe, 41.
Hearn, 160.
Keene, 125, 136 (Imtiaz Mahal).
Von Orlich, II, 24 (palaces of King's wives).
Asar (1904), chap. II, 34-5.

(*l*) 1729, 2218, 2223, 2260, 2261, 2396, 2397, 2548, 2549, 2550, 2551, 2554, 2555, 2556.

No. 15. (*a*) Rang Mahal.

(*b*) South of Khuwabgah and Baithak.

(*c*) Archæological Department.

(*d*) I*a*.

(*e*) 1048-1058 A.H. (1639-1648 A.D.).

(*f*) None.

(*g*) Good, but the building has suffered much during the last hundred years.

[1] The old picture of the east wall of the Fort in the Museum shows this building in its original condition.

(*h*) "Protected Monument."

(*j*) The building measures some 153′ 6″ north and south by 69′ 3″ east and west, and is so called from the coloured decoration with which its internal walls were originally adorned. It was the largest of the apartments of the Imperial Seraglio and in the time of Shah Jahan was known as the Imtiyaz Mahal (Palace of distinction). It consists of a main hall with smaller end rooms while a marble water channel runs down the centre of the building with a central marble basin of singularly effective design. On the west side there is a range of underground rooms. The building is said to have been originally ceiled with silver, then with copper, and finally with wood. Between the building and the back of the Diwan-i-Am lay a garden surrounded with arcades and a central tank. The latter was exposed to view in 1911.

(*k*) *Annual* (1904-05), 17; (1905-06), 29-31; (1907-08), 3, 23-30; (1908-09), railing near, 2.
Carr Stephen, 236-237.
Catalogue, 39 *et seq.*, J. 6, J. 23, J. 24.
Cole, (1st Report) XXV.
Crane, 150.
Fall of Moghul Empire, 177 (Imtiaz Mahal).
Fanshawe, 41.
Fergusson, II, 311, 312.
Hearn, 158-9.
Tavernier, I, 93 (harem).
Von Orlich, II, 24 (Palaces of King's wives).
Asar (1904), chap. II, 35-7.
Salih, Fol. 582-3.

(*l*) 1180, 1184, 1186, 1527, 1627, 1628, 1629, 1676, 1677, 1678, 1696 1721, 1722, 1723, 1724, 1725, 1834, 1835, 2228, 2338, 2393, 2399, 2400 2408, 2469, 2500, 2501, 2563, 2568-2572.

No. 16. (*a*) Marble Basin.

(*b*) In the centre of the large tank in front of the Rang Mahal.

(*c*) Archæological Department.

(*d*) I*a*.

(*e*) 1048-1058 A. H. (?) (1639-1648 A.D.).

(*f*) None.

(*g*) Good.

(*h*) "Protected Monument."

(*j*) This tank is of one piece of marble, taken from the Makrana quarries by Shah Jahan. It measures 10′ 2″ × 9′ 6″ × 2′ 3″. Its former position is doubtful. It would appear from some accounts that it stood immediately in front of the Rang Mahal in the shallow basin in front of that building, while another account places it in front of the Moti Mahal, the pavilion which formerly stood in the centre of the east terrace of the Hayat Bakhsh garden. It was brought from the

Queen's Gardens, whither it was removed, presumably after the Mutiny, and placed in its present position in 1911.

(*k*) *Annual* (1907-08), 27.
Auckland, 96.
Oriental Annual (1835), 101.
Asar (1904), chap. II, 45.

(*l*) 2409, 2410.

No. 17. (*a*) Tasbih Khana, Khuwabgah and Baithak.

(*b*) On the south of the Diwan-i-Khas.

(*c*) Archæological Department.

(*d*) I*a*.

(*e*) 12th Zilhajjah 1048 A.H. (16th April 1639 A.D.)—24th Rabi I 1058 A.H. (18th April 1648 A.D.).

(*f*) On the southern arch of the Khuwabgah.

سبحان الله این چه منزلهاست رنگین و نشیمن هاست دلنشین قطعهٔ بهشت برین چون گویم که قدسیان همت بلند بتماشایش آرزو مند اگر ساکنان اطراف و اکناف بسان بیت العتیق بطوافش آیند رواست و اگر نظارگیان انفس و آفاق مثل حجر اسود به تقبیل آستان رفیع الشانش شتابند سزا آغاز قلع والا که از کاخ گردون برتراست و رشک سد اسکندر و این عمارت دلکشا و باغ حیات بخش که در منازل چون روح در بدن ست و شمع در انجمن و نهر اطهر که آب صافیش به بینا آئینه جهان نماست و دانا را از عالم غیب پرده کشا و آبشا رها که گوی سپیدهٔ صبحدم ست یا لوحهٔ اسرار لوح و قلم و فوارها که هر کدامش پنجهٔ نورست

On the northern arch of the Khuwabgah.

بمصافحهٔ آسمانیان مائل یا لالي متلالي ست بانعام زمینیان نازل و حوض که همه از اب زندگاني پر بصفا رشك نور و چشمه خوردوازدهم ذي الحجه سال جلوس دوازدهم اقدس مطابق هزار و چهل و هشت هجري بعالمیان نوید کامراني داد و انجامش که بصرف پنجاه لک روپیه صورت پذیرفت بست و چهارم ربیع الاول سال بست و یکم جلوس همایون موافق سنه هزار و پنجاه و هشت بفر قدوم میمنت لزوم گیتي خدیوگیهان خداوند باني این مباني آسماني شهاب الدین محمد صاحبقران ثاني شاهجهان بادشاه غازي در فیض بر روی جهانیان بگشاد -

Translation.

"God is pure! How beautiful are these painted mansions and charming residences. They are a part of the high heaven. I may say the high-souled holy angels are desirous of looking at them; if the residents of different parts and directions of the world should come to walk round them, as [they walk] round the old house [*kaba*][1] it would be allowable; or if the beholders of the two worlds should run to kiss their highly glorious threshold as [they kiss] the black stone [of the *kaba*], it would be proper. The commencement of this great Fort, which is higher than the palace of the heavens and is the envy of the wall of Alexander; and of this pleasant edifice; and of the Hayat Bakhsh (life bestowing) garden, which is to these buildings as the soul is to the body, and the lamp to an assembly; and of the pure canal, the limpid water of which is to the person possessing sight as a mirror showing the world, and to the wise, the unveiler of the secret world; and of the water-cascades, each of which you

[1] The mosque at Mecca.

may say is the whiteness of the dawn, or a tablet containing secrets of the Table and Pen [of Fate]; and of the fountains, each of which is a hand of light inclined to shake hands with the inhabitants of heavens, or is a string of bright pearls made to descend to reward the inhabitants of the earth; and of the tank, full to the brim of the water of life and in its purity the envy of light and the spring of the sun, announced on the 12th Zilhajjah in the 12th year of the holy ascension, corresponding to 1048 A.H., the tidings of happiness to men. The completion of it, at the expense of fifty lacs of rupees, by the power of the auspicious feet of the sovereign of the earth, the lord of the world, the originator of these heavenly buildings, Shihabuddin Muhammad, the second lord of felicity, Shah Jahan, the King, the champion of the faith, opened on the 24th Rabiu-l-Awwal in the 21st blessed year of the ascension, corresponding to 1058 A. H., the door of grace to the world."

(*g*) Excellent.

(*h*) "Protected Monument."

(*j*) The Tasbih Khana consists of three rooms facing the Diwan-i-Khas; the row of three rooms behind the former are known as the Khuwabgah, and the adjoining hall, half the width of the Khuwabgah is known as the Baithak, or Tosha Khana. The walls of the Khuwabgah are ornamented with an inlaid marble dado, while the north and south walls of the central room are provided with arched screens. The inscriptions on the arches are the work of Sadullah Khan, the *wazir* of Shah Jahan "the most able and upright minister that ever appeared in India" (Elphinstone), and who died in 1656 A.D. The verses on the wall, referred to in *Carr Stephen*, p. 235, have unfortunately disappeared. On the northern marble screen is a representation of the *Mizan-i-Adl* (Scales of Justice), which are suspended over a crescent surrounded with stars and clouds.

The two apartments on the west side have recently been furnished in the Mughal manner to assist visitors in revisualising the internal appointments of the Palace.

(*k*) *Annual* (1905-06) 30; (1907-08) 30 (King's private apartments).
As. Res., IV, 425 (Tusbeah Khanah).
Carr Stephen, 234.
Catalogue, 40, J. 21.
Cole (1st report), XXV.
Fanshawe, 37-38.
Hearn, 156.
Keene, 135.
Tavernier I, 101 (little chamber).
Von Orlich, II, 25 (Scales of justice).
Asar (1904), chap. II, 38-41, 43.

(*l*) 1699.

No. 18.

(*a*) Burj-i-Tila (Golden Tower) or Musamman Burj (Octagonal tower).

(*b*) Adjoining the eastern wall of the Khuwabgah.

(*c*) Archæological Department.

(*d*) I*a*.

(*e*) 1048-1058 A. H. (1639-1648 A.D.).

(*f*) On the western arch of the Musamman Burj.

(۱) اے بندبپائے و قفل بردل هشدار * وے دوخته چشم پائے درگل هشدار

(۲) عزم سفر مغرب و رو در مشرق * اے راه روے پشت بمنزل هشدار

Translation.

(1) "O! thou who hast fetters on thy legs, and a padlock on thy heart, beware! and O! thou who hast thine eyelids sewn up and feet in the mire, beware!"

(2) "Bound towards the west and having thy face to the east, O traveller who hast turned thy back on thy destination, beware!"

(*g*) Excellent.

(*h*) "Protected Monument."

(*j*) Three sides of the octagon have been cut off by the Khuwabgah. Four of these five sides are covered with marble screens and in front of the fifth, the central one, there is a small covered balcony. A "Musamman Burj" is also found in the palaces at Agra and Lahore and was generally used as the *jharoka* or 'showing place' wherein the King appeared daily to his subjects gathered on the low ground below. This ceremony was known as the *darshan* and was rigorously observed by the earlier Mughal Emperors, it being the only sign by which the people knew who was on the throne. The dome on this building is not the original one, but was erected after the Mutiny. The original dome was of different section, as may be seen from old photos taken prior to 1857, and covered with gilded copper.

(*k*) *Annual* (1905-06), 29-31.
Bernier, 267 (tower covered with plates of gold).
Cole (1st Report), XXV, CXCVIII.
Carr Stephen, 236.
Catalogue, 39 *et seq.*, J. 1, J. 56-7.

Fall of Moghul Empire, 183.
Fanshawe, 38.
Fergusson, II, 311.
Havell, 128. (Golden Pavilion.)
Hodges, 118.
Hearn, 156-158.
Prinsep, 27.
Asar (1904), chap. II, 41.

(*l*) 1526, 1527, 1901, 2332, 2495 (*jharoka* near to south of), 2503, 2505, 2564 (*jharoka* near).

No. 19. (*a*) Balcony.

(*b*) In front of Musamman Burj, overlooking the river.

(*c*) Archæological Department.

(*d*) I*a*.

(*e*) 1223 A.H. (1808-9 A.D.).

Khas Mahal, Lal Qila

Diwan-i-Khas, Lal Qila

(*f*) On the arches of the balcony.

(۱) ثنا و حمد سزاوار مالک الملکی * که کرد بادشه دهر همچو شاهنشه
(۲) کزاب وجدشه ابن شهنشه تا تیمور * جهان پناه فلک بارگه ستاره سپه
(۳) معین دین و ابوالنصر اکبر غازی * شه جهان و جهانگیر عهد ظل الله
(۴) بروے برج مثمن زنو مرتب ساخت * نشیمنے که درو چشم دوخت مهر و مه
(۵) بسید الشعرا کرد حکم تاریخش * که بر سفید بماند نوشته حرف سیه
(۶) نوشت مصرع تاریخ این بنا سید * بود نشیمنے عالی آساس اکبرشه
سنه ۱۲۲۳

Translation.

(1) "Praise and commendation are due to the Lord of the world (God) who made the King of the age one like the Emperor,"

(2) "Who is descended from a royal father and grand-father up to Timur, and is the protection of the world, having sky-like mansions and soldiers as (numerous as) stars,"

(3) "Muinu-d Din Abu-n Nasr Akbar, the champion of the faith, the king of the world, the world conqueror of the age, and the shadow of God,

(4) "On the face of the octagonal tower built anew, such a seat that the Sun and the Moon fixed their eyes on it."

(5) "The poet-laureate was ordered to find its date, in order that black letters may remain written on the white (ground)."

(6) "The chief (poet) wrote down as the chronogram of this buil ing 'The seat of exalted foundation is of Akbar Shah.' The year 1223."

(*g*) Excellent.

(*h*) "Protected Monument."

(*j*) The balcony was added by Akbar II who also engraved the inscription upon it, its miniature dome being of the curved Bengali type. It is interesting to note that Their Imperial Majesties King George V and Queen Mary appeared from this balcony to the multitude gathered below, December 1911, thus reviving the old *darshan* ceremony.

(*k*) *Carr Stephen*, 236.
Cole, 1st Report, XXV.
Fanshawe, 38.
Hearn, 156-158.
Keene, 136.
Asar (1904), chap. II, 41.

(*l*) 1526, 1527, 2332, 2505.

No. 20. (*a*) Diwan-i-Khas, or the "Hall of Private audience."

(*b*) On the east wall of the Fort between the Hammam and Musamman Burj.

(*c*) Archæological Department.

(*d*) I*a*.

(*e*) 1048-1058 A. H. (1639-1648 A. D.).

(*f*) Over the corner arches of the northern and southern walls, under the cornice, the following verse is written in duplicate:—

اگر فردوس بر روے زمین است * همین است و همین است و همین است

Translation.

"If there is a paradise on the face of the earth, it is this, it is this, it is this."

(*g*) Excellent.

(*h*) "Protected Monument."

(*j*) The Diwan-i-Khas was also known as the Shah Mahall or the Royal palace. It had two courtyards in front of it on the west, both enclosed by arcaded colonnades. The entrance to the courtyard nearest the Diwan-i-Khas and known as the *Jilau Khana* or "Abode of splendour" was on the west, and was kept screened by a red curtain (the *Lal Parda*). In this court the *Umaras* and nobles of highest rank were wont to wait on the Emperor. This Court, together with the lesser court which lay immediately to the west, was removed after the Mutiny, but from old plans, and ample evidence forthcoming in excavations, it has been possible to lay out the present lawns and shrubberies so as to demarcate with accuracy their former alignment.

The hall is 90′ in length, 67′ in width and stands on a plinth 4′ 6″ in height. Fergusson considers it "if not the most beautiful, certainly the most highly ornamented of all Shah Jahan's buildings." The central chamber measures 48′ by 27. The ceiling is flat and supported by engrailed arches. *Pietra dura* work is freely used on the lower portions of the arch piers, the upper portions being treated with gilding and painting. A marble water channel (the *Nahr-i-Bihisht*), 12′ in width, runs through the centre of the hall. The marble dais is said to have supported the famous peacock throne of Shah Jahan, removed by Nadir Shah in 1739. Over the arches at the northern and southern ends of the central chamber will be noticed the famous inscription of which the text is given above.

This building is perhaps bound up more closely than any other with the history of the Mughal Empire. The favourite resort of the Emperor who built it, it witnessed in turn the heyday and decline of the Empire. In it Nadir Shah received the submission of Muhammad Shah (Mughal Emperor 1719-1748 A. D.) in 1739 and deprived him of the most valuable treasures of his ancestors. It saw come and go the depredatory hordes of Jats, Marathas and Rohillas which harassed in turn the last Emperors of the house of Timur, and the blinding of the aged Shah Alam by the brigand Ghulam Qadir. In it Lord Lake was thanked for delivering the now tottering Empire from the house of Scindhia, while in May 1857 the mutineers chose it as the spot wherein to proclaim Bahadur Shah II once more Emperor of Hindustan, all unwitting that but some 7 months later he was to be tried in the same spot for his life.

(*l*) *Annual* (1906-07), 30.

Archer, I, III *et seq.*

A. S. I., IV 70.

As. Res. IV. 425 (Dewaun Khana), 427.

Auckland, 11.

Baxter, 29.

Bernier, 268 (*Gosel-Kane*), 266 (*Gosel Kanay*).

Carr Stephen, 227-232.

Catalogue, 39, *et seq.*, J. 7, J. 8, J. 22, J. 41, J. 43, J. 56.

Cities, 145.

Cole (1st Report), XXIV, CXCVI; (2nd report), CXII; (3rd report), XXI, CXLI.

Cooper, 25, 30, 44, 122.

Crane, 149.
C. S. Range, 252.
Fall of Moghul Empire, 11, 47, 160, 176, 179 *et seq*, 189.
Fanshawe, 33-37.
Fergusson, II, 311.
Gardens, 79, 124.
Havell, 86.
Hearn, 149-151.
Heber, II, 303.
Hoffmeister, 283.
Keene, 129, 131-135.
Manucci, II, 10, 361, 400, 422, 461; IV, 423.
Mundy, 38 *et seq*.
Oriental Annual (1835), 101; (1840) 25.
Pennell, 142.
Prinsep, 24, 46.
Roberts, II, 224.
Saladin, 577.
Sleeman, II, 276.
Thevenot, III, 42.
Tour, 151 (square enclosure paved with white marble).
Von Orlich, II, 24.
Wilson, 46.
Asar (1904), chap. II, 41-42.
Badshah Namah, I, part II, 237; II, 220.
Khazanah, 104.
Maasir, III, 464.
Salih, Fols. 579-580.

(*l*) 933, 934, 1179, 1526, 2229, 2470, 2495, 2505, 2506, 2560, 2561, 2562, 2573.

No. 21. (*a*) Nahr-i-Bihisht (Stream of Paradise).

(*b*) Passing from the Shah Burj through the Hammam, Diwan-i-Khas, Khuwabgah and Rang Mahal.

(*c*) Archæological Department.

(*d*) I*a*.

(*e*) 1048-1058 A.H. (1639-1648 A.D.).

(*f*) (See the inscription on the Khuwabgah, p. 16.)

(*g*) Good.

(*h*) "Protected Monument."

(*j*) A canal is mentioned in the inscription on the arches of the Khuwabgah. It has been termed the Nahr-i-Athar (pure canal), but the Nahr-i-Bihisht is probably meant, *Athar*, not being used as its name, but simply as an attribute.

(*k*) *Annual* (1904-05), 15 (channel); (1907-08) 26-27; (1910-11) for an account of history of the Canal, see "Shah Jahan's Fort, Delhi."
A. S. I., I, 219.
As. Res., IV, 418, 424 (aqueduct).
Auckland, 16, 17, 87. (Feroze Shah's Canal.)

Bernier, 257 (canal).
Carr Stephen, 228.
Cooper, 36.
C. S. Range, 257.
Fanshawe, 37.
Hearn, 157.
Heber, II, 288.
Keene, 7, 124 (masonry canal).
Manucci, I, 184; II, 463.
Roberts, II, 221.
Tavernier, I, 97 (channel).
Turks in India, 140.
Von Orlich, II, 23 (canal).
Wilson, 46.
Asar (1904), chap. II, 45, 53-54.
Salih, Fol. 579.

(*l*) 2262, 2686, 2689.

No. 22. (*a*) Hammam (Baths).
(*b*) To the North of Diwan-i-Khas.
(*c*) Archæological Department.
(*d*) I*a*.
(*e*) 1048-1058 A.H (1639-1648 A.D.).
(*f*) None.
(*g*) Excellent.
(*h*) "Protected Monument."
(*j*) The entrance to the baths faces the north wall of the Diwan-i-Khas, the two rooms on either side being said by tradition to have been used as baths for the royal children. The baths consist of three main apartments divided by corridors, the pavements, reservoirs, vapour slabs and walls, waist high, being of marble inlaid with vari-coloured stones. The apartment facing the river was known as the 'Aqab-i-Hammam, the apartment wherein garments were removed, and contains three fountain basins, one for the use of the rose water spray being of special interest. The marble lattice work of the window still exists, as do some of the old panes of coloured glass, too vivid in tone to be artistic. In the next apartment, there is a central basin only. This could be used for the hot or cold bath as desired. A marble couch of pleasing design still remains to show the character of the fittings such chambers contained. The westernmost compartment, used for the hot bath only, possesses a vapour slab of singular beauty, the heating arrangements being in the west wall. Light was admitted to these two apartments by stained glass windows of the type seen in the easternmost apartment. The Hammam were a favourite resort of the Mughal Emperors and in them business of a most important nature was often transacted. Sir Thomas Roe visited Jahangir in the Hammam in the palace at Agra. In the cold season they were also used, being warmed by means of stoves. Saiyyid Ahmad states that the Hammam were never warmed

after the reign of Shah Jahan and Aurangzeb, and adds that 125 *maunds* of firewood are required to heat them.

(*k*) *Annual* (1904-05), 17, 18; (1908-09), 2 (railing near).
As. Res., IV, 429.
Carr Stephen, 232-233.
Cities, 148.
Cole (1st Report), XXV, CXCVII.
Crane, 151.
Fanshawe, 38-39.
Hearn, 152-153.
Hoffmeister, 284.
Keene, 130.
Oriental Annual (1835), 102, 103.
Orlich, II, 25.
Pennell, 143.
Tour, 170.
Asar (1904), chap. II, 43-44.

(*l*) 2406, 2407.

No. 23. (*a*) Moti Masjid (Pearl Mosque).
(*b*) Immediately to west of the Hammam.
(*c*) Archæological Department.
(*d*) I*a*.
(*e*) 1070 A.H. (1659-60 A.D.).
(*f*) None.
(*g*) Excellent.
(*h*) "Protected Monument."
(*j*) The mosque was built by Aurangzeb at a cost of 160,000 rupees of the time. It was used as a private chapel of the Emperors of Delhi, while the female members of the household also attended prayers in it. The main entrance is in the eastern wall of the enclosure, and it is furnished with copper plated doors. There was also a passage in the northern wall of the enclosure, which was intended for the use of ladies. The mosque was damaged during the Mutiny and the original section of domes as they now stand does not resemble the original ones, which were covered with gilded copper plates. The *pietra dura* work has been considerably repaired.

(*k*) *Annual* (1903-04), 5, 22.
A. S. I., IV, plate X (Plan).
As. Res., IV, 429.
Baxter, 29.
Carr Stephen, 233.
Cities, 147.
Cole (1st Report), XXV, CXCVIII.
Cooper, 46.
Crane, 151.
C. S. Range, 260.
Fanshawe, 39.

Fergusson, II, 320.
Havell, 205.
Hearn, 14, 150.
Heber, II, 304 (private mosque).
Hoffmeister, 284.
Hodges, 119.
Pennell, 144.
Prinsep, 24.
Saladin, 576.
Tavernier, I, 101 (small well-built mosque).
Wilson, 46.
Asar (1904), chap. III, 73.
Alamgir Namah, 467-470.
(*l*) 928, 929, 2200.

No. 24. (*a*) Hayat Bakhsh (life bestowing) garden.
(*b*) To the north of the Moti Masjid.
(*c*) Archæological Department.
(*d*) I*a*.
(*e*) 1048-1058 A.H. (1639-1648 A.D.).
(*f*) None.
(*g*) Good. It has only been possible to reconstruct half of the garden to date, the remaining portion of it being occupied by barracks.
(*h*) "Protected Monument."
(*j*) The garden, as it now stands, has with its causeways and water channels been considerably reconstructed. In 1902 it lay buried under an accumulation of earth and debris and roads, and the causeway and channels had almost entirely disappeared. The work of its reconstruction was put in hand in 1904 and finished in 1911.
(*k*) *Annual* (1903-4), 21-2; (1904-5), 17; (1908-9), 1-3; (1909-10), 1 *et seq.*
Auckland, 11.
Cole (1st Report), XXV.
Crooke, 335.
Fanshawe, 23, 25, 39.
Fergusson, II, 310 (garden), 311.
Hearn, 155.
Heber, II, 303.
Keene, 136.
Manucci, II, 463.
Oriental Annual (1835), 101.
Orlich, II, 25.
Tour, 170-1.
Asar (1904), chap. II, 45-46.
Miftah, 254.
Salih, Fols, 580-2.
(*l*) 1185, 1365, 1406, 1407, 1408, 1631, 1657, 1658, 1697, 1865, 1937, 1938, 2199, 2224, 2394, 2395, 2405, 2553, 2564, 2574.

No. 25. (*a*) Hira Mahal.

(*b*) North of the Hammam.

(*c*) Archæological Department.

(*d*) II *a*.

(*e*) About 1258 A.H. (1842 A.D.).

(*f*) None.

(*g*) Good.

(*h*) "Protected Monument."

(*j*) A small marble pavilion measuring 22′ 3″ north and south by 19′ 4″ east and west with three open arches on each face, built by Bahadur Shah II. The work shows the contrast in the quality of late Moghal Architecture, as compared with that of the period of Shah Jahan. North of this building, and facing the main eastern causeway of the Hayat Bakhsh garden, stood the Moti Mahal (see old picture of the last wall of the Fort in the Delhi Museum). This was removed after the Mutiny and a battery erected on its site. This battery was removed in 1913, traces of the foundation of the Moti Mahal being disclosed.

(*k*) *Hearn*, p. 154.

Asar (1904), chap. III, 101.

(*l*) 1630, 2262, 2689.

No. 26. (*a*) Shah Burj.

(*b*) North of the Hira Mahall at the north-east corner of the Fort.

(*c*) Archæological Department.

(*d*) II*a*.

(*e*) 1048-1058 (1639-1648 A.D.).

(*f*) None.

(*g*) Fair, but has suffered considerably from occupation during the last 50 years.

(*h*) "Protected Monument."

(*j*) It is also called the "northern tower." The main portion now consists of two storeys only, the dome having disappeared after the Mutiny. The marble pavilion to the south is of singular beauty, although already showing signs of the decadence in architecture which culminated in reign of Aurangzeb. It measures some 69′ 2″ east and west by 33′ north and south. The centre of the north wall is occupied by a marble water cascade of pleasing design which slopes into a 'scalloped' marble basin. For many years after the Mutiny the building served as an officer's residence, but in 1904 its conservation was taken up, the marble cascade being reconstructed and modern additions removed. The earthquake of the same year so damaged the structure that it was necessary to take it almost all down and rebuild it. The grass terrace between this pavilion and the Hammam was laid out as it now exists in 1911. The *Nahr-i-Bihisht* (see p. 21), the famous canal which supplied the many fountains and water channels of the palace, also served this building and thence proceeded along the entire length of the east wall. The ceiling of the domed chamber behind the marble pavilion is decorated with glass work, and a small marble tank exists in the centre of the floor. The first storey chamber above it is surrounded by a pillared arcade. Old drawings show that the *chhatri* or pavilion on the roof said to have been removed to Meerut must have been very similar to that on the summit of the Asad Burj. In 1784, Jawan Bakht, the eldest son of Shah Alam, made his escape from this *Burj* by a ladder of turbans, and eluding the vigilance of his father's minister made his way to the English at Lucknow.

(*k*) *Annual* (1903-4), 22; (1904-5), p. 17; (1905-6), 1; (1907-8), 2; (1908-9), 1; (1909-10), 1 *et seq.*, 25 *et seq.*
As. Res., IV, 429.
Carr Stephen, 237.
Catalogue, 40 *et seq.*, J. 28, J. 55, J. 58.
Fall of Moghal Empire, 140.
Fanshawe, 39.
Fergusson, II, 311.
Hearn, 154.
Heber, II, 303-304.
Keene, 137.
Manucci, II, 463.
Oriental Annual (1837), 160 (Plate).
Asar (1904), chap. II, 48-9.

(*l*) 932, 1131, 1132, 1341, 1405, 1682, 1698, 1900, 2225, 2226, 2227, 2327, 2402, 2403, 2404, 2566.

No. 27. (*a*) Pavilion.
(*b*) Immediately north-west of the Shah Burj and on the north wall of the Fort.
(*c*) Military.
(*d*) II*b*.
(*e*) Late Mughal period.
(*f*) None.
(*g*) Fair. The modern additions should be removed and the building placed under the control of the Public Works Department.
(*h*) After this has been done it should be declared a "Protected Monument."
(*j*) The function of this building is unknown, but tradition says this quarter of the Fort was occupied by the residences of the King's sons in the earlier days. The building is now known as the 'Tea house.'

No. 28. (*a*) Sawan and Bhadon pavilions.
(*b*) To the north and south of the central tank in the Hayat Bakhsh garden.
(*c*) Archæological Department.
(*d*) I*a*.
(*e*) 1048-1058 A.H. (1639-1648 A. D.).
(*f*) None.
(*g*) Excellent.

(*h*) Protected.

(*j*) The pavilions, which measure 48′ 4″ by 35′ 3″, are built in white marble throughout. The northernmost contains a central tank with candle-niches, the other being supplied with a shallow central channel only. The water is intended to flow from them over candle-niches into the water causeway of the Hayat Bakhsh garden. The buildings have been considerably repaired during the last ten years, while the tanks have also been opened up. *Sawan* and *Bhadon* are the two rainy months in the Hindu calendar, and it is not known whether the buildings were so called on account of their water cascades, 'which represented the fall of rain,' or because they were used during the rainy season. It is also uncertain which is the 'Sawan' and which the 'Bhadon.'

(*k*) *Annual* (1903-04), 22; (1907-08), 2.
Cole (1st Report), CXCIX; (2nd Report), CXII.
Fanshawe, 39.
Fergusson, II, 311 (pavilions and kiosks).
Hearn, 155.
Keene, 137.
Asar (1904), chap. II, 46-8.

(*l*) 929, 930, 931, 937, 938, 1124, 1125, 1126, 1127, 1128, 1528, 2557, 2567.

No. 29. (*a*) Zafar Mahal Tank.

(*b*) In the centre of the Hayat Bakhsh garden.

(*c*) Archæological Department.

(*d*) I*a*.

(*e*) 1048-1058 A.H. (1639-1648 A.D.) (upper portion of parapet 1837-1857 A.D.).

(*f*) None.

(*g*) Good.

(*h*) Protected.

(*j*) The tank measures 158′ 3″ by 153′ and is surrounded with a scalloped border. The upper portion of its parapet was not included in the original work of Shah Jahan, and was probably added by Bahadur Shah II. The greater portion of it has been recently reconstructed.

(*k*) *Hearn*, 153-6.
Keene, 136.

(*l*) 2552.

No. 30. (*a*) Zafar Mahal.

(*b*) In the centre of the tank. (No. 29.)

(*c*) Archæological Department.

(*d*) II*a*.

(*e*) 1842 A.D. (Hearn).

(*f*) None.

(*g*) Poor.

(*h*) "Protected Monument."

(*j*) Built by Bahadur Shah II, the last Mughal Emperor. It stands in the centre of the large tank in the Hayat Bakhsh garden, and was called after him Zafar Mahal, Zafar being his poetical name. It is of red sandstone and of but poor design, consisting of a central hall with small rooms at the north and south sides. It was reached by means of a bridge, which has now disappeared, while the central hall has lost its roof. It was used as a military swimming bath for many years.

(k) *Annual* (1903-1914), 22; (1904-1905), 17.
Hearn 155-156.
Keene 136.
Asar (1904), chap. III, 100-101.

(l) 925, 936, 1129, 1130, 2337, 2552.

No. 31. (a) *Baoli* (stepped well).

(b) On the parade ground west of the Hayat Bakhsh's garden.

(c) Archæological Department.

(d) II*a*.

(e) Late Afghan (?).

(f) None.

(g) Fair.

(h) Unnecessary.

(j) The *Baoli* consists of an octagonal shaft 21′ 4″ in diameter and 46′ 10″ deep, and an adjoining tank measuring 20′ 0″ by 20′ 0″. At a depth of 27′ 5″ an arch in the northern wall permits water from the well to run into the tank to a specified height. This is so arranged in order that the well-proper should retain its natural depth of water, while bathers might use the tank in safety. At the north and west of the tank are flights of steps with arched apartments at either side. Both the well and the tank are now roofed with corrugated iron sheeting, and supply water to the gardens within the Archæological area. The whole is enclosed by a modern iron railing.

No. 32. (a) Mosque (unnamed).

(b) South of *Chhatta Chauk*, in the Supply and Transport enclosure.

(c) Military.

(d) II*b*.

(e) 1837-1857 A.D.

(f) None.

(g) Poor; the modern additions require to be removed and repairs effected.

(h) Should be declared protected.

(j) The mosque measures 42′ 6″ by 24′ 0″ and was erected by Bahadur Shah II, the last Mughal Emperor. There is no courtyard to the mosque; the prayer chamber covered by a flat roof consists of two aisles, each with five arches and is now used as a godown by the Supply and Transport Department.

(l) *S.* 22.

CITY (SOUTH OF CHANDNI CHAUK).

(NOTE.—The name of the *Muhalla* or quarter in which the monument or monuments are situated is given in the centre of the page in Capitals.)

DARYAGANJ.

No. 33. (*a*) Sonehri Masjid (Golden Mosque) I.

(*b*) About a hundred yards to south of the Delhi Gate of the fort.

(*c*) Archæological Department.

(*d*) II *a*.

(*e*) 1164 A. H. (1751 A.D.).

(*f*) On the central arch.

(۱) شکر حق در عہد احمد شاہ غازي بادشاہ * خلق پرور دادگر شاہان عالم را پناہ

(۲) مسجدی کردہ بنا نواب قدسي منزلت * باد دایم فیض عام آن ملایک سجدہ گاہ

(۳) سعي نواب بہادر صاحب لطف و کرم * ساخت تعمیری چنین جاوید عالي دستگاہ

(۴) چاہ و حوض صاف صحنش آبروی زمزم است * ہر کہ از آبش طہارت کرد شد پاک از گناہ

(۵) سال تاریخش چہ خرم یافت از إلہام غیب * مسجدی بیت المقدس مطلع نور الہ

Translation.

(1) "Thanks be to God! in the reign of Ahmad Shah, who is a champion of the faith, a king, a cherisher of the people, a doer of justice, and a protection to the kings of the world."

(2) "Nawwab Qudsi (of divine) dignity built this mosque; may the common favour of that place of adoration of angels be everlasting."

(3) "The exertions of the courteous and benevolent Nawwab Bahadur (named) Jawid, of exalted power, constructed such an edifice."

(4) "The clean well and tank of its court are an honour to Zamzam[1]; whoever washed himself with its water became clean of his sins."

(5) "How beautifully! Khurram obtained the year of its foundation, from the invisible inspiration; '(it is) the mosque of Jerusalem, the rising place of the divine light.'"

(*g*) Good. The minarets are slightly out of the perpendicular but it is not supposed that they are sufficiently so to be in any danger of falling.

(*h*) Protected Monument.

(*j*) The mosque measures some 50′ 0″ east and west by 15′ 0″ north and south and is one of the three mosques in Delhi bearing this name. It consists of a main prayer chamber with two minarets and three domes, a courtyard without walls, and a gateway towards the east. The domes were originally covered with copper gilt plates, but when the mosque was repaired by Bahadur Shah II in 1852, he covered the ruined domes with sandstone. In the inscription on its central arch two personages are referred to: one Nawwab Qudsiya Begam, who built it, and the other Nawwab Bahadur, under whose supervision the work of construction was carried out.

---

[1] Zamzam is a famous well at Mecca, held in great sanctity by Muhammadans.

Nawwab Qudsiya Begam, the mother of Ahmad Shah, was originally a dancing girl. She was introduced into Muhammad Shah's *harem* in the beginning of his reign, and received the title of Udham Bai, and for some time remained the favoured one in the sight of the Emperor. But her good fortune deserted her, she lost all her former influence and station and eventually was not allowed to see her own son Ahmad Shah. When, however, he ascended the throne, she became once more influential, till at last she surpassed all the Begams. She possessed a *mansab* of 50,000 and owing to her intimacy with Nawwab Bahadur Jawid Khan she became supreme and practically took over the reins of government, the Emperor being ruler only in name. At last her high and undue aspirations brought about the downfall of her son with whom she was imprisoned and blinded. Notwithstanding her humble origin, she had much to commend her and was extremely generous to the young children and Begams of the deceased Emperor Muhammad Shah.

Jawid Khan was the chief eunuch of Muhammad Shah, and had the entire management of the *harem* and the entrée to the women's apartments. He could neither read nor write, but on the accession of Ahmad Shah he so influenced that Emperor that he appointed him Darogha of the Diwan-i-Khas[1] with a *mansab* of 6,000. In the days of his former master he had carried on a secret intimacy with Ahmad Shah's mother. He now openly governed the realm in concert with her, and contrary to the custom of the *harem*, remained in the women's apartments all night. His audacity excited the hatred and jealousy of the nobles and other officers who conspired and killed him.

(*k*) *Asar* (1904), chap. III, 37.
Carr Stephen, 275.
Fanshawe, 43.
Hearn, 15, 162.
Keene, 16.
Rodgers, 94.

(*l*) *S. I.*

PARADE GROUND.

No. 34. (*a*) Grave (unknown).

(*b*) Behind Sonehri Masjid of Jawid Khan.

(*c*) Archæological Department.

(*d*) III *a*.

(*e*) C. 1748 A. D.

(*f*) None.

(*g*) Good.

h) Unnecessary.

(*j*) The tomb is marked by a ruined masonry enclosure not more than one foot in height. The grave possesses a white marble *tawiz* in excellent condition. Local tradition assigns this tomb to Bagwa Begam, a daughter of Muhammad Shah. Before the Mutiny the spot where the tomb is found was called the Bagwa Bari, after the name of the same Bagwa Begam.

k) *Asar* (1847), chap. III, p. 39.

---

[1] See Bernier.

No. 35. (*a*) Grave.

(*b*) Near the Sonehri Masjid to the east.

(*c*) Not known.

(*d*) III*b*.

(*e*) 1141 A. H. 6th Rajab (5th February 1729 A.D.).

(*f*) "Throne verse", then "Darud" and after that

.... بیست و نه ساله و چهار ماه سنه ۱۱۴۱ هجري بتاریخ ششم رجب

Translation.

"........Aged twenty-nine years and four months, on the sixth Rajab of the year 1141 Hijra."

(*g*) Fair.

(*h*) Unnecessary.

(*j*) The inscription is written round the *Tawiz*, and partly obliterated. The name of the deceased is not known.

No. 36. (*a*) Zinat-ul-Masajid.

(*b*) Near the Khairati Ghat or Masjid Ghat close to the city wall.

(*c*) Archæological Department.

(*d*) II*a*.

(*e*) C. 1707 A.D.

(*f*) None.

(*g*) Fair.

(*h*) "Protected monument" (?)

(*j*) This mosque was built by Zinatu-n-nisa Begam, the daughter of Alamgir Aurangzeb with a neighbouring tomb in which she was buried. The latter was removed when the mosque was used for military purposes after the Mutiny of 1857. There was an inscription on the tomb, dated 1122 A. H. (1710-11 A. D.). The mosque is situated on a commanding position and consists of a prayer chamber with seven arches and three domes; there are two large minars and a court-yard and central tank on the river side. There are, beneath the courtyard, thirteen rooms, terminating on the south and north with two arched entrances leading up to the court of the mosque. It is built of red sandstone, with the exception of the domes which are banded with black and white marble. For many years after the Mutiny the mosque was used as a bakery for troops.

(*k*) *Annual* (1902-3), 25.
A. S. I., I, 225; IV, 70.
As. Res. IV, 70, 423.
Carr Stephen, 261.
Cole (1st Report), XXVI, CXCXIX.
Fanshawe, 68.
Hearn, 16, 163.
Ind. Ant. XXV (1901), 79.
Keene, 16.
Rodgers, 93.
Asar (1904), chap. III, 78.

FAIZ BAZAR.

No. 37. (*a*) Mosque (unnamed).

(*b*) At the point where the Faiz Bazar and Daryaganj roads meet.

(*c*) Waqf, Mutawalli Yatimkhana.

(*d*) III.

(*e*) Late Mughal.

(*f*) None.

(*g*) Fair.

(*h*) Unnecessary.

(*j*) The mosque is of no especial interest. It is said to have been built by one Kallu, tobacco seller.

No. 38. (*a*) Dargah Shah Sabir Bakhsh, mosque and Musafirkhana.

(*b*) On Faiz Bazar Road.

(*c*) Waqf, Mutawalli Shah Amir Husain, a descendant of the founder.

(*d*) III.

(*e*) 1133 A. H. (1720-1 A.D.).

(*f*) None.

(*g*) Good.

(*h*) Unnecessary.

(*j*) The whole group of buildings is known after the name of Shah Sabir Bakhsh a saint of the time of Akbar II. The Musafirkhana bears, on the outside of its back wall, a modern inscription dedicating it to Mahbub Ali Khan, the Nizam of Hyderabad, but the building is really older. There are several other inscriptions but none of them of any historical interest. On the arches of the mosque are inscribed extracts from the Quran, but on the central one the date 1133 A. H. is also to be found. At the head of the graves, built into the wall, there is an inscribed slab of stone containing quotations from the Quran and an extract from the Munajat of Shaikh Fariduddin Attar. This inscription is said to have been written and sent by Bahadur Shah II.

Shah Sabir Bakhsh was a well-known saint of his time and belonged to a family long noted for its piety. He died on the 14th Rabi I of the year 1237 A. H. (7th December 1821 A. D.) during the reign of Bahadur Shah II.

(*k*) *Asar* (1847), chap. IV, 40—42.

(*l*) *Mazarat*, part II, 25-26.

No. 39. (*a*) Sonehri Masjid (Golden mosque) II, also called Qazi-Zadon-ki-Masjid.

(*b*) On the north side of the Faiz Bazar.

(*c*) Waqf, Mutawalli Hashmatullah in Hyderabad State service.

(*d*) II*b*.

(*e*) 1157 A.H. (1744—5 A.D.).

(*f*) On the central arch.

(۱) شکر حق کز یمن فیض سید عرفان پناہ * شاہ بہیکہ آن مرشد کامل ولایت دستگاہ

(۲) در زمان شاہ اسکندر نشان جمشید قدر * معدلت گستر محمد شاہ غازی بادشاہ

(۳) روشن الدولہ ظفر خان صاحب جود وکرم * کرد تعمیر طلای مسجد عرش اشتباہ

(۴) مسجدی کند رفضای صحن قدرش آسمان * کرده از خط شعاع مهر جاروبی پگاه

(۵) حوض صاف او نشان از چشمه کوثر دهد * هر که از آبش وضو سازد شود پاک از گناه

(۶) سال تاریخش رسایی یافت از الهام غیب * مسجد چون بیت اقصی مهبط نور الله

سنه ۱۱۵۷

Translation.

1 "Thanks be to God, that by the blessings of the grace of the *Sayyid*, a protection of the knowledge (of God), Shah Bhik who is a perfect and holy teacher;"

2 "In the reign of a king glorified like Alexander and dignified like Jamshid, the spreader of justice (named) Muhammad Shah, the champion of the faith and the king,"

3 "Raushan-ud-Daula Zafar Khan, the Lord of beneficence and bounty, built this golden mosque resembling heaven."

4 "Such a mosque that its dignified open courtyard the sky sweeps every morning with the pencil of the sun's rays."

5 "Its clear tank represents the stream of Paradise, whoever performed ablutions with its water became pure of his sins."

6 "The date of its foundation Rasai obtained from the invisible inspiration; '(It is a) mosque like the mosque of Jerusalem where the light of God descends'. The year 1157."

(*g*) Good (but has been spoilt by coats of whitewash).

(*h*) Unnecessary.

(*j*) The second Sonehri mosque in Shahjahanabad, and built by Raushan-ud-Daula Zafar Khan. It measures some 55′ 0″ north and south by 19′ 0″ east and west. Its domes were originally covered with copper gilt plates, which were afterwards placed on those of the Sonehri mosque near the Kotwali. The mosque was much dilapidated, but was repaired by Qazi Muhammad Faizullah.

The inscription on the central arch records the erection of the mosque by Raushan-ud-Daula Zafar Khan, in the reign of Muhammad Shah for Shah Bhik.

Raushan-ud-Daula's real name was Khuwaja Muzaffar. He belonged to the family of Naqshbandi Khuwajas. His grandfather Khuwaja Muhammad Nasir came to India during the reign of Shah Jahan, and was killed defending the palace gate of Sultan Shuja after the battle of Khajwa, fought between that prince and Aurangzeb. Abdul Qadir, the father of Muzaffar, is of no historical importance. He passed his life as a *Darwesh* and died during the reign of Farrukhsiyar. Muzaffar began his career in the service of Rafiushshan, the third son of Shah Alam Bahadur Shah I, when he rose to the rank of 1,500 and 500 horse, and obtained the title of Zafar Khan. After the prince was killed he left the service and joined Shah Bhik. When it was rumoured that Farrukhsiyar was marching from Patna to meet Jahandar Shah, he joined the former at the instance of Shah Bhik, and by the favour of Sayyid Husain Ali Khan of Barha was appointed the 3rd *Bakhshi*, and granted the rank of 5,000 and 5,000 horse and the title of "Zafar Khan Bahadur Rustam Jang." After Farrukhsiyar's victory over Jahandar Shah he was promoted to the rank of 7,000 and 7,000 horse and was given the title of Raushan-ud-Daula. During the reign of Muhammad Shah, Raushan-ud-Daula ingratiated himself with the Emperor's *Koka*(1) (a foster sister). She had great influence with the Emperor, and

(1) Name of the *koka* not given in the *Maasir*.

Raushan-ud-Daula made much money by bribes. During the reign of Muhammad Shah another title, that of 'Yar wafadar' (sincere friend), was given him. He was also known by the name of "Turrah Baz Khan" (the Khan fond of the tassel) because he, followed by his servants, wore a large number of tassels on his turban. He is said to have had no good qualities, save that he was extremely courteous and treated mendicants with great munificence. He died in the year 1149 A. H. (1736-7 A.D.).

Sayyid Muhammad Said (better known as Sayyid Miran Bhik), was a Sayyid by caste and a successor of Shah Abul Maali. The original home of his ancestors was Tirmiz, whence the head of his family, Sayyid Zaid, came with a large army to India with the intention of making a religious war against the infidels. They first stayed at Siwana, where the local Raja killed the Sayyid whilst at prayer; his sons waged war against the Raja with success, and took up their residence there. Shams-ud-Din Iltutmish the Emperor of Delhi, having heard of the excellent qualities and respectability of the brothers gave his daughter to one of them in marriage.

Shah Bhik is said to have performed a considerable number of miracles. He was born on the 9th of Rajab 1046 A. H. (27th March 1627 A.D.), and died at the age of 84 on the 5th of Ramazan 1131 A. H. (22nd July 1719 A.D.). He had a large number of disciples, one of whom was Raushan-ud-Daula, who built his tomb at Gharam.

(*k*) *Carr Stephen*, 273-274.
Asar, (1904), chap. III, p. 90.
Khazina, part I, 489-494.
Maasir II, 333-336.

(*l*) S. 63.

DELHI GATE.

No. 40. (*a*) Nabi Bakhsh's Mosque.

(*b*) Close to the Delhi Gate and Octroi Station.

(*c*) Waqf, Mutawalli, Salimuddin Saqqa.

(*d*) III.

(*e*) Late Mughal.

(*f*) On the central arch.
Muhammadan creed and

نبی بخش سقالی بانی مسجد

Translation.

"Nabi Bakhsh the water-carrier (was) the founder of the mosque."

(*g*) Good.

(*h*) Unnecessary.

(*j*) The building is of no special interest. It is said to have been rebuilt by Nabi Bakhsh Saqqa (water-carrier); it stood originally on the site of the present Octroi Station.

No. 41 (*a*) Delhi Gate.

(*b*) The southern gate of Shahjahanabad.

(*c*) Municipality.

(*d*) IIa.

(*e*) 1638—1649 A. D.

(*f*) None.

(*g*) Fair.

(*h*) Should be declared a "Protected Monument."

(*j*) So called the Delhi Gate because it opens towards the old cities of Delhi. Built in local stone and of simple design. The fourteen gates of Shahjahanabad are as below—

II.—Mori Gate to north; demolished in 1867, and the grounds behind the gate opened out. (See *A. S. res.* IV, 419.)

III.—Kabul Gate to west; the rest of the above remark applies to this gate. (See *A. S. res.* IV, 419; *Sleeman* II, 222.)

IV.—Lahore Gate[1], to west. (See *A. S. res.* IV, 419, 424; *Archer* I, 125; *Heber* II, 305.

V.—Ajmer Gate, to south-west.

VI.—Turkman Gate, to south.

VII.—Kashmir Gate, to north.

VIII.—Khairati Gate, to east.

IX.—Raj Ghat Gate, to east on river face.

X.—Calcutta Gate, to north-east, now no longer in existence; built in 1852.

XI.—Kela Ghat Gate, to north-east, on river face.

XII.—Nigambodh Gate, to north-east, on river face.

XIII.—Pathar Ghati Gate, destroyed.

XIV.—Badar Rau Gate, to north-east.

The *khirkis* or wickets constructed for the convenience of residents of the different *muhallas* may be enumerated as follows:—

I.—Khirki Zinat-ul-masjid, under the mosque of that name.

II.—Khirki Nawwab Ahmad Bakhsh Khan.

III.—Khirki Nawwab Ghazi-ud-din Khan.

IV.—Khirki Nasirganj.

V.—Khirki Nai.

VI.—Khirki Shahganj.

VII.—Khirki Ajmer Gate.

VIII.—Khirki Sayyid Bhola.

IX.—Khirki Baland Bagh.

X.—Khirki Farrash Khanah.

XI.—Khirki Amir Khan.

XII.—Khirki Khalil Khan.

XIII.—Khirki Bahadur Ali Khan.

XIV.—Khirki Nigambodh.

(*k*) *Archer*, I. 105 (glacis round the city walls); 125 (Agra Gate).

A. S. I., I, 224—5 (and also all city gates).

As. res. IV, 419, 424.

Catalogue, 40, J. 17.

C. S. Range, 243.

Orlich, II, 20.

Heber, II, 290, 306 (Agra Gate).

(1) The Lahore Gate is no longer in existence.

Cooper, 33 (City gates).
Hearn, 67.
Fanshawe, 8, 43, 183, 184, 222.
Keene, 16.
Pennel, 147.

(*l*) S. 15.

No. 42. (*a*) Jain temple.
(*b*) At the Delhi Gate.
(*c*) Lala Isridas, servant, Treasury, Delhi.
(*d*) III.
(*e*) Late Mughal (?)
(*f*) The Samvat year on the oldest image is 1830 as far as I know.

On the images to the visitor's left are inscribed the Samvat years, 1960, 1935, 1935, and on those to his right the years 1930, 1930, 1935. On other three images the date is: Samvat 1967, Falguna Sukla, 3.

(*g*) Good.
(*h*) Unnecessary.
(*j*) There are 24 images of *tirthankaras* in the sanctum. Those of black marble are of Neminatha. Among the images to the visitor's left, the middle one is of Adinatha, that to the left is of Neminatha and that to the right is of Saptrshi.

The temple has some carved ornament representing creepers and flowers. The roof is painted. It is said that after the foundation of the Jain temple near the Fort (No. 333) a dispute arose in the Jain community, resulting in the foundation of two sects. One [remained in possession of the old building, the other erected the temple under reference.

JATWARA, NEAR DELHI GATE.

No. 43. (*a*) Gaddiyan's Mosque.
(*b*) Katra Hakim Muhsin Khan.
(*c*) Waqf, Mutawalli Abdul Hafiz.
(*d*) III.
(*e*) Late Mughal.
(*f*) None.
(*g*) Good.
(*h*) Unnecessary.
(*j*) The building is of no special interest.

CHHATTA LAL MIYAN.

No. 44. (*a*) Qassaban's (Butchers') Mosque.
(*b*) Close to the city wall.
(*c*) Waqf, Mutawalli, people of the Muhalla.
(*d*) III.

(e) Late Mughal.
(f) None.
(g) Good.
(h) Unnecessary.
(j) The building is of no special interest.

No. 45. (a) Mosque (known as the Chhoti Masjid) I.
(b) In the *Muhalla*.
(c) Waqf, Mutawalli, Ahmad Husain.
(d) III.
(e) Late Mughal.
(f) None.
(g) Fair.
(h) Unnecessary.
(j) The building which measures 25′ 0″ north and south by 10′ 0″ east and west, is of no special interest.

No. 46. (a) Mosque Bhatyariwali.
(b) *Muhalla* Chauhan.
(c) Waqf, Mutawalli, Ali Ahmad Khan.
(d) III.
(e) Late Mughal.
(f) None.
(g) Good.
(h) Unnecessary.
(j) The building which measures some 20′ 0″ north and south by 12′ 8″ east and west, is of no special interest.

MUHALLA DHOBIAN.

No. 47. (a) Masjid Dhobian (washermen's mosque).
(b) Near Delhi Gate.
(c) Waqf, Mutawalli, Ahmad Husain and Allahdiya.
(d) III.
(e) Late Mughal.
(f) None.
(g) Good.
(h) Unnecessary.
(j) The building measures 24′ 3″ north and south by 11′ 0″ east and west, is of no special interest.

KUNCHA-I-SADULLAH KHAN.

No. 48. (a) Unchi Masjid I.
(b) On the Phul-ki-Mandi Road.

(c) Waqf.
(d) III.
(e) Late Mughal.
(f) None.
(g) Good.
(h) Unnecessary.
(j) The building measures some 23′ 0″ square. It is of no special interest.

TIRAHA BAIRAM KHAN.

No. 49. (a) Mosque Daiwali.
(b) In the Muhalla.
(c) Waqf, Mutawalli, Maulvi Misbahuddin.
(d) III.
(e) 1064 A. H. (1653—1654 A. D.).
(f) On the Central Arch.

(۱) شکر اللّٰه که گشت این مسجد * از شرف سجده گاه اهل نظر
(۲) سال تاریخ او خرد گفتا * گشته آباد کعبهٔ دیگر
سنه ۱۰۶۴

Translation.

(1) "Thanks be to God that this mosque, through its glory, became a place of adoration to the saintly persons."
(2) "Wisdom said the year of its foundation 'Another Kaba has been populated.' The year 1064."
(g) Fair.
(h) Unnecessary.
(j) A large building measuring some 44′ 0″ by 16′ 0″. It has no historical or any other interesting event connected with it.
(k) *Asar* (1847), chap. III, 31.
(l) S. 4.

No. 50. (a) House of Jawwad-ud-Daulah Arif Jang Dr. Sir Sayyid Ahmad, Khan Bahadur, K.C.S.I.
(b) Near Auliya Mosque.
(c) Sayyid Ross Masud.
(d) III.
(e) Late Mughal.
(f) None.
(g) Fair.
(h) Unnecessary.
(j) Sayyid Ahmad Khan was a well-known and recognised leader of the Indian Muhammadans towards the close of the 19th century. The original home of his ancestors was Arabia, whence they removed to Herat. They came to India during the reign of Akbar, from which time they enjoyed Royal titles and dignity. During the reign of Alamgir II, the

grandfather of Sayyid Ahmad Khan received the title of Jawwad-ud-Daulah and the rank of one thousand foot and five hundred horse After the death of his grandfather, his father Sayyid Muhammad Muttaqi-Khan Bahadur, enjoyed the same rank of Mansab at the time of Shah Alam II, and after the death of the latter the same hereditary title was conferred upon him. After the abolition of the Mughal rule in India Sayyid Ahmad Khan was treated with favour by the British Government, which recognized his services by conferring upon him the K.C.S.I.

Sayyid Ahmad Khan is chiefly known for the disinterested devotion with which he applied himself to the cause of his community and the good of the general public. In 1877 he founded the M. A. O. College at Aligarh. He so successfully directed his efforts, by his own example and instruction as to infuse his co-religionists with a new spirit and with loyalty to the Government. He died in 1898 at Aligarh and is buried within the precincts of the college, near the mosque.

He is equally known for his literary pursuits. His famous work Asaru-s-Sanadid, the first book written on the Archæology of Delhi, was much appreciated in England and the degree of L.L.D. was conferred upon him. He was elected an Honorary Member of the Royal Asiatic Society of London in the year 1864.

No. 51. (a) House of Nawwab Dabir-ud-Daulah Amin-ul-Mulk Khuwaja Farid-ud-Din Ahmad Khan Bahadur Muslih-i-Jang.

(b) Near the Auliya Mosque.

(c) Shaikh Nasir Ali.

(d) III.

(e) Late Mughal.

(f) None.

(g) Fair.

(h) Unnecessary.

(j) The house originally belonged to Mahdi Quli Khan, but was afterwards purchased by Nawwab Dabir-ud-Daula. The Nawwab was a man of considerable importance in the last century. He was deputed by the British East India Company as their Ambassador to the Court of the King of Persia when the ambassador of the latter was killed in a brawl in Bombay. He acquitted himself of his charge to the entire satisfaction of his employers and on return from Persia was appointed to a political agency at Ava. After this, in later times, he held the office of Prime Minister of Akbar II. He was the maternal grandfather of Sayyid Ahmad Khan, the author of Asaru-s Sanadid.

(k) Asar, (1847), chap. III, p. 31 ; and see preface (1904).

No. 52. (a) Masjid Khajur wali I (Mosque of palm-tree).

(b) Near Kamrai-Bangash.

(c) Waqf, Mutawalli, Anjuman-al-Islam.

(*d*) III.
(*e*) Late Mughal.
(*f*) On the entrance.

این هر شش دوکانها مع چاه و بالاخانه وقف مسجد اند -

Translation.

"All these six shops with the well and the upper storey are dedicated to the mosque."

(*g*) Good.
(*h*) Unnecessary.
(*j*) The mosque measures 33′ 9″ north and south by 14′ 4″ east and west. On the entrance to the mosque there is an inscription as above, but it has no historical value.

No. 53. (*a*) Rang Mahal.
(*b*) In the ***Muhalla.***
(*c*) Maulvi Maslahuddin.
(*d*) III.
(*e*) Mughal.
(*f*) None.
(*g*) Ruinous.
(*h*) Unnecessary.
(*j*) The Rang Mahal and the other adjacent buildings have undergone a total change. They were built by a descendant of Bairam Khan, Khan Khanan, the brother-in-law of Humayun and Regent of the empire till Akbar could act for himself. Only a very small portion of the Mahal now remains.

MUHALLA REKAB.

No. 54. (*a*) Mosque (unnamed).
(*b*) In the ***Muhalla.***
(*c*) Waqf, Mutawalli, Karim Bakhsh, butcher.
(*d*) III.
(*e*) Late Mughal (?).
(*f*) None.
(*g*) Good.
(*h*) Unnecessary.
(*j*) The building measures 26′ 0″ north and south by 11′ 0″ east and west. It is of no special interest.

HAVELI MIR KHAN.

No. 55. (*a*) Mosque, called Shish Mahal-ki-Masjid.
(*b*) Muhalla Teliyan.
(*c*) Waqf, Mutawalli, Muhammad Awan.
(*d*) III.
(*e*) Late Mughal.

(*f*) None.
(*g*) Poor.
(*h*) Unnecessary.
(*j*) The building measures 18′ 0″ north and south by 10′ 9″ east and west. It is of no special interest.

No. 56. (*a*) Rang Mahal of Mirza Ilahi Bakhsh.
(*b*) In the *Muhalla.*
(*c*) Nawwab Malka Jahan Begam and Nawwab Badshah Jahan Begam, daughters of Mirza Suraiya Jah, the son of Mirza Ilahi Bakhsh.
(*d*) III.
(*e*) Late Mughal.
(*f*) None.
(*g*) Fair.
(*h*) Unnecessary.
(*j*) The Mahal is said to have been built by Prince Mirza Jamshid Bakht, otherwise known as Mirza Kura, son of Shah Alam II. It was purchased by Ilahi Bakhsh and was inherited by Suraiya Jah.

No. 57. (*a*) Chandni Mahal.
(*b*) In the *Muhalla.*
(*c*) Nawwab Malka Jahan and Badshah Jahan Begam.
(*d*) III.
(*e*) Late Mughal.
(*f*) None.
(*g*) Poor.
(*h*) Unnecessary.
(*j*) It is said to have been built in the time of the Muhammad Shah, and was in the possession of Prince Salim Shah, son of Akbar II. One of the princes, Mirza Gauhar, acquired it through his sister Husaini Begam, the wife of Prince Salim Shah. It was afterwards sold to Mirza Suraiya Jah.

No. 58. (*a*) Shish Mahal.
(*b*) In the *Muhalla.*
(*c*) Nawwab Malka Jahan and Badshah Jahan Begam.
(*d*) III.
(*e*) Late Mughal.
(*f*) None.
(*g*) Ruinous.
(*h*) Unnecessary.
(*j*) It is said to have been built in the time of the Emperor Muhammad Shah, and was then possesed by one Mirza Khurshid Irani. Afterwards it was sold by auction and purchased by Mirza Suriya Jah. Only the southern wall of the Mahal is now extant.

KUNCHA-I-BAQAULLAH.

No. 59. (*a*) House of Mirza Khujista Bakht, son of Shah Alam II.
(*b*) In the *Muhalla*.
(*c*) Bishambar Nath Basheshwar Nath.
(*d*) III.
(*e*) 1246 A.H. (1830-1 A.D.).
(*f*) None.
(*g*) Good.
(*h*) Unnecessary.
(*j*) The house of Mirza Khujista Bakht, son of Shah Alam II and brother of Akbar II. The date of its erection is known as مکان خجستہ بنیاد (The house of auspicious foundation.)
(*k*) *Asar* (1847), chap. III, 30.

KUNCHA-I-CHELAN.

No. 60. (*a*) Mosque (unnamed).
(*b*) Rang Mahal.
(*c*) Waqf, Mutawalli, Khalil-ur-Rahman.
(*d*) III.
(*e*) Late Mughal.
(*f*) None.
(*g*) Good.
(*h*) Unnecessary.
(*j*) The mosque measures 26′ 3″ north and south by 19′ 0″ east and west. It is said to have been built by Mufti Mir Lal a man of great fame and learning. His real name was Sayyid Rahmat Ali Khan, and he had the title of Siraj-ul-Ulama Ziya-ul-Fuqaha.
(*k*) *Asar*, (1847), chap. IV, 127-128.

No. 61. *a*) Kaharwali Mosque.
(*b*) Near Gali Auliya.
(*c*) Waqf, Mutawalli, Badrul Islam.
(*d*) III.
(*e*) Late Mughal.
(*f*) None.
(*g*) Good.
(*h*) Unnecessary.
(*j*) The mosque is said to have been built by one Rahimullah Khan. It measures 37′ 9″ north and south by 10′ 10″ east and west. It is of no special interest.

No. 62. (*a*) Aqa Masita's Mosque.
(*b*) Near the "Comrade" office.
(*c*) Waqf, Mutawalli, Hafiz Ghiyas-ud-din.

(*d*) III.
(*e*) Late Mughal.
(*f*) None.
(*g*) Excellent.
(*h*) Unnecessary.
(*j*) The building measures 40′ 0″ north and south by 11′ 9″ east and west. It is of no special interest.

No. 63. (*a*) Mosque of Kale Khan.
(*b*) In the Muhalla.
(*c*) Waqf, Mutawalli, Mir Abdul Wahhab.
(*d*) III.
(*e*) Late Mughal.
(*f*) None.
(*g*) Good.
(*h*) Unnecessary.
(*j*) The building measures 29′ 2″ north and south by 12′ 8″ east and west. It is of no special interest.

PHUL-KI-MANDI.

No. 64. (*a*) Auliya Mosque.
(*b*) On the Phul-ki-Mandi Road.
(*c*) Waqf, Mutawalli, Hafiz Alahuddin.
(*d*) III.
(*e*) 1261 A. H. (1845 A.D.).
(*f*) None.
(*g*) Good.
(*h*) Unnecessary.
(*j*) The building measures 28′ 0″ north and south by 13′ 0″ east and west. It is of no special interest.
(*k*) *Asar*, (1847), chap. III, 31.

KUNCHA-I-FAULAD KHAN.

No. 65. (*a*) Khuwaja Mir Dard's Mosque.
(*b*) In Barah Dari.
(*c*) Waqf, Mutawalli, Mir Nasir Said, a descendant of Mir Dard.
(*d*) III.
(*e*) Late Mughal. (?)
(*f*) None.
(*g*) Fair.
(*h*) Unnecessary.
(*j*) The mosque was originally built by Khuwaja Mir Dard, a poet and saint. It was rebuilt some 45 years ago.

No. 66. (*a*) Hakim Agha Jan's mosque.

(*b*) Chhatta Agha Jan.

(*c*) Waqf, Mutawalli, Yusuf Beg.

(*d*) III.

(*e*) Mughal.

(*f*) None.

(*g*) Fair.

(*h*) Unnecessary.

(*j*) The mosque is said to have been built by Ihtiman Khan *Kotwal*, brother of Faulad Khan, in whose *Kuncha* (street) it lies. Its plinth is buried.

Ihtiman Khan *Kotwal* was a noble of the court of Shah Jahan. He rose from the rank of 1,200 and 500 *sawars* to 2,200 and 800 *sawars*, and twice held the post of *thanidar*. On this account he was probably called "Kotwal". He died in the year 1056 A. H. (1646 A. D.).

(*k*) *Maasir*, Vol. I, 160-162.

KUNCHA-I-NAHAR KHAN.

No. 67. (*a*) Mosque (unnamed).

(*b*) In the *Muhalla*.

(*c*) Waqf, Mutawalli, Abdul Qadir.

(*d*) III.

(*e*) Late Mughal.

(*f*) None.

(*g*) Good.

(*h*) Unnecessary.

(*j*) It is said to have been built by one Pirji Hasan Askari. The building measures 31' 6" north and south by 13' east and west. It is of no special interest.

KUNCHA-I-MAHR PARWAR.

No. 68. (*a*) Mosque (unnamed).

(*b*) In the *Muhalla*.

(*c*) Waqf, Mutawalli, Mirza Yaqub Beg.

(*d*) III.

(*e*) Late Mughal.

(*f*) None.

(*g*) Good.

(*h*) Unnecessary.

(*j*) A small building of no special interest.

KUNCHA-I-DAKHNI RAO.

No. 69. (*a*) Mosque (unnamed.)

(*b*) Near Church.

(*c*) Waqf.

(*d*) III.

(*e*) Late Mughal.
(*f*) None.
(*g*) Good.
(*h*) Unnecessary.
(*j*) The building measures 20′ 0″ north and south by 11′ 6″ east and west It is of no special interest.

NAQQAR KHANA ROAD.

No. 70. (*a*) Mosque (unnamed).
(*b*) Near the house of Nawwab Patodi.
(*c*) Waqf, Mutawalli, Mirza Bulaqi.
(*d*) III.
(*e*) Late Mughal.
(*f*) None.
(*g*) Good.
(*h*) Unnecessary.
(*j*) A large mosque with three domes and a spacious courtyard, with a tank at its eastern side. It stands on a raised piece of ground, and is entered from an eastern door, on either side of which are 10 stone steps leading to the courtyard of the mosque.
(*l*) S. 7.

KHIRKI OR HAVELI KHANDAURAN.

No. 71. (*a*) Mosque (unnamed).
(*b*) In the *Muhalla*.
(*c*) Waqf, Mutawalli, Wahid Ali.
(*d*) III.
(*e*) Late Mughal.
(*f*) None.
(*g*) Good.
(*h*) Unnecessary.
(*j*) The original mosque was built by one Agha Jan, but it was badly damaged and it has now been rebuilt. The building is small and of no special interest.

GALI GONDNI WALI.

(NEAR KALAN MAHAL.)

No. 72 (*a*) Mosque, Gondniwali I.
(*b*) In the *Muhalla*.
(*c*) Waqf, Mutawalli, Sarfraz Khan.
(*d*) III.
(*e*) Late Mughal.
(*f*) None.

(*g*) Good.
(*h*) Unnecessary.
(*j*) The original mosque was ruined; it has been recently rebuilt. It measures some 30′ 0″ north and south by 12′ 6″ east and west. It is of no special interest.

MUHALLA GARHAIYA
or
HAVELI NAWWAB AHMAD ALI KHAN.

No. 73. (*a*) Mosque (unnamed).
(*b*) In the *Muhalla*.
(*c*) Waqf, Mutawalli, Wazir Husain.
(*d*) III.
(*e*) (Date unknown.)
(*f*) None.
(*g*) Good.
(*h*) Unnecessary.
(*j*) The mosque is said to have been very old, but has been rebuilt.

KATRA GOKAL SHAH.

No. 74. (*a*) Mosque (unnamed).
(*b*) In the *Muhalla*.
(*c*) Waqf, Mutawalli, Hafiz Abdul Aziz.
(*d*) III.
(*e*) Late Mughal (?)
(*f*) None.
(*g*) Good.
(*h*) Unnecessary.
(*j*) The building measures 26′ 4″ north and south by 9′ 7″ east and west. It is of no special interest.

MATYA MAHAL.

No. 75. (*a*) Matya Mahal Mosque.
(*b*) In the *Muhalla*.
(*c*) Waqf, Mutawalli, Muhammad Karamullah.
(*d*) III.
(*e*) Date unknown.
(*f*) None.
(*g*) Good.
(*h*) Unnecessary.
(*j*) The original mosque was small, but it was rebuilt and extended by one Munshi Agha Jan, about the year 1248 A.H. (1832—1833 A.D.). Adjoining it, towards the north-west, is a large well called Banjaron-ki-baoli (stepped well) which is supposed to belong to the pre-Mughal

period. The condition of the well is much changed, a large portion of it having become commingled with the mosque.

No. 76. (*a*) Mosque (unnamed).

(*b*) In the compound of Nawwab Azizabadi-ki-haveli.

(*c*) Waqf, Mutawalli, Khurshid Ali Khan.

(*d*) III.

(*e*) Middle Mughal (?)

(*f*) None.

(*g*) Good.

(*h*) Unnecessary.

(*j*) A fairly large mosque with one dome and two minarets. It was badly ruined but one Maulvi Sadr-ud-Din Khan, the *Sadaru-s-sadur* of Shahjahanabad repaired and constructed a well in it. The *haveli* or the enclosure within which it lies possesses some historical interest, as it contains the ruins of some ancient buildings which are supposed to be the remains of the Matya Mahal after which the whole *muhalla* is named. Local tradition avers that the Matya Mahal was built as a temporary residence for Shah Jahan, while the fort was being built. It was, in later times, given to one Nawwab Azizabadi Begam who was in the *harem* of one of the Mughal princes, and was for this reason called Azizabadi-ki-haveli. Bahadur Shah II gave it to one of his grandsons, and after the Mutiny, when all the houses belonging to the Royal family were confiscated and sold, it was bought by Nawwab Dojana: the compound is now also known by the name of its present owner.

(*k*) *Asar*, (1847), chap. III, 20, 22.

(*l*) *S.* 5.

MUHALLA AZAM KHAN-KI-HAVELI.

No. 77. (*a*) Mosque Kunwewali.

(*b*) In the *Muhalla*.

(*c*) Waqf, Mutawalli, Munshi Yaqub Ali.

(*d*) III.

(*e*) 1266 A. H. (1849—50 A. D.).

(*f*) On the central arch.

(۱) اولیا نام زن صالحه کز دنیا * رفت و بر بستر آرام ته خاک بخفت

(۲) چو ز مال و زر او گشت بنا مسجد نو * دل من سال بنایش سبب تحسین گفت

Translation.

(1) "The saintly woman named Auliya departed from the world and slept on the bed of comfort, under ground."

(2) "As a new mosque was built out of her property and money, my heart spake the year of its foundation 'cause of praise.'"

(*g*) Good.

(*h*) Unnecessary.

(j) The mosque is small, and of but little importance historically. The inscription states that it was built by a woman named Auliya in the year 1266 A. H. (1849-50 A. D.).

No. 78. (a) Mosque (unnamed).
(b) Inside the *Muhalla*.
(c) Waqf, Mutawalli, Ahmad Husain.
(d) III.
(e) (Date unknown).
(f) None.
(g) Good.
(h) Unnecessary.
(j) Said to be the oldest mosque in the *Muhalla*. It is only a small building measuring some 14′ 0″×16′ 0″.

KALAN MAHAL.

No. 79. (a) Mosque, Jamanwali.
(b) Close to Kalan Mahal.
(c) Waqf, Mutawalli, Shafi-ul Hasan.
(d) III.
(e) Late Mughal.
(f) None.
(g) Good.
(h) Unnecessary.
(j) A small building of no special interest said to have been constructed originally by one Hakim Mina; it has been rebuilt.

MOCHION-KI-GALI.

No. 80. (a) Mosque (unnamed).
(b) In the *Muhalla*.
(c) Waqf, Mutawalli, Abdul Sattar.
(d) III.
(e) (Date unknown.)
(f) None.
(g) Fair.
(h) Unnecessary.
(j) The mosque, which is only a small structure, is of considerable antiquity, but has been rebuilt. On its central arch there is an inscription containing the *Kalima* only.

ROAD FROM JAMI MASJID TO DELHI GATE.

No. 81. (a) Mosque (unnamed).
(b) Between Kamra-i Bangash and Chitli Qabr.
(c) Waqf, Mutawalli, Yatim Khana.

(*d*) III.
(*e*) (Date unknown.)
(*f*) None.
(*g*) Good.
(*h*) Unnecessary.
(*j*) The original mosque, said to have been of considerable antiquity, was ruined. It has been rebuilt.

No. 82. (*a*) Mosque (unnamed).
(*b*) Between Kamra-i-Bangash and Chitli Qabr.
(*c*) Waqf, Mutawalli, Hafiz Ghiyas-ud-din.
(*d*) III.
(*e*) (Date unknown.)
(*f*) None.
(*g*) Good.
(*h*) Unnecessary.
(*j*) The original mosque is said to have been of some antiquity, but it was rebuilt by one Maulvi Muhammad Ishaq. It is a small building of no special interest.

No. 83. (*a*) Kamra-i-Bangash.
(*b*) See above.
(*c*) Shaikh Nasir Ali.
(*d*) III.
(*e*) Late Mughal.
(*f*) None.
(*g*) Fair.
(*h*) Unnecessary.
(*j*) This house was built by Faizullah Khan Bangash at the cost of a large sum of money. Bangash is the name of a hill in North-West Frontier near Kohat, and the people coming also from that place to Delhi were known as "Bangash."

The first coming of the "Bangash" into India was during the time of Shah Alam I. In the time of Muhammad Shah they rose to power, Nawwab Muhammad Khan Ghazanfar Jang Bangash being made governor of Farrukhabad, Agra and Allahabad, the territory over which his son Ahmad Khan Ghalib Jang afterwards ruled as an independent Nawwab.

Faizullah Khan was the son of Neknam Khan, one of the principal adherents of Muhammad Khan. He held the post of "Superintendent of buildings." Rabia Begam, the chief wife of Muhammad Khan, was architecturally inclined and took Faizullah Khan into her favour. Through him she erected a large number of *serais*, mosques, bridges and palaces, etc., many of which are still extant. After the death of Muhammad Khan, when Rabia Begam became all powerful, Faizullah Khan was appointed to manage her estate at Delhi, and to watch her interests at court.

(*k*) *Asar* (1847), chap. III, 30.

MUHALLA CHITLI QABR.

No. 84. (*a*) Grave of Mir Muhammadi Sahib.
(*b*) In the Khanqah of Mir Muhammadi.
(*c*) Nawwab Mirza.
(*d*) III.
(*e*) 1242 A.H. (1826-27 A.D.).
(*f*) None.
(*g*) Good.
(*h*) Unnecessary.
(*j*) The real name of this saint was Maulana Imaduddin, but he is known by the name of Mir Muhammadi. Mirza Salim, the son of Akbar II, was his disciple and had great faith in him. When the saint died in the year 1242 A.H., Mirza Salim buried him in his own house, now known as the Khanqah of Mir Muhammadi. His grave, with two others, is built on a raised platform: the grave towards the extreme east is that of Mir Muhammadi, the centre one being that of Mirza Salim, while the one on the extreme west is that of Husaini Begam, the wife of Mirza Salim. The *urs* of Mir Muhammadi used to be celebrated but is now discontinued.
(*k*) *Asar* (1847), chap. III, 24.
Mazarat, part II, page 23.

No. 85. (*a*) Grave of Sayyid Jalal-ud-Din.
(*b*) In a shop close to Chitli Qabr.
(*c*) Nawwab Buddhan.
(*d*) III.
(*e*) Date unknown.
(*f*) None.
(*g*) Good.
(*h*) Unnecessary.
(*j*) Sayyid Jalal-ud-Din is said to have been a nephew of Sayyid Raushan Shahid. His *urs* is celebrated on the 8th Shaban.

No. 86. (*a*) Chitli Qabr.
(*b*) In the *Muhalla*.
(*c*) Waqf, Mutawalli, Muhammad Said-ud-Din *alias* Bundi Jan.
(*d*) III.
(*e*) Date unknown.
(*f*) None.
(*g*) Good.
(*h*) Unnecessary.
(*j*) The *Muhalla* and *Bazar* are called after this tomb. Traditionally it is said to be the tomb of Sayyid Raushan Shahid. The author of *Asar-us-Sanadid* says that it has been here for more than 500 years. On its northern arch there is a modern inscription referring to *Asar-us-Sanadid* and stating that the tomb has been here since the year 793 A.H. (1391 A.D.). The name 'Chitli Qabr' has been given to it because it

had ornamentation of different colours. The annual '*urs*' is celebrated on the 27th of Rajab.

(*k*) *Asar* (1847), chap. III, 24.
Mazarat, part II, 24.

(*l*) S. 2.

HAVELI OF MIR HASHIM.

No. 87. (*a*) Shah Afaq's Mosque.

(*b*) In the *Muhalla*.

(*c*) Waqf, Mutawalli, Hashmat Ali.

(*d*) III.

(*e*) Late Mughal.

(*f*) None.

(*g*) Good.

(*h*) Unnecessary.

(*j*) The mosque was originally the *Tasbih Khana* of one Shah Afaq, but was afterwards converted by him into a mosque. It is of no special interest.

DUGDUGI SHAH KALLAN.

No. 88. (*a*) Khanqah of Shah Ghulam Ali.

(*b*) On the road from the Turkman Gate to Chitli Qabr.

(*c*) Shah Abul Khair.

(*d*) III.

(*e*) Late Mughal.

(*f*) See below.

(*g*) Fair.

(*h*) Unnecessary.

(*j*) The enclosure consists of a mosque, a house, a *Tasbih Khana* and a few apartments. In the courtyard there are four graves: three on a raised platform and one below it on the east. On the platform, the centre grave is that of Shah Ghulam Ali, on the east is that of Mirza Mazhar-i-Janjanan, the *pir* or spiritual guide of Shah Ghulam Ali, and on the west is that of Shah Abu Said, the disciple of the latter. The grave below the platform is that of Maulvi Rahim Bakhsh, a disciple of Shah Abu Said who held the supervision of the Khanqah when Shah Abu Said went on pilgrimage to Mecca. The inscription at the head of this grave is only a quotation from the Quran.

The mosque and the graves have been recently repaired. The inscriptions are as follows:—

(1) مزار حضرت مرزا جانجانان مظهر شهید قدس سره سنه ۱۱۹۵ تاریخ دهم محرم -

(2) مزار حضرت شاه عبد الله معروف بشاه غلام علي قدس سره سنه ۱۲۴۰ تاریخ ۲۲ صفر

(3) مزار حضرت شاه ابو سعید احمدي قدس سره سنه ۱۲۵۰ تاریخ یکم شوال

Translation.

(1) The tomb of His Holiness Mirza Janjanan Mazhar, the martyr, may his tomb be purified; dated 10th Muharram of the year 1195 (6th January 1781).

(2) The tomb of His Holiness Shah Abdullah known as Shah Ghulam Ali, may his tomb be purified; dated 22nd Safar of the year 1240 (16th October 1824).

(3) The tomb of His Holiness Shah Abu Said Ahmadi, may his tomb be purified; dated the 1st Shawwal of the year 1250 (31st January 1835).

Mirza Mazhar-i-Janjanan Shahid was a very well-known poet and saint of his time. He was Sayyid by caste and also connected with the house of Timur.

(*k*) *Asar* (1847), chap. III, 24.
Mazarat, part II, 19—23.

MUHALLA SUIWALAN.

No. 89. (*a*) Mosque (unnamed).
(*b*) In the *Muhalla*.
(*c*) Waqf, Mutawalli, Maulvi Abdul Ghani.
(*d*) III.
(*e*) Late Mughal.
(*f*) None.
(*g*) Good.
(*h*) Unnecessary.
(*j*) The building measures some 33′ 0″ feet north and south by 16′ 9″ east and west. It is of no special interest.

No. 90. (*a*) Mosque of Patli Gali.
(*b*) In the *Muhalla*.
(*c*) Waqf, Mutawalli, Hajji Bulaqui.
(*d*) III.
(*e*) Late Mughal.
(*f*) None.
(*g*) Good.
(*h*) Unnecessary.
(*j*) The building measures some 27′ 0″ north and south by 16′ 0″ east and west. It is of no special interest.

MUHALLA SUIWALON-KA-HAUZ.

No. 91. (*a*) Grave of Sayyid Daud.
(*b*) On the north of Hauz Wali Mosque.
(*c*) Owners unknown.
(*d*) III.
(*e*) Date unknown.

(*f*) None.
(*g*) Fair.
(*h*) Unnecessary.
(*j*) There are two graves here; the eastern one with the headstone is that of Sayyid Daud the Khalifa of Shah Turkman Biyabani. The grave is of considerable antiquity and has evidently been repaired from time to time. Its platform which is now almost buried is of inlaid marble. The tawiz and the headstone have been white-washed.
(*k*) *Mazarat*, part II, 25.

No. 92. (*a*) Hauz Wali Mosque I.
(*b*) Near Hauz.
(*c*) Waqf, Mutawalli, Imdad Husain.
(*d*) III.
(*e*) Late Mughal.
(*f*) None.
(*g*) Good.
(*h*) Unnecessary.
(*j*) The mosque which measures 36′ 0″ north and south by 26′ 0″ east and west is said to have been built by Nawwab Azam Khan (see No. 93). It is of no special interest.

No. 93. (*a*) Barah Dari and Hauz of Nawwab Azam Khan.
(*b*) In the *Muhalla*.
(*c*) Muhammad Yaqub Jute wala, etc.
(*d*) III.
(*e*) Late Mughal.
(*f*) None.
(*g*) Ruinous.
(*h*) Unnecessary.
(*j*) The house is said to have been built by Nawwab Azam Khan, son of Nawwab Amir Khan Umdat-ul-Mulk who possessed a great influence in the court of Muhammad Shah and was a formidable rival to Qamruddin Khan, the Prime Minister, and Nawwab Asaf Jah Bahadur. To please the latter chiefs the Emperor sent Amir Khan away from the court, appointing him as governor at Allahabad.. But here also his restless and ambitious nature asserting itself, and he schemed against his enemies at court in concert with Safdar Jang, but was killed by one of his own servants on the 23rd Zilhajjah in the year 1159 A.H. (6th January 1747), before he could attain his ends. Nothing is known about Azam Khan, his son.
(*k*) *Bayan-i-Waqii*, *Elliot* VIII, 131.

GANJ MIR KHAN.

No. 94. (*a*) Pipalwali Mosque I.

(*b*) Behind Nawwab Azam Khan's house.
(*c*) Waqf, Mutawalli, Masta Dallal.
(*d*) III.
(*e*) Late Mughal.
(*f*) None.
(*g*) Excellent.
(*h*) Unnecessary.
(*j*) The building measures 30′ 0″ north and south by 18′ 0″ east and west. It is of no special interest.

TURKMAN GATE.

No. 95. (*a*) Graves of some unknown saints.
(*b*) Near the Gate and Police Station.
(*c*) Owners unknown.
(*d*) III.
(*e*) Unknown.
(*f*) None.
(*g*) Ruinous.
(*h*) Unnecessary.
(*j*) The graves are said to be those of some unknown saints. They are now marked by white-washed stones and bricks.

No. 96. (*a*) Turkman Gate of Shahjahanabad.
(*b*) South-western gate of the city.
(*c*) Government.
(*d*) II *a*.
(*e*) C. 1658 A.D.
(*f*) None.
(*g*) Fair.
(*h*) Unnecessary.
(*j*) The gate is so called because it lies near the tomb of Shah Turkman. (See also paragraph (*j*) No. 41.)
(*k*) *As. Res.*, IV, 419.
A. S. I., I, page 219.
Carr Stephen, 244.
Cooper, 33, (gates of Shahjahanabad).
C. S. Range, 248.
Hearn, 67, 177, 257.
Keene, 34.
(*l*) S. 16.

No. 97. (*a*) Mosque (unnamed).
(*b*) Near the gate.
(*c*) Waqf, Mutawalli, Shaikh Nanne.
(*d*) II *b*.

(*e*) 1087 A.H. (1676 A.D.).
(*f*) On the central arch.

بسم الله الرحمن الرحيم - لا اله الا الله محمد رسول الله -

بنائے مسجد صالح بہادر بن حسین سلطان بدور سنہ ۱۹ عالمگیر ... سنہ ۱۰۸۷

Translations.

"In the name of God, the most merciful, the most compassionate. There is no God but Allah and Muhammad is His prophet."

"The foundation of the mosque of Salih Bahadur, son of Husain Sultan [was laid] in the 19th year of the reign of Alamgir. The year 1087."

(*g*) Good.
(*h*) Unnecessary.
(*j*) The mosque consists of a prayer chamber with 3 domes and 3 arches and a courtyard with an apartment on the south. The inscription records that it was built by Salih Bahadur, son of Husain Sultan, in 1087 A. H. (1676 A. D.) the 19th year of the reign of Alamgir Aurangzeb. Salih Bahadur was appointed, in the 46th year of the reign of Aurangzeb, to succeed *Khanazad Khan* as the *Faujdar* of Jalandar.
(*k*) *Alamgir*, 487.
(*l*) S. 17.

MUHALLA GUDARYA.

(NEAR TURKMAN GATE.)

No. 98. (*a*) Gudarya Mosque.
(*b*) In the *Muhalla*.
(*c*) Waqf, Mutawalli, Hafiz Abdul Hamid.
(*d*) III.
(*e*) Date unknown.
(*f*) None.
(*g*) Good.
(*h*) Unnecessary.
(*j*) The mosque is recently rebuilt. On its central arch there is a modern Urdu inscription referring to its reconstruction. It is of no special interest.

MUHALLA QABRUSTAN.

No. 99. (*a*) Qalandar Beg's Mosque.
(*b*) In the *Muhalla*.
(*c*) Waqf, Mutawalli, Hajji Muhammad Inayat Beg
(*d*) III.
(*e*) Date unknown.
(*f*) None.
(*g*) Fair.
(*h*) Unnecessary.
(*j*) The mosque, as its name shows, was built by one Qalandar Beg.

No. 100. (*a*) Hafiz Daud's Mosque.

(*b*) In the ***Muhalla.***

(*c*) Waqf, Mutawalli, Sayyid Muhammad Yaqub.

(*d*) III.

(*e*) Date unknown.

(*f*) None.

(*g*) Good.

(*h*) Unnecessary.

(*j*) The original mosque is said to have been of considerable antiquity, but it has been rebuilt.

No. 101. (*a*) Pulaowali Mosque.

(*b*) In the ***Muhalla.***

(*c*) Waqf, Mutawalli, Amir Ali.

(*d*) III.

(*e*) Late Mughal.

(*f*) None.

(*g*) Fair.

(*h*) Unnecessary.

(*j*) It is so called from the ***Pulao*** tree which stands in its courtyard. The leaves of this tree are said to be a sure medicine against fever. It is also known by the name of the mosque of Mir Mendhu, who probably built it.

No. 102. (*a*) Tomb of Shah Turkman.

(*b*) In the ***Muhalla.***

(*c*) Waqf, Mutawalli, Shams-ud-Din.

(*d*) III.

(*e*) 637 A. H. (1240 A. D.).

(*f*) None.

(*g*) Good.

(*h*) Unnecessary,

(*j*) The tomb which lies within a graveyard consists of four walls only without a roof. There are, within the enclosure, a few more unimportant brick built graves, which are said to be those of the disciples of the saint. The grave of Shah Turkman is of white marble, together with a small surrounding pavement of the same material; this is, however, later work.

Shah Turkman was a saint of great repute. His real name was Shams-ul-Arifin, and he was also called Biyabani because he generally lived in the forest (Biyaban) and did not like society. He died on the 24th of Rajab(1) of the year 637 A. H. (19th February 1240 A. D.). His ***urs*** is celebrated.

(*k*) ***Keene,*** 34.

Asar (1904), chap. III, 25.

Mazarat, Part II, 19.

(*l*) S. 8.

(1) Mirat-i-Aftab Numa and Akhbaru-l Akhyar.

No. 103. (*a*) Grave of Haidar Raza.

(*b*) In the graveyard belonging to the tomb of Shah Turkman.

(*c*) Waqf, Mutawalli, Shams-ud-Din.

(*d*) III.

(*e*) 1203 A. H. (1788-89 A. D.).

(*f*) On the headstone of the grave. A pious ejaculation, then—

(۱) نوجوان حیدر رضی بیك الدرین قبر کہن * از ازل پاکیزہ دین بو دست وہم پاکیزہ خو

(۲) چون بضرب گولہ در...... شد شہید * با شہیدان رفت در جنت و لیکن سرخرو

(۳) سال فوتش را چو موزون از خرد جستم بگفت * داورا کن با حسین ابن حیدر حشر او

سنہ ۱۲۰۳ ہجری نبوی

Translation.

(1) "The youthful Haidar Raza Beg, who is (buried) in this old grave, was from eternity of pious religion and also of pious habits."

(2) "When killed by a shell as a martyr at .... he went to paradise with honour in the company of martyrs."

(3) "When I sought the chronogram of his death in verse, from wisdom, it said 'O God! make his resurrection with Husain, son of Haidar (Ali)'. The year 1203 of the flight of the Prophet."

(*g*) Good.

(*h*) Unnecessary.

(*j*) The grave is built of white marble and red sandstone. Haidar Raza seems to have professed the Shia faith, as on the *Tawiz* there are religious formulæ exclusively believed by Shias and found only on their graves.

No. 104. (*a*) Grave of Bi Mamola.

(*b*) In the graveyard belonging to the tomb of Shah Turkman.

(*c*) Waqf, Mutawalli, Shams-ud-Din.

(*d*) III.

(*e*) 1242 A. H. (1826-27 A.D.).

(*f*) On the headstone. The *Kalima*, then—

بتاریخ چہاردہم ذیقعد سنہ ۱۲۴۲ ہجری بی ممولا نوراللہ مضجعہا قفس عنصری را شکستہ
باشیانہ فردوس پرواز نمود

Translation.

"On the fourteenth of Ziqad of the year 1242 Hijra, Bi Mamola (Mamola literally=a wagtail), may God lighten her grave, having broken the elemental cage flew to the nest in paradise (died)."

(*g*) Good.

(*h*) Unnecessary.

(*j*) The grave is built of marble and red sandstone.

No. 105. (*a*) Grave of Tahqiq Khan.

(*b*) To south of the mosque of Qalandar Beg.

(c) Archæological Department.
(d) II a.
(e) 1078 A.H. (1667-68 A.D.).
(f) On the grave stone. A pious ejaculation and

مرقد اسحاق بیگ مخاطب تحقیق خان ۱۰۷۸ اللهم اغفرله والدیه

Translation.

"The sleeping place (grave) of Ishaq Beg, known as Tahqiq Khan 1078. O God! pardon him and his parents."

(g) Good.
(h) Unnecessary.
(j) The grave is built in bricks and lime. The Tawiz consists of a white marble slab and bears the above quoted inscription.
(l) S. 3.

ROAD FROM TURKMAN GATE TO CHITLI QABR.

No. 106. (a) Hajji Amanullah's Mosque.
(b) Near the *Khanqah* of Shah Ghulam Ali.
(c) Waqf, Mutawalli, Abdul Sattar.
(d) III.
(e) 1199 A. H. (1784—5 A. D.).
(f) On the central arch.

(۱) . . . .
(۲) ... خرد گفت از سال او * زهے مسجد پر ز نور خدا

Translation.

(1) . . . .
(2) "...... wisdom said of its date, 'what a good mosque, full of Divine light'"
(g) Good.
(h) Unnecessary.
(j) A small building only.

No. 107. (a) Hafiz Nizam Ali Attar's Mosque.
(b) Near the Dargah of Mir Muhammadi.
(c) Waqf, Mutawalli, Abdul Ghani.
(d) III.
(e) Late Mughal.
(f) None.
(g) Good.
(h) Unnecessary.
(j) A small building of no special interest.

BAZAR CHITLI QABR.

No. 108. (*a*) Sayyid Rafai's Mosque.

(*b*) Near Chitli Qabr.

(*c*) Waqf, Mutawalli, Hakim Sharif Hasan.

(*d*) III.

(*e*) Date unknown.

(*f*) None.

(*g*) Good.

(*h*) Unnecessary.

(*i*) This mosque is of considerable antiquity but as Sayyid Rafai generally lived in it and repaired it, it is known after him. Sayyid Rafai was a saint of great repute. He held meetings in honour of the Prophet which were attended by his chief disciples, the restriction being that there should be no women present. The disciples attended the meetings with knives and struck each other in their religious frenzy, but none of them suffered harm. If by chance any one was wounded, the wound is said to have been healed at once by the application of the saliva of the Sayyid. He died about the year 1233 A.H. (1817-18 A. D.).

The mosque has been recently added to, and the additions have been commemorated by an inscription on its central arch.

الله اکبر

محمد احسان الرحمن ابن مرحومی محمد یوسف الرحمن خان حسب وصیت اهلیه
مرحومه خود دکاکین پخته و حمام و متوضا و حجره و زینه وغیر ذلک بر قطعه زمین متعلقه مسجد
رفاعی بنا کرد و براے مصارف مسجد وقف نمود سنه ۱۳۰۶ ﻫ -

Translation.

"God is great."

"Muhammad Ihsanu-r-Rahman son of the late Muhammad Yusufu-r Rahman Khan, according to the parting advice of his deceased wife built masonry shops, a bath, a place for making ablutions, an apartment and a staircase, etc., on the plot of land belonging to the Rafai mosque, and dedicated them for the expenses of the mosque. The year 1306 A.H. (1888-89 A. D.)".

(*k*) *Asar* (1847), chap. III, 23.

BHOJLA PAHARI.

No. 109. (*a*) Mosque (unnamed).

(*b*) *Gali* Ramji Das.

(*c*) Waqf, Mutawalli, Tajammul Husain.

(*d*) III.

(*e*) Late Mughal.

(*f*) None.

(*g*) Good.

(*h*) Unnecessary.

(*i*) A small building of no historical importance.

No. 110. (*a*) Mosque (unnamed).
(*b*) *Gali* Ramji Das.
(*c*) Waqf, Mutawalli, Mahmud Beg.
(*d*) III.
(*e*) Late Mughal.
(*f*) None.
(*g*) Good.
(*h*) Unnecessary.
(*j*) A small building of no special interest.

No. 111. (*a*) Mosque (unnamed).
(*b*) In the Andheri *Gali*.
(*c*) Waqf, Mutawalli, Amanullah Khan.
(*d*) III.
(*e*) Late Mughal.
(*f*) None.
(*g*) Good.
(*h*) Unnecessary.
(*j*) A small building of no special interest.

No. 112. (*a*) Ustad Karim Bakhsh's Mosque.
(*b*) In *Gali* Jhotwali.
(*c*) Waqf, Mutawalli, Sayyid Ahmad.
(*d*) III.
(*e*) Late Mughal.
(*f*) None.
(*g*) Good.
(*h*) Unnecessary.
(*j*) A small building of no historical importance.

No. 113. (*a*) Gadh Kaptan's Mosque.
(*b*) In the *Muhalla*.
(*c*) Waqf, Mutawalli, Hajji Inayat Husain and Pirji Firoz Husain.
(*d*) III.
(*e*) 1235 A. H. (1819-20 A. D.).
(*f*) On the outer entrance.

الله

مسجد حنفیه

بانی محمد امیر الدین گڈه کپتان سنه ۱۲۳۵ مرمت کننده میاں سراج الدین سنه ۱۳۲۳ -

Translation.

Allah.

Mosque of Hanafis.

"Founder (of the mosque) Muhammad Amir-ud-din Gadh Kaptan (Captain of the fort), the year 1235; repairer Miyan Siraj-ud-din, the year 1323 (1905-06 A.D.)."

(*g*) Good.
(*h*) Unnecessary.
(*j*) The building measures 32′ 0″ north and south by 14′ 7″ east and west. It is not known who this Amir-ud-din Gadh Kaptan was.

GALI MASHALCHIYAN.

No. 114. (*a*) Mosque (unnamed).
(*b*) In the *Muhalla.*
(*c*) Waqf.
(*d*) III.
(*e*) Mughal.
(*f*) None.
(*g*) Good.
(*h*) Unnecessary.
(*j*) The mosque is said to have been of the time of Shah Jahan, but has been recently repaired. It is of no historical importance. There is an inscription on the central arch bearing the *Kalima* and 1229 (?) (1813-14 A.D.) as date, but people say that it has nothing to do either with the erection of the mosque or its repair. The stone was found somewhere and for the sake of respect to the *Kalima* was affixed here.

IMLI KI PAHARI.

No. 115. (*a*) Mosque of Imli ki Pahari.
(*b*) In the *Muhalla.*
(*c*) Waqf, Mutawalli, Hafiz Abdul Hamid.
(*d*) III.
(*e*) Late Mughal.
(*f*) None.
(*g*) Good.
(*h*) Unnecessary.
(*j*) A small building of no special interest.

No. 116. (*a*) Yak Burji (one domed), Mosque I.
(*b*) In the *Muhalla.*
(*c*) Waqf, Mutawalli, Hamid Alam.
(*d*) III.
(*e*) Date unknown.
(*f*) None.
(*g*) Good.
(*h*) Unnecessary.
(*j*) The Mosque is domeless and has probably received its name by reason of the domed tomb of Shah Muhammad Ali Waiz which stands near it. It is a small building of no particular interest.

No. 117. (*a*) Tomb of Shah Muhammad Ali Waiz.

(*b*) Close to the Yak Burji Mosque.

(*c*) Waqf, Mutawalli, Iwaz Ali.

(*d*) III.

(*e*) 1131 A.H. (1718-19 A.D.).

(*f*) None.

(*g*) Poor.

(*h*) Unnecessary.

(*j*) The tomb has a large dome under which lie three graves, two being side by side, within a stone railing. One of them is that of Shah Muhammad Ali, and the other is said to be that of his brother Asadullah There is a third grave on a level with the ground, of which nothing is known. Probably it is that of one of the disciples of Shah Muhammad Ali.

The Shah was a man of great piety, who had devoted himself to preaching and imparting religious instruction at Gujrat. The oppressive treatment of Chanpat Singh (the Governor) of Gujrat obliged him to depart and he left with his friends for Delhi, where he is said to have been imprisoned in the *Chobi* mosque (1) in the fort by Farrukh Siyar at the instigation of Chanpat Singh. The Emperor was admonished in a dream for this improper act, and in consequence he set the Shah with his companions at liberty. The latter then took up his abode in the Jami Masjid and employed himself again in teaching and preaching. He died in 1131 A.H. (1718-19 A. D.). He is said to have been the spiritual guide of Alamgir II.

(*k*) *Mazarat*, part II, 24.

GALI SURKH POSHAN.

No. 118. (*a*) Unchi Masjid II.

(*b*) In the *Muhalla*.

(*c*) Waqf, Mutawalli, Ziya-ud-din.

(*d*) III.

(*e*) Late Mughal.

(*f*) None.

(*g*) Good.

(*h*) Unnecessary.

(*j*) A century or so ago the mosque was known as that of one Shah Surkh Posh, who, probably had built it. The street, in which the mosque lies, is still known after the name of Surkh Posh. The mosque was rebuilt and extended recently. It is a small building of no particular interest.

HAVELI BAKHTAWAR KHAN.

No. 119. (*a*) Mosque and Madrasa of Husain Bakhsh.

(*b*) In the *Muhalla*.

(1) This mosque was built of wood and stood in the Hayat Baksh gardens. *Asar* (1904) states that the *Chobi* Masjid was built by Ahmad Shah in 1164-A.H. (1750-51 A.D.). Possibly the wooden building of Ahmad Shah was erected on the site of an earlier structure in which Farrukh Siyar imprisoned the saint.

(c) Waqf, Mutawalli, Hajji Muhammad Ismail.
(d) III.
(e) 1268 A. H. (1851-52 A. D.).
(f) On the gateway—

دارالهدی والوعظ سنه ۱۲۶۸ الوقف لایملک

Translation.

"The house for guidance and preaching; the year 1268. The Waqf (pious dedication) is the property of none."

(g) Good.
(h) Unnecessary.
(j) The building was erected by one Husain Bakhsh. It consists of a mosque, and galleries wherein the school is held, and apartments occupied by students or teachers of the school.

CHHATTA SHAIKH MANGLU.

No. 120. (a) Maulvi Mahbub Ali's Mosque.
(b) In the *Muhalla*.
(c) Waqf, Mutawalli, Hafiz Muhammad Ismail.
(d) III.
(e) Late Mughal.
(f) None.
(g) Good.
(h) Unnecessary.
(j) The mosque measures 48′ 0″ north and south by 13′ 6″ east and west. It is of no special interest.
Mahbub Ali was a Maulvi of repute, and a pupil of Shah Abdul Aziz, a well-known Maulvi of Delhi.
(k) *Asar* (1847), chap. IV, 108.

CHITLA DARWAZA.

No. 121. (a) Burhiya's Mosque I.
(b) In the *Muhalla*.
(c) Waqf, Mutawalli, Qasim Ali.
(d) III.
(e) Late Mughal.
(f) None.
(g) Good.
(h) Unnecessary.
(j) It is said that the mosque was built by a certain *Burhiya* (an old woman).

No. 122. (a) Mosque (unnamed).
(b) In Garhaiya.
(c) Waqf, Mutawalli, Abdul Hadi.
(d) III.

(*e*) Late Mughal.
(*f*) None.
(*g*) Good.
(*h*) Unnecessary.
(*j*) It is said that the mosque was built by one of the ancestors of the family now known as Ali Jan Wale.

KUNCHA-I MIR ASHIQ.

No. 123. (*a*) Mosque Chhoti (Small) II.
(*b*) In the ***Muhalla***.
(*c*) Waqf, Mutawalli, Hafiz Abdul Wahhab.
(*d*) III.
(*e*) Date unknown.
(*f*) None.
(*g*) Good.
(*h*) Unnecessary.
(*j*) A small building of no special interest.

No. 124. (*a*) Mosque Bari (Big).
(*b*) In the ***Muhalla***.
(*c*) Waqf, Mutawalli, Hafiz Nuruddin.
(*d*) III.
(*e*) Late Mugha
(*f*) None.
(*g*) Good.
(*h*) Unnecessary.
(*j*) A small building of no special interest.

GALI KEDAR NATH.

No. 125. (*a*) Temple of Babu Gulab Das.
(*b*) In the ***Muhalla***.
(*c*) Ramji Das.
(*d*) III.
(*e*) Late Mughal (?)
(*f*) None.
(*g*) Excellent.
(*h*) Unnecessary.
(*j*) The temple was built by Raja Kedar Nath, after whose name the street, in which the temple lies, is known. An interesting story is related about the father of Kedar Nath explaining the mystery of the latter's greatness and wealth. It is said that he sold roasted maize in the fort, when the throne of Delhi was occupied by a minor prince and the State affairs were directed by his maternal uncle as a vice-regent (?). The uncle once resolved to do away with the prince by means of poison, and the father of Kedar Nath by chance heard of this plan. He at once informed the

mother of the prince of the matter, who immediately fled with him to Agra. The prince conferred great favours on the son of the maize seller who had saved his life and gave him the title of Mirza Raja Kedar Nath. In the main shrine are images of Rama, Sita and Lakshmana. In front is an image of Hanumat and a ling of Siva.

N.B.—I have followed Prof. Kielhorn in giving the crude form, *viz.*, Hanumat as it is incorrect to use Nom. Sing. of it, *viz.*, Hanuman after 'of' that is to call 'of Hanuman' as is done by some scholars.

GALI MURGHAN.

No. 126. (*a*) Mosque (unnamed).
(*b*) In the ***Muhalla***.
(*c*) Waqf, Mutawalli, Fida Ali.
(*d*) III.
(*e*) Late Mughal.
(*f*) None.
(*g*) Good.
(*h*) Unnecessary.
(*j*) A small building of no particular interest.

No. 127. (*a*) Temple (unnamed).
(*b*) In the ***Muhalla***.
(*c*) Babu Bansi Dhar.
(*d*) III.
(*e*) Unknown.
(*f*) None.
(*g*) Ruinous.
(*h*) Unnecessary.

No. 128. (*a*) Sivalaya([1]) (unnamed).
(*b*) In the ***Muhalla***.
(*c*) Lachchhu.
(*d*) III.
(*e*) 1858 A.D.
(*f*) There is an inscription on the outer wall of the temple written in modern Devanagari characters.
It is in three lines. It runs :—

(1) कुवा सिवाला श्री नाराय अर्पण
Kuva sivala sri Narayana arpana

(2) नाई चुनाका बेटा बहादर सं १९१५ का
Nai Chunnaka beta Bahadara Sam 1915 Ka-

(3) र्तिक वदो ५ *
rtika vadi 5 *

([1]) Throughout the Delhi temples five or six images are found generally in close juxtaposition, not even separate niches being assigned to them. I think it is convenient to give my explanation at once and I hope it will be a satisfactory one.

Explanation of a Sivalaya :—

Those temples have been styled Sivalayas where circumstantial evidence points to the God Siva as being the prime object of worship. In No. 237 for example it is apparent from the inscription that the temple was specially built to enshrine the ling of Siva and the image of Parvati, and, therefore, it should be called a Sivalaya. In some temples several images are kept in the niches, and to a non-Hindu it may at times be difficult to say whether a temple is a Sivalaya or one dedicated to some other god.

There are in Delhi a few temples intended for the worship of other deities of the Brahmanical religion and these cannot be called Sivalayas.

The result of study of these temples in Delhi would seem to show that the worship of Siva was far more prevalent than that of any other deity. In fact it almost excluded all other forms.

Translation.

"This well and Sivalaya is dedicated to Sri Narayana (by) barber Bahadara, son of Chunna. Sam (*i.e.*, Samvat) 1915 (A. D. 1858) 5th day of the dark fortnight of the (month of) Kartika".

Explanation:—The word Narayana in the present instance is a generic term and means god in general. It cannot be taken as the name of the particular God Narayana since as a matter of fact we see that the God enshrined is Siva and not Narayana.

After the asterisk follows an Urdu inscription of the same meaning and date.

It appears from enquiries that the barber erected a new temple on the old site. There was a feud and the stone was afterwards inserted by him.

MUHALLA CHURIWALAN.

No. 129. (*a*) Mosque, Hammamwali.
(*b*) In the *Muhalla.*
(*c*) Waqf, Mutawalli, Sayyid Muhammad Hasan Imam-i Idgah.
(*d*) III.
(*e*) Late Mughal.
(*f*) None.
(*g*) Good.
(*h*) Unnecessary.
(*j*) A small building of no particular interest.

No. 130. (*a*) Jutewalan's Mosque.
(*b*) In the *Muhalla.*
(*c*) Waqf, Mutawalli, Faiyaz.
(*d*) III.
(*e*) Late Mughal.
(*f*) None.
(*g*) Good.
(*h*) Unnecessary.
(*j*) The mosque has been recently rebuilt and extended. It consists of a prayer chamber, a courtyard and a tank, and apartments on the northern side and over the prayer chamber. It is of no special interest.

No. 131. (*a*) Sivalaya (unnamed).
(*b*) *Gali* Kashmiriyan.
(*c*) Rupnatha and Sivanarayana.
(*d*) III.
(*e*) The temple is about 100 years old.
(*f*) There is a modern inscription above the outer door with the words (that the temple was erected or belongs to (?))—"Pandit Bisana Narayana Hakasara."

(1) पंडित बिशन नारायन (*sic*).
Pandit Bisana Narayana.

(2) हाकसर
Haksara.

(*g*) Good.
(*h*) Unnecessary.
(*j*) In the temple is a ling of Siva and the images of Parvati and Nandi.

MUHALLA BADLIYAN.

No. 132. (*a*) Temple of Chowdhari.
(*b*) In the *Muhalla*.
(*c*) Bhagvandasa and Jhabbumala.
(*d*) III.
(*e*) It is said to be about 100 years old (?).
(*f*) None.
(*g*) Good.
(*h*) Unnecessary.
(*j*) In the temple are images of Parvati and Ganapati and the ling of Siva.

KUNCHA-I-SAR BULAND KHAN.

No. 133. (*a*) Sivalaya (unnamed).
(*b*) In the *Muhalla*.
(*c*) Kallumala.
(*d*) III.
(*e*) Late Mughal.
(*f*) None.
(*g*) Good.
(*h*) Unnecessary.
(*j*) In the temple are two lings, one image of Parvati, one of Ganapati, one of Brahmadeva and one of Nandi.

BULBULI KHANA.

No. 134. (*a*) Munshi Sher Ali's Mosque.
(*b*) In the *Muhalla*.
(*c*) Waqf, Mutawalli, Majidu-d-Din.
(*d*) III.
(*e*) 1091 A. H. (1680-81 A. D.).
(*f*) On the central arch there is an inscription bearing the *Kalima* and the date 1091 A. H.
(*g*) Good.
(*h*) Unnecessary.
(*j*) The mosque is very small one and consists of a prayer chamber with three arches and a courtyard.

No. 135. (*a*) Tomb of Raziya Sultan.
(*b*) In the *Muhalla*.
(*c*) Unknown.

(*d*) II *b*.

(*e*) Date unknown.

(*f*) None.

(*g*) Fair.

(*h*) Should be declared a "Protected Monument."

(*j*) The tomb consists of four walls without a roof. In the centre of the enclosure there are two graves on a raised platform. At the head of one of them is a small masonry pillar used as a stand for lamps: this is said to be the grave of Raziya; the other is said to belong to her sister Sajiyah, who is unknown to history. At the south-east corner of the enclosure are two other unknown graves of minor importance. In the western wall is a recess or *mihrab*, showing that the place may also be used as a mosque.

Raziya Sultan was the only woman who ascended the throne of Delhi. She was the daughter of Iltutmish and was so endowed with the qualities befitting a king that he nominated her in his own lifetime as his successor, remarking to the nobles who raised objections to this measure, "that none of his sons were more competent to guide the state than she was." She ruled with authority for a little more than three years (1236-1239 A. D.) and rode on horseback like a man, unveiled and armed with a bow and quiver. She was eventually suspected of an intimacy with one of her slaves, Amir Jalalu -d-Din Yaqut, an Abyssinian by birth. The nobles of the state revolted against her in consequence, and Malik Altuniya, the governor of Sirhind killed the Abyssinian, imprisoned Raziya, and soon after espoused her. Meanwhile Muizzu-d-Din Bahram Shah had ascended the throne and Malik Altuniya with Raziya led an army to Delhi to regain possession of the kingdom. But fortune did not favour them and Sultan Raziya and Altuniya were defeated. They fled to Kaithal when their remaining forces abandoned them and they fell into the hands of villagers who killed them. The date of their defeat was 24 Rabi I 638 A. H. (13th October 1240 A. D.) and Raziya Sultan was killed the day after the battle. According to the Arab historian Ibn-i-Batuta, Sultan Raziya was killed by a peasant, who after murdering and burying her, carried some of her garments to the market for sale. He was caught and taken before the Magistrate, confessed that he had killed Raziya and told his guards where he had buried her; they exhumed the body, washed it, and wrapping it in a shroud, buried it again in the same place. A small shrine was erected over her grave which is visited by pilgrims and considered a place of sanctity. It is situated on the banks of the Jumna, about one *Farsang* from Delhi.

(*k*) *Asar* (1904), chap. II, 25—26.
A. S. I., IV, 69.
As. Res. IV, 69.
Carr Stephen, 77—78.
Fanshawe, 66, 269, 295.
Hearn, 176-177 (Queen Riziyat).
Keene, 36.
Rodgers, 86.
Tabaqat-i-Nasiri, *Tazjiyatu-l-Amsar*, *Travels of Ibn Batuta* } *Elliot*, Vol. II, 332 *et seq*; Vol. III, 37, 38, 592.

(*l*) S. 20.

No. 136. (*a*) Mosque (unnamed).
(*b*) In the *muhalla*.
(*c*) Waqf, Mutawalli, Miyanjan.
(*d*) III.
(*e*) Late Mughal.
(*f*) None.
(*g*) Good.
(*h*) Unnecessary.
(*j*) The mosque is said to have been built by one Muhammad Shafi, who was a relative of Sayyid Hasan Rasul Numa. The building is a small one of no particular interest.

No. 137. (*a*) Nawwab Maulvi Qutbu-d-Din's Mosque.
(*b*) In the *Muhalla*.
(*c*) Waqf, Mutawalli, Daud Beg and Aiyub Beg.
(*d*) III.
(*e*) 1148 A. H. (1735-36 A. D.).
(*f*) The inscription is written on a loose piece of stone housed in the mosque.

سال مکان بزرگ ساخته با زیب و زین * مدرسه و مسجدے کرده بنا شاه حسین

Translation.

" The chronogram of the big house which has been built with elegance and beauty (is) ' A mosque and school are built by Shah Husain '."

(*g*) Good.
(*h*) Unnecessary.
(*j*) It was repaired by Nawwab Maulvi Qutbu-d-Din after whom it is now known. There is also on the back wall of the prayer chamber, an inscription to the effect that the mosque is that of Nawwab Maulvi Qutbu-d-Din Khan Sahib. It is not known who Shah Husain was.

KALAN MASJID OR KALI MASJID.

No. 138. (*a*) Kalan Masjid.
(*b*) Near the Turkman gate.
(*c*) Waqf, Mutawalli, Managing Committee Fathpuri.
(*d*) II *b*.
(*e*) 10th Jumada II 789 A. H. (28th June 1387 A.D.).
(*f*) On the east entrance—

بسم الله الرحمن الرحیم - بفضل و عنایت آفریدگار در عهد دولت پادشاه دین دار الواثق
بتائید الرحمن ابوالمظفر فیروز شاه السلطان خلد ملکه این مسجد بنا کرده بنده زاده درگاه جونا نجه
مقبول المخاطب خانجهان ابن خانجهان خدائے بر آن بنده رحمت کند هر که در مسجد بیاید
بدعای خیر بادشاه مسلمانان و این بنده بفاتحه و اخلاص یاد کند حق تعالی ان بنده را بیامرزد
بحرمت النبي و آله مسجد مرتب شد بتاریخ دهم جمادي الآخر سنه تسع و ثمانین و سبعمایه

Translation.

"In the name of God, the most merciful, the most compassionate. By the grace and kindness of the Creator, in the reign and sovereignty of the religious king, strong by the help of the merciful (named) Abul

Muzaffar Firoz Shah Sultan may his kingdom be perpetuated this mosque was built by the son of the slave of the threshold, Junan Shah Maqbul entitled Khan Jahan son of Khanjahan, may God be merci ful to that slave. Any one coming to the mosque should pray for the benefit of the King of the Musalmans and recite the Fatiha and the Ikhlas for this slave, and may God forgive that slave. In honour of the Prophet and his posterity this mosque was finished on the 10th Jumada II of the year 789."

(*g*) Good, but might be kept cleaner and the surroundings opened up.

(*h*) Should be declared Protected Monument with the agreement of the owners.

(*j*) The mosque is commonly known as *Kali* Masjid, or black mosque, but this designation, though there are reasons for believing it to be one of long standing, may be a corruption of *Kalan* Masjid, *i.e.*, large mosque. It may also have been so called on account of its external plaster having weathered to a dark colour.

The mosque is built on somewhat high ground and with the exception of Jami Masjid is the most prominent structure in the city of Shahjahanabad. It consists of two storeys; the first or basement storey, the middle of which is a solid mass, forming the floor of the mosque, is 28 feet in height, consisting of a number of small double apartments, which were possibly built for the very purpose they now answer, namely, that of assisting, by the rent they yield, in defraying the expenses of the mosque. The upper storey, to the level of the battlements, is 38 feet high, making a total height of 66 feet. The mosque is built of the common quartzose sandstone found in the immediate neighbourhood of Delhi. This stone, which is in masses of various sizes, those towards the base being of considerable dimensions, is unhewn and cemented by *chunam* with which the whole of the edifice is externally plastered. The mosque possesses a square courtyard surrounded by a cloister. On the west side of the court is the main body of the mosque or prayer chamber, consisting of five arches three aisles in depth, supporting fifteen domes in all; there are five domes over the northern and five over the southern arcades, and four over the eastern rooms, besides the dome over the main entrance, thus making a total of thirty domes. There were, in the courtyard, 4 brick built graves, two of which are said to have been those of Khan Jahan, the prime minister of Firoz Shah Tughlaq, and Khan Jahan, the son. These graves were removed in 1857.

The main entrance to the mosque, which is towards the east, is reached by 30 steps and contains the above-quoted inscription, written in *naskh* characters, and refers to the construction of the mosque during the reign of Firozshah by Junan Shah who bore the title of Khan Jahan.

Firoz Shah Tughlaq was the third Emperor of his line. He successfully ruled for more than 27 years 752-790 (1351-1388 A.D.) and was one of the most enlightened rulers that India has seen. Irrigation by canals was his hobby. He founded a new city of Delhi called Firozabad after himself, and endowed many hospitals and colleges. He constructed many other buildings, and conscientiously repaired the buildings, erected by the kings before him.

Junan Shah was the son of a Hindu convert named Kattu, who embraced Islam in the time of Muhammad Tughlaq and was given the name 'Maqbul' by the Emperor, at whose hands he afterward received a great honour an high rank. Firoz Shah, on ascending the throne, made him *Wazir* and gave him the title of Khan Jahan. The title and office of wazir was, after his death, bestowed upon his son Junan Shah, who discharged his duties as a minister under Firoz Shah for 20 years. He had all the affairs of the kingdom committed to his charge. Towards the end of the reign of Firoz Shah, Khan Jahan Junan Shah incurred the enmity of Prince Muhammad Khan, afterwards Muhammad Shah, which resulted in his total downfall. He was compelled to leave his house and fly for life into Mewat where he sought refuge with Koka Chauhan at Mahari. The prince, now entrusted with full powers by the Sultan, sent one Sikandar Khan with an army against Khan Jahan. When this force reached Mahari, Koka Chauhan seized Khan Jahan and sent him prisoner to Sikandar Khan, who killed him and carried his head to court. Khan Jahan Junan Shah is known to have built, in and near Delhi, some six or seven mosques which will be dealt with in their proper order.

(*k*) *Annual* (1902-3), 77.
A. S. I., I, 219-221; *IV*, 69.
As. Res. I, 220; IV, 69; XXXIX, 80.
Auckland, 16.
Carr Stephen, 148-154.
Catalogue, 39, J. 4.
Cole, (1st report), XXVIII.
Cooper, 55 *et seq.*
Fanshawe, 65.
Fergusson, II, 219.
Hearn, 67, 122, 199.
Heber, II, 295-6.
Keene, 35, 151.
Rodgers, 88.
Asar (1904), chap. III, 39.
Shams Siraj Afif, 394 *et seq.*
Tarikh-i-Mubarak Shahi } Elliot, III, 367 *et seq.* IV, 15-16.
„ „ *Firoz Shahi* }

(*l*) S. 14, S. 21.

MUHALLA AQAB KALAN MASJID.

No. 139. (*a*) Mosque of Naqibu-l-Auliya.
(*b*) In the *Muhalla.*
(*c*) Waqf, Mutawalli, Hafiz Mumtaz Beg.
(*d*) III.
(*e*) Late Mughal.
(*f*) None.
(*g*) Good.
(*h*) Unnecessary.
(*j*) The mosque is said to have been built by one Naqibul-Auliya. It is of no special interest.

No. 140. (*a*) Beriwali Mosque.
(*b*) In the *Muhalla.*

(c) Waqf, Mutawalli, Mahfuz Beg and Hajji Bahadur.
(d) III.
(e) Late Mughal.
(f) None.
(g) Good.
(h) Unnecessary.
(j) The mosque which measures 25′ 8″ north and south by 18′ 16″ east and west is said to have been built by one Hajji Qubba, who is buried in the courtyard of the mosque.

HAVELI NAWWAB MUZAFFAR KHAN.

(NEAR THE TURKMAN GATE.)

No. 141. (a) Gate (unnamed).
(b) See above.
(c) Pandit Jwala Nath.
(d) III.
(e) Mughal.
(f) None.
(g) Fair.
(h) Unnecessary.
(j) The gate was the main entrance to the house of Sayyid Muzaffar Khan, a nobleman of the Court of Shah Jahan. He encountered and killed Khan Jahan Lodi when the latter rebelled against the Emperor in the year 1040 A.H. (1630-31 A. D.) and was rewarded with a *mansab* of 5,000 and 5,000 horse, and received the title of Khan Jahan.
The gate was the central entrance to the old house which is now in ruins, and is now occupied by the *Muhalla*.
(k) *Badshah Namah*, I, 348 *et seq.*
Elliot, VII, 20—22.
(l) S. 13.

GALI SINGHI WALI.

AQAB KALAN MASJID.

No. 142. (a) Ghulam Chishti's Mosque.
(b) In the *Muhalla*.
(c) Waqf, Mutawalli, Rasul Bakhsh.
(d) III.
(e) 1195 A. H. (1781 A.D.).
(f) On the *Mihrab*—

مسجد مولوي صحب الله ساکن دهلي بمساحت زمين مسجد معه چاه غلام چشتي
يکصد و چهل و چهار ذرعه معماري و دو صد و ده ذرعه زمين قبرستان مملوکه مرزا لالن بيگ ولد
محمد بيگ بنام مسجد مندرجه بالا که اجاره غلام چشتي بفاصله جانب مشرق بست و هشت
قدم واقع است سنه ۱۱۹۵ هجري بسبيل الله وقف کرده شد

Translation.

"The mosque of Maulvi Muhibbullah, resident of Delhi, and the piece of land belonging to the mosque and measuring 144 yards (*Memari*) with the well of Ghulam Chishti, and 210 yards of land used as a graveyard belonging to Mirza Lalan Beg, son of Muhammad Beg have been dedicated in the way of God in the year 1195 Hijra for the aforesaid mosque from which the farm of Ghulam Chishti lies twenty-eight paces towards east."

(*g*) Good.
(*h*) Unnecessary.
(*j*) The mosque is small and of no special importance. It is not known who those referred to in the inscription were.

MUHALLA GHOSIYAN.

Aqab Kulan Masjid.

No. 143. (*a*) Chanda Ghosi's Mosque.
(*b*) In the *Muhalla*.
(*c*) Waqf, Mutawalli, Chanda Ghosi.
(*d*) III.
(*e*) Late Mughal.
(*f*) None.
(*g*) Good.
(*h*) Unnecessary.
(*j*) The mosque has been rebuilt by one Chanda Ghosi. It is a small building of no particular interest.

GALI DAKOTAN.

Aqab Kalan Masjid.

No. 144. (*a*) Mominan's Mosque.
(*b*) In the *Muhalla*.
(*c*) Waqf, Mutawalli, Abdu-r Rahman.
(*d*) III.
(*e*) 1206 A.H. (1791-92 A.D.).
(*f*) On the central arch—

سنہ ۱۲۰۶ ہجری

مسجد حنفیہ مومناں متعلقہ مسجد ۵۰ گز زمین اور دوکان مع چبوترہ

Translation.

"The year 1206 Hijra."

"The mosque of Hanafi Momins (weavers). Belonging to mosque 5 yards of land and a shop with a platform."

(*g*) Good.
(*h*) Unnecessary.
(*j*) The mosque is a small one and has three arches.

KUNCHA-I-GOKAL SHAH.

No. 145. (*a*) Hafiz Habibullah's Mosque.

(*b*) In the *Muhalla.*

(*c*) Waqf, Mutawalli, Pirji Ashraf Ali.

(*d*) III.

(*e*) Late Mughal.

(*f*) None.

(*g*) Good.

(*h*) Unnecessary.

(*j*) The mosque lies in a *Muhalla* commonly known as Kuncha-i-Gokal Shah; but it is said that this designation should be really "Kuncha-i-Aqil-Khan," *i.e.*, "street of Aqil Khan," who was an important personage in the reign of Aurangzeb.

In the northern corner of the courtyard of the mosque lies the grave of Hafiz Habibullah, after whom the mosque is known. The *Tawiz* of the grave is of white marble inscribed with extracts from the Quran.

BAZAR SITA RAM.

No. 146. (*a*) Kalesvaranatha's Temple.

(*b*) In the *Bazar.*

(*c*) It is said to be about 125 or 150 years old?

(*d*) III.

(*e*) Late Mughal.

(*f*) None.

(*g*) Good.

(*h*) Unnecessary.

(*j*) The temple is a small one and much frequented by the Hindus. Kalesvaranatha (a name of Siva) is supposed to favour his devotees and it appears from the number of old bells that many worshippers have received answers to their prayers. There are 104 bells in all. It is believed that barren women who visit the shrine will bear children.

The gates of the main shrine, in which are images of Parvati, Ganapati, Brahmadeva, Kartikasvami and Nandi, are of brass. In a niche on the right is an image of Bhairva and on the left one of Hanumat.

No. 147. (*a*) Khuwaja Turab's Mosque.

(*b*) In the *Muhalla.*

(*c*) Waqf, Mutawalli, Managing Committee, Fathpuri.

(*d*) II *b*.

(*e*) 1063 A. H. (1652-53 A. D.).

(*f*) On the central arch—

در سال ۲۶ جلوس حضرت ظل الله شاهجهان بادشاه غازي صاحبقران ثاني که موافق سنه
۱۰۶۳ هجري بود باني اين مسجد رچه خراجه طرب توفيق اتمام اين معبد شريف يافته وجه
محصول شش دوکان متعلقه انرا برکسانے که در اوقات خمسه باقامت امر امامت و اذان
قيام نمايند وقف گردانيد -

Translation.

"In the 26th year of the reign of His Majesty, the shadow of God Shah Jahan, the King, the champion of the faith, and the second lord of the happy conjunction, corresponding to 1063 Hijra, the founder of this mosque and well, Khuwaja Turab, having obtained the favour (of God) for completing this eminent place of worship dedicated the rent of six shops belonging to it for such men that should perform the duties of leading the prayers and calling for it five times (a day)."

(*g*) Good.
(*h*) Unnecessary.
(*j*) The mosque, which measures 36′ 0″ north and south by 13′ 9″ east and west, is a solidly constructed building of red sandstone and has a large courtyard, a portion of which is paved with the same material. There are 3 domed compartments.

It is interesting to find a building of this earlier style of architecture within the walls of Shahjahanabad. The inscription also refers to a pious endowment made of the rent of six shops belonging to the mosque, in favour of the Imam and Muazzin. The shops referred to lie towards the north of the mosque, but they have for many years ceased to be its property.

(*l*) S. 19.

No. 148. (*a*) Pipalwali Mosque II.
(*b*) Kuncha-i Sharif Beg.
(*c*) Waqf, Mutawalli, Karim Bakhsh.
(*d*) III.
(*e*) Late Mughal.
(*f*) None.
(*g*) Good.
(*h*) Unnecessary.
(*j*) A small building of no particular interest.

No. 149. (*a*) Sivalaya (unnamed).
(*b*) Kuncha-i-Sharif Beg.
(*c*) Bhola Nath (?)
(*d*) III.
(*e*) Late Mughal.
(*f*) None.
(*g*) Good.
(*h*) Unnecessary.
(*j*) In the temple are enshrined images of Parvati, Kartikasvami, Ganesa and Nandi, besides the ling of Siva. In the niche facing the visitor are images of Rama, Sita and Lakshmana. They are of white marble. In another niche is an image of Bhairava besmeared with red lead.

No. 150. Kashmiriyan's Temple.

(*b*) Kuncha-i-Sharif Beg.
(*c*) Ganga Sahai (Jagat Narayana).
(*d*) III.
(*e*) Late Mughal.
(*f*) None.
(*g*) Good.
(*h*) Unnecessary.
(*j*) In the temple are enshrined images of Parvati, Kartikasvami, Nandi, Rama, Sita and Lakshmana and the ling of Siva.

IMLI MUHALLA.

No. 151. (*a*) Temple (unnamed).
(*b*) Kuncha-i-Harjas Mal.
(*c*) Saran Lal.
(*d*) III.
(*e*) About 80 years old.
(*f*) None.
(*g*) Good.
(*h*) Unnecessary.
(*j*) The temple is a small building of no particular interest. It was built by Visvambharanath, grandfather of Saran Lal.

No. 152. (*a*) Sivalaya usually called the temple of Uma-Mahesvara (Uma=Parvati and Mahesvara=Siva).
(*b*) Gali Lehsva.
(*c*) Baijanatha.
(*d*) III.
(*e*) About 85 years old.
(*f*) None.
(*g*) Good.
(*h*) Unnecessary.
(*j*) In the temple are images of Mahadeva, Parvati, Ganapati, Kartikasvami, Nandi and Hanumat, with the ling of Siva. To the visitor's left there is another image of Hanumat besmeared with red lead.

No. 153. (*a*) Kaseran's Temple.
(*b*) Chauk Shah Mubarik.
(*c*) Jotiprasada Kasera.
(*d*) III.
(*e*) Late Mughal.
(*f*) There is a modern inscription over the gate of the temple. It runs :—

(१) श्री
Sri
(२) मंदिर
Mandira

(३) स्वामी दीनदयालजी महाराज का

Savami Dinadayalaji Maharajaka

(४) पंचायती कसेरोंका बना

Panchayati Kaseronka Bana

(५) संवत्

Samvat

(६) १९६०

1960

(*j*) The temple is dedicated to Svami Dina Dayala. There is no image in it. It is lighted on Sundays and Mondays when the lamps are worshipped. It was rebuilt in Samvat 1960 (1903 A.D.) as will be seen from the inscription.

No. 154. (*a*) Sivalaya (unnamed).
(*b*) *Gali* Kashmirian.
(*c*) Birabhavana Natha.
(*d*) III.
(*e*) Late Mughal.
(*f*) None.
(*g*) Good.
(*h*) Unnecessary.
(*j*) In the temple are images of Parvati, Ganges, Kartikasvami and Nandi with the ling of Siva.

No. 155. (*a*) Qannauji Rai's Temple.
(*b*) Kuncha-i Patiram.
(*c*) Rai Bahadur Kanhayalala.
(*d*) III.
(*e*) It is said to be more than 250 years old (?)
N.B.—The inscription in Naskh characters in the well which has yet to be deciphered may, perhaps, throw light on the date.
(*f*) The inscription has already been referred to.
(*g*) Good.
(*h*) Unnecessary.
(*j*) Qannauji Rai is said to have built the temple. The inscription referred to above may make it clear, if it contains any name. The local tradition affirms the well to be the work of a *banjara.*
In the main shrine are images of Rama, Sita and Lakshmana. In front of them there is a ling and images of Parvati, Ganapati, Kartikasvami and Nandi. There is an image of Hanumat to the visitor's left and that of Bhairava to the right.
The temple was repaired in Samvat 1901 (1844 A.D.)

No. 156. (*a*) Sivalaya (unnamed).
(*b*) Kuncha-i-Pati Ram.

(*c*) Jagadish Rai.
(*d*) III.
(*e*) Late Mughal.
(*f*) None.
(*g*) Good.
(*h*) Unnecessary.
(*j*) The Sivalaya proper consists of a small pavilion in the centre of a house. It has been rebuilt. Within are images of Parvati, Ganapati, Kartikasvami and Nandi.

No. 157. (*a*) Sivalaya (unnamed).
(*b*) Jatavara *Mahalla* or Kunde Vala, close to a well on road-side.
(*c*) Lala Bala Prasad.
(*d*) III.
(*e*) Late Mughal.
(*f*) None.
(*g*) Poor.
(*h*) Unnecessary.
(*j*) The Sivalaya is now in a dilapidated condition. Even the ling has disappeared and only small pillars are lying here and there. The temple however, can still be traced. The ling is said to have disappeared about 15 or 20 years ago.

MUHALLA NAMDEWALAN.

No. 158. (*a*) Mosque (unnamed).
(*b*) In the *Muhalla.*
(*c*) Waqf, Mutawalli, Ramzani.
(*d*) III.
(*e*) Late Mughal.
(*f*) None.
(*g*) Good.
(*h*) Unnecessary.
(*j*) The mosque is a small building of no particular interest.

AJMER GATE.

No. 159. (*a*) Mochiyan's Mosque. In Dr. Vogel's list given as Mosque of Khalil.
(*b*) Near Ajmer Gate.
(*c*) Waqf, Mutawalli, Husain Bakhsh.
(*d*) II *b*.
(*e*) 1110 A. H. (1698-99 A. D.).
(*f*) On the northern arch—

(۱) حبذ [۱] مسجدے که شد ز شرف * سجده گاه گدا و شاهنشاه
(۲) شد بنایش بعهد عالمگیر * بطفیل نبي رسول الله
(۳) گفت تاریخ این حرم هاتف * کرد کعبه بنا خلیل الله

Translation.

(1) "What a beautiful mosque, which by reason of its eminence became a place of worship for a beggar and an emperor."

(2) "Its foundation was laid in the reign of Alamgir (Aurangzeb), through the favour of the Prophet, the messenger of God."

(3) "The invisible crier spake the date of this sanctuary. 'Khalil-ullah built Kaba.'"

(*g*) Good.

(*h*) Unnecessary.

(*j*) The mosque, which measures some 35′ 9″ north and south by 12′ 9″ east and west, is situated on raised ground and is reached from the road by a flight of steps. The prayer chamber consists of three domed compartments. There are three arched entrances towards the east and one towards the north. The latter has the above inscription written over it in black letters on a white piece of stone. The courtyard is paved with red sandstone and contains a tank.

No. 160.

(*a*) Ajmer Gate.
(*b*) In south-west wall of the city.
(*c*) Municipality.
(*d*) II*a*.
(*e*) 1644—1649 A. D.
(*f*) None.
(*g*) Fair.
(*h*) Should be declared a Protected Monument.
(*k*) *Archer* I, 125.
A. S. I., I (1862-63), 224-225.
As. Res., IV, 418, 419.
Baxter, 32.
C. S. Range, 248.
Tour, 162.
Carr Stephen, 244.
Keene, 34.
Fanshawe, 6, 65, 248.
Hearn, 44, 257.

No. 161.

(*a*) Unchi Mosque III.
(*b*) Kuncha-i-Shah Tara.
(*c*) Waqf, Mutawalli, Rafiuddin Beg.
(*d*) III.
(*e*) Late Mughal.
(*f*) None.
(*g*) Good.
(*h*) Unnecessary.
(*j*) The mosque, which is reached by means of 9 steps from the road, is a smal building of no particular interest.

No. 162. (*a*) Qabronwali Mosque.

(*b*) Kuncha-i-Shah Tara.

(*c*) Waqf, Mutawalli, Hafiz Abdul Karim.

(*d*) III.

(*e*) 1201 A.H. (1786-87 A.D.)

(*f*) On the central arch—

(۱) برد پاینده خان دلیر جنگ خطاب * رفت برد از فنا سوے بقا اسباب

(۲) رابعه بیگم اهلش این بنا بنمود * همچو قطب فلک به ارض اختر بحساب

۱۲۰۱

Translation.

(1) "Painda Khan, entitled Diler Jang, departed and carried goods from mortality to eternity."

(2) "Rabia Begam, his wife, built this (mosque) like the polar star of the sky on the earth and a star in reckoning (date) 1201."

(*g*) Good.

(*h*) Unnecessary.

(*j*) The mosque, which measures 20′ 6″ north and south by 13′ 10″ east and west, consists of a prayer chamber of three compartments roofed by domes. The courtyard has arched rooms on either side. The above inscription is on the central arch of the prayer chamber, and inscribed on a piece of white marble.

(*l*) S. 25.

No. 163. (*a*) Painda Khan's grave.

(*b*) Kuncha-i Shah Tara, in the compound of the mosque Qabronwali.

(*c*) Waqf, Mutawalli, Hafiz Abdul Karim.

(*d*) III.

(*e*) 1201 A.H. (1786-87 A.D.).

(*f*) On the head-stone of the grave—

(۱) پاینده خاني شرف دهر که ذاتش * موصوف باوصاف حسن بود کماهي

(۲) خانی که بلندی سزد قدر رفیعش * بگذاشت به چرخ برین دار ملاهي

(۳) اسپهبد سر کرده که میداد جبینش * امروز بمغفوري فرداش گواهي

(۴) از بحر فنا رخت بدر برد جهان را * بگذاشت در امواج چو کشتي ماهي

۱۲۰۱

(۵) تاریخ چو جستم اخرت نیك بحالي * حشرش بحسین ابن علي باد الهي

Translation.

(1) " Painda Khan, an honour to the age, whose person was endowed with as excellent qualities as they ought to be."

(2) " The Khan, as his exalted rank deserves eminence, left this vain world for the high heavens."

(3) " The victorious general whose forehead was a witness, to-day, (in this world) of his to-morrow's salvation (*i.e.*, salvation in the next world)."

(4) " From the perishable sea (world) he took out his goods (and) left the world as the fisherman's bark on the waves."

(5) "When I found the chronogram 'Akhirat' very happily O God! May his resurrection be with Husain, son of Ali."
(g) Good.
(h) Unnecessary.
(j) The grave is of white marble and contains the above inscription written on the head-stone. The wife of Painda Khan erected the mosque (*see* No. 163), in the courtyard of which the grave lies.

ROAD FROM AJMER GATE TO QAZI KA HAUZ.

No. 164. (a) The Koclewalan's (charcoal sellers') Mosque.
(b) Kuncha-i Shah Tara.
(c) Waqf, Mutawalli, Muhammad Ishaq and Abdul Rashid.
(d) III.
(e) Late Mughal.
(f) None.
(g) Good.
(h) Unnecessary.
(j) Shah Tara, in whose Kuncha the mosque lies, was one of the daughters of Nawwab Qamru-d-din Khan. Like her other sisters her residence was a portion of the house of the Nawwab. It is now transformed into a Kuncha or street, which bears her name. Near the mosque are traces of a gateway which was probably an entrance to her house. The building is a small one and of no particular interest.

No. 165. (a) Gate (unnamed).
(b) The gate serves as the entrance to the *Muhalla* Karori.
(c) Amar Nath and Abul Hasan, etc.
(d) III.
(e) Late Mughal.
(f) None.
(g) Poor.
(h) Unnecessary.
(j) The gate was the principal entrance to the Ganj of the Nawwab Wazir, which is now known by the name of *Muhalla* Karori.

No. 166. (a) Gate (unnamed).
(b) Entrance to the Kuncha-i-Rajna Begam.
(c) Muhammad Ahmad and Abdul Hamid.
(d) III.
(e) Muhammad Shah's reign.
(f) None.
(g) Ruinous.
(h) Unnecessary.
(j) Rajna Begam is in all probability a corruption of Rasi-un-Nisa Begam, the name of another daughter of Nawwab Qamruddin Khan. This

gate was the entrance to her house, also a portion of the house of Nawwab Qamruddin Khan.

(*l*) S. 26.

No. 167. (*a*) Gate (unnamed).

(*b*) Entrance to the Kuncha-i Fathu-n-Nisa Begam.

(*c*) Lala Jai Diyal.

(*d*) III.

(*e*) Muhammad Shah's reign.

(*f*) None.

(*g*) Good.

(*h*) Unnecessary.

(*j*) Fathu-n-Nisa Begam was the third daughter of Nawwab Qamruddin Khan. This gate led to her house and formed a portion of the house of the Nawwab. The site of the house is now occupied by a *Muhalla* known after her name.

MUHALLA QAZI KA HAUZ.

No. 168. (*a*) Mosque of Qazi Ka Hauz.

(*b*) In the *Muhalla*.

(*c*) Waqf, Mutawalli, Abdul Ghaffar.

(*d*) III.

(*e*) 1131 A.H. (1718-19 A.D.).

(*f*) On the entrance to a house within the enclosure of the mosque.

باغ نبي الله ١١٣١

Translation.

"The garden of Nab-i-ullah 1131."

(*g*) Good.

(*h*) Unnecessary.

(*j*) The mosque, which measures some 49′ 0″ north and south by 22′ 0″ east and west, is said to be very old, but was rebuilt and extended by one Mufti Karimullah. In its south-east corner is a house on the entrance of which is an inscription referring to a garden, and dated 1131 A.H. It seems probable that the ground, where the house now stands, was once a garden and that the present mosque was reconstructed at the same time as the garden was made and the inscription on its entrance was put up.

No. 169. (*a*) Mosque (unnamed).

(*b*) Kuncha-i-Fathu-n-Nisa Begam.

(*c*) Waqf, Mutawalli, Muhammad Murtaza.

(*d*) III.

(*e*) Late Mughal.

(*f*) None.

(*g*) Good

(*h*) Unnecessary.

(*j*) A small building of no particular interest. In the courtyard of the mosque there is a tomb of one Sayyid Baqa-ullah.

BAZAR SIRKI WALAN.

No. 170. (*a*) Lal Masjid I. In Dr. Vogel's list given as mosque of Mubarak Begam, known as Randi Ki Masjid.

(*b*) Near Qazi Ka Hauz.

(*c*) Waqf, Mutawalli, Muaiyadul Islam Committee.

(*d*) II *b*.

(*e*) 1238 A.H. (1822-23 A.D.)

(*f*) On the central arch—

(۱) مبارک بیگم این مسجد بنا کرد * که باشد برتر از چرخ مقوس

(۲) کم از بیت المقدس نیست شانش * بگو این ثانی بیت مقدس

۱۲۳۸

Translation.

(1) "Mubarak Begam built this mosque which is superior to the arched sky."

(2) "Its dignity is not less than that of Jerusalem; call this a second Jerusalem, 1238."

(*g*) Good.

(*h*) Unnecessary.

(*j*) The mosque is built of red sandstone and measures 29′ 0″ north and south by 14′ 0″ east and west. It is two storeyed, the first storey which forms the floor of the mosque, consists of arched rooms used as shops; the upper storey consists of a courtyard and prayer chamber of 3 compartments roofed by domes, and having 3 arched entrances. The central arch bears the inscription given above, and inscribed on a piece of white marble.

There are, however, several other inscriptions written on the arches of a lower apartment and the entrance to the mosque. They are all modern, and excepting one which refers to the repair of the mosque, etc., are only of a religious character. The mosque is reached by 15 steps from the road.

Mubarik Begam who built the mosque was the mistress of an Englishman. She came into possession of his property and from it she built the mosque and a neighbouring house, now occupied by the Police Station.

(*l*) S. 18.

No. 171. (*a*) Gate (unnamed).

(*b*) Entrance to the Nawwab Haveli of Badal Beg Khan.

(*c*) Mr. Mohammad Rafiq, etc.

(*d*) III.

(*e*) Late Mughal.

(*f*) None.

(*g*) Fair.

(*h*) Unnecessary.

(*j*) The gate is an entrance to the above Haveli.

No. 172. (*a*) Sirki Walan's Mosque.

(*b*) Near the gate of the Haveli of Nawwab Badal Beg Khan.

(*c*) Waqf, Mutawalli, Mirza Muhammad Beg Khan.

(*d*) III.

(*e*) Probably of the same date as the house of Badal Beg Khan.

(*f*) None.

(*g*) Good.

(*h*) Unnecessary.

(*j*) The mosque is two storeyed and measures 33′ 0″ north and south by 15′ 0″ east and west, the first or basement storey, which forms the floor of the mosque, consisting of apartments, now used as shops and which are a source of income to the mosque. The upper storey consists of a courtyard and prayer chamber with three arched entrances roofed by domes. The mosque is reached by a flight of 11 steps from the road.

No. 173. (*a*) Gate (unnamed).

(*b*) Entrance to the Haveli of Nawwab Badal Beg Khan.

(*c*) Muhammad Islamullah.

(*d*) III.

(*e*) 1270 A. H. (1853-54 A. D.).

(*f*) On the gate—

هوالحکیم

نهادہ بنا احسن الله خان * سر راہ بد انسان در دلکشا

که غالب پئے سال تاریخ او * رقم زد در دلکشا حبذا

فقیر محمد امیر رضوي ۱۲۷۰

Translation.

"He is Doctor."

(1) "Ahsanullah Khan laid the foundation of such a charming gate, by the road,"

(2) "That Ghalib for its chronogram wrote 'what a beautiful and charming gate.'"

"Faqir Muhammad Amir Rizvi. 1270."

(*g*) Fair.

(*h*) Unnecessary.

(*j*) The gate is one of the two entrances to the Haveli of Nawwab Badal Beg Khan. It was built by Hakim Ahsanullah Khan, the court phycisian of Bahadur Shah II when he acquired the house. The inscription was composed by Ghalib, the well known poet of Delhi of the last century, and was written by F. Muhammad Amir Rizavi. Badal Beg Khan was styled "Turki Jang." He came into India from Samarqand in the beginning of the reign of Shah Alam II (1173—1221 A. H.=1759—1806 A. D.) and was given the post of Risal-i-dar in the service of Amir-ul-Umara Mirza Najaf Khan.

Hakim Ahsanullah Khan came from Hirat, his family being obliged to leave that place on account of differences with the Governor. Medicine was not the hereditary profession of the family but it was adopted by his father. Ahsanullah Khan was held in considerable repute and honour. He was appointed royal physician by Akbar II who honoured him with the title of Umdat-ul-Mulk Haziqu-z-Zaman, while Bahadur Shah II not only continued his post and rank but also added to his titles the epithets "Ihtiram-ud-daula Sabit Jang." The Hakim possessed much influence with Bahadur Shah II and it is said that the Emperor did nothing without first consulting him. He had a house at Mehrauli.

No. 174. (*a*) Hakim Ahsanullah Khan's house.

(*b*) Haveli of Nawwab Badal Beg Khan.

(*c*) Muhammad Islamullah Khan.

(*d*) III.

(*e*) Time of Muhammad Shah.

(*f*) None.

(*g*) Good.

(*h*) Unnecessary.

(*j*) The house was built by Nawwab Qamruddin Khan. It was originally of considerable extent, reaching as far as the Ajmer gate and affording accommodation to the whole family and dependants of the Nawwab. After the death of Qamruddin Khan the house was divided into several portions; the one now under discussion came into the possession of Nawwab Badal Beg Khan after whom it is still known. It afterwards belonged to Hakim Ahsanullah Khan, who built a Hammam in its enclosure.

Wazirul-Mulk Itimad-ud-daulah Qamruddin Khan was the son of Itimadu-d-daulah Amin Khan, the son of Mir Jumla. Qamruddin Khan was offered the post of minister by Muhammad Shah in the sixth year of the reign, Nizamul-Mulk, appointed Wazir after the death of Itimadu-d-daulah Amin Khan, having vacated the post in disgust with the Emperor and his court. He held the office until his death. He was shot in the battle against Ahmad Shah Abdali at Sirhind.

(*k*) *Shahjahan Namah*, Inayat Khan, *Muntakhabu-l-Lubab*, Khafi Khan; *Tarikh-i-Hindi*, Rustam Ali; *Tarikh-i-Ahmad Shah*. } *Elliot*, *VII*, 108—109, 505—7, 525, 531; *VIII*, 45, 50, 55—56, 106—108.

No. 175. (*a*) Hammam (Bath).

(*b*) Haveli of Nawwab Badal Beg Khan, in the compound of the house of Hakim Ahsanullah Khan.

(*c*) Muhammad Islamullah Khan.

(*d*) III.

(*e*) 1268 A. H. (1852 A. D.).

(*f*) On a piece of marble on one of the inner walls—

هو الحکیم

تب گشت این حمام دلخواه * بتعمیر فقیر احسن الله

محمد امیر رضوی ۱۲۶۸

Translation.

"He is Doctor."

"This fascinating bath was finished by the construction of Faqir Ahsanullah. Muhammad *Amir* Rizvi. 1268."

On a piece of red stone built into the outside wall—

هوالطاهر

(۱) بدهلي احسن الله خان بنا کرد * یکی گرما به قدسي نشیمن

(۲) پے سالش که یارب جاودان باد * بفرق باني خود سایه افگن

(۳) بشستم روے لفظ انگاه گفتم * شده تعمیر این حمام احسن

سمت ۱۹۰۹ سنه ۱۸۵۲ ع سنه ۱۶ ج سنه ۱۲۶۸ ه

Translation.

"He is Holy."

(1) "Ahsanullah Khan built in Delhi a bath which is a celestial seat."

(2) "For the year of it, which, O God! may ever remain casting shade on the head of its founder,"

(3) "I washed the face of the word and then said, 'This excellent bath has been constructed.'"

"Sammat 1909; 1852 A.D; 16 regnal year; 1268 A. H."

(*g*) Good.

(*h*) Unnecessary.

No. 176. (*a*) Gate (unnamed).

(*b*) Entrance to the Haveli of Abdurrahman Khan.

(*c*) Karamallah *alias* Nanne Khan Sahib.

(*d*) III.

(*e*) 1221 A.H. (1806-07 A.D.).

(*f*) On the archway—

حویلي عبدالرحمن خان صاحب

سنه ۱۲۲۱

Translation.

"House of Abdur-Rahman Khan Sahib."

"The year 1221."

(*g*) Fair.

(*h*) Unnecessary.

(*j*) The gateway is a large one and has the above quoted inscription, written in black letters on a small piece of white marble. Abd-ur-Rahman Khan was a respectable and wealthy citizen of Shahjahanabad.

No. 177. (*a*) Gate (Lal Darwaza).

(*b*) See above.

(*c*) Babu Ali Mirza.

(*d*) III.

(*e*) Late Mughal period.

(*f*) None.

(*g*) Fair.

(*h*) Unnecessary.

(*j*) The gate was built by one Mirza Mughal Beg Khan as an entrance to his house.

No. 178. (*a*) Mirza Mughal Beg Khan's Mosque.
(*b*) Lal Darwaza.
(*c*) Waqf, Mutawalli, Ahmad Mirza.
(*d*) III.
(*e*) Late Mughal period.
(*f*) None.
(*g*) Good.
(*h*) Unnecessary.
(*j*) The mosque, which is a small building of no particular interest, was built by Mirza Mughal Beg Khan.

KUNCHA-I PANDIT.

No. 179. (*a*) Khojan Sahib's Mosque.
(*b*) *Gali* Azizu-d Din.
(*c*) Waqf, Mutawalli, Nasir Ahmad.
(*d*) III.
(*e*) 1165 A. H. (1751-52 A. D.).
(*f*) On the outer entrance—

(۱) محمد عربي کا بروے هر دوسرا ست * کسے که خاک درش نیست خاک برسر او

(۲) چراغ و مسجد و محراب و منبر * ابو بکر و عمر عثمان و حیدر

بنائے مسجد مرزا محمد جان برکي در سنه یکهزار و یکصد و شصت و پنج هجري

Translation.

(1) "Muhammad of Arabia is an honour to both the worlds; may dust be on the head of him who is not the dust of his threshold."
(2) "Abu Bakr, Umar, Usman, and Haidar are lamp, mosque, Mihrab and pulpit."
"The foundation of the mosque of Muhammad Jan Birki (inhabitant of Birka, a city in Persia) (was laid) in the year one thousand one hundred and sixty-five Hijra."
(*g*) Good.
(*h*) Unnecessary.
(*j*) The mosque measures 26′ 9″ north and south by 12′ 6″ east and west.

No. 180. (*a*) Miyanji Sahib's Mosque.
(*b*) In the *Muhalla*.
(*c*) Waqf, Mutawalli, Maulvi Muhammad Ismail.
(*d*) III.
(*e*) Original building, Shahjahan's reign (?). Recent mosque, late Mughal period.
(*f*) None.
(*g*) Good.
(*h*) Unnecessary.
(*j*) The original building said to have been erected during the period of Shahjahan is now below the level of the surrounding ground; the present mosque has been constructed over it.

No. 181. (*a*) Sawar Khan's Mosque.
(*b*) *Gali* Sawar Khan.
(*c*) Waqf, Mutawalli, Abdur Rahman.
(*d*) III.
(*e*) 1209 A. H. (1794—95 A. D.).
(*f*) On the entrance.

مسجد علي محمد خان حنفي
سنه ۱۲۰۹

Translation.

"The mosque of Ali Muhammad Khan Hanafi. The year 1209."
(*g*) Good.
(*h*) Unnecessary.

MUHALLA NIYARYAN.

No. 182. (*a*) Mosque (unnamed).
(*b*) In the *Muhalla.*
(*c*) Waqf, Mutawalli, Manzur Ali.
(*d*) III.
(*e*) Late Mughal.
(*f*) None.
(*g*) Good.
(*h*) Unnecessary.
(*j*) A small building of no particular interest.

FASILEN FARRASHKHANA.

No. 183. (*a*) Mosque (unnamed).
(*b*) Rajji Ka Katra.
(*c*) Waqf, Mutawalli, Muhammad Amir.
(*d*) III.
(*e*) Late Mughal.
(*f*) None.
(*g*) Good.
(*h*) Unnecessary.
(*j*) A small building of no particular interest.

MUHALLA FARRASHKHANA.

No. 184. (*a*) Khirki (Postern) Farrashkhana. (*See* Nos. 41 and 343.)
(*b*) South-west Postern of Shahjahanabad.
(*c*) Government.
(*d*) II*a*.
(*e*) 1644—1649 A. D.
(*f*) None.
(*g*) Fair.
(*h*) Should be declared a "Protected Monument."
(*k*) *Carr Stephen*, 244.
Keene, 34.
(*l*) S. 79.

No. 185. (*a*) Anarwali (pomegranate) Mosque I.
(*b*) Ghanta Kakwan.
(*c*) Waqf, Mutawalli, Hafiz Shihab-ud-din.
(*d*) III.
(*e*) 1071 A. H. (1660-61 A. D.)
(*f*) On the central arch—

(۱) این مسجدے که کعبه ارباب طاعتست * اسلام تا بپاست اساسش بجا بود
(۲) هر کس ز روے عجز گریزد بدر گهش * کــز بیمش از گناه نباشد روا بود
(۳) خیر النساء که بانی این قبله دعاست * روے دلش همیشه بسوے خدا بود
(۴) ز اولاد برگزیدهٔ یحی هاشمیست * ان سـیده که صالحه بـیریا بود
(۵) سال بنائے او چو طلب کردم از خرد * گفتا بگو که مسجد خیر النساء بود
۱۰۷۱

Translation.

(1) "This mosque which is the Kaba of religious persons; may its foundation be extant as long as Islam exists."
(2) "Whoever submissively runs to its threshold, if he has no fear of sin, it may be permissible."
(3) "Khairu-n Nisa who is founder of this Qibla of prayer, has ever the face of her heart towards God."
(4) "That Sayyid lady who is good and artless, is one of the selected descendants of Yahya Hashmi."
(5) "When I asked wisdom the date of its foundation, it replied, 'Say it is the mosque of Khairu-n Nisa.' 1071."

(*g*) Good.
(*h*) Unnecessary.
(*j*) The mosque which is only a small building was built by Khairu-n Nisa, who was a descendant of Yahya Hashmi. The prayer chamber has three arched entrances, on the central arch of which there is a white marble inscription. The mosque takes its name from the pomegranate tree which stands in the enclosure.

No. 186. (*a*) Mir Madari's Mosque.
(*b*) *Gali* Mir Madari.
(*c*) Waqf, Mutawalli, Mir Fukhru-d-Din.
(*d*) III.
(*e*) Late Mughal period. (?)
(*f*) None.
(*g*) Good.
(*h*) Unnecessary.
(*j*) The mosque, which is of no particular interest, has been rebuilt.

No. 187. (*a*) Mosque (unnamed).
(*b*) Ihata Hajjan Sahib.
(*c*) Waqf, Mutawalli, Ahmad Mirza.
(*d*) III.
(*e*) Shahjahan's reign. (?)

(*f*) None.
(*g*) Good.
(*h*) Unnecessary.
(*j*) The mosque, which is only a small building of no particular interest, was built by one Khuwaja Khumar Shah in the enclosure of his house. He is said to have been a saint in the time of Shahjahan.

No. 188. (*a*) Gate (unnamed).
(*b*) Entrance to the Ihata Hajjan Sahib.
(*c*) Nawwab Mirza.
(*d*) III.
(*e*) Shahjahan's reign. (?)
(*f*) None.
(*g*) Fair.
(*h*) Unnecessary.

No. 189. (*a*) Akhund Ji's Mosque.
(*b*) *Gali* Akhundji.
(*c*) Waqf, Mutawalli, Maulvi Muhammad Umar Akhund.
(*d*) III.
(*e*) Late Mughal.
(*f*) None.
(*g*) Good.
(*h*) Unnecessary.
(*j*) On the central arch of the mosque there is a modern inscription stating that it was originally built in 1105 A.H. (1693—94 A.D.) and reconstructed in the year 1308 A.H. (1890—91 A. D.)

No. 190. (*a*) Mosque (unnamed).
(*b*) Katra Dhobiyan.
(*c*) Waqf, Mutawalli, people of the *Muhalla*.
(*d*) III.
(*e*) Late Mughal.
(*f*) None.
(*g*) Good.
(*h*) Unnecessary
(*j*) A small building of no particular interest.

No. 191. (*a*) Mirza Fakhrullah Beg's Mosque.
(*b*) Near the bridge.
(*c*) Waqf, Mutawalli, Muhammad Mirza.
(*d*) III.
(*e*) Late Mughal period.
(*f*) None.
(*g*) Good.

(h) Unnecessary.
(j) The mosque has been rebuilt. It is a small building of no particular interest.

No. 192. (a) Mosque (unnamed).
(b) Katra Hindu.
(c) Waqf, Mutawalli, people of the *Muhalla*.
(d) III.
(e) Late Mughal.
(f) None.
(g) Good.
(h) Unnecessary.
(j) A small building of no particular interest.

No. 193. (a) Hakims' Mosque.
(b) Gali Chah Shirin.
(c) Waqf, Mutawalli, Hakim Ahmad Said Khan.
(d) III.
(e) Late Mughal.
(f) None.
(g) Good.
(h) Unnecessary.
(j) A small building of no particular interest.

No. 194. (a) Mosque (unnamed).
(b) *Gali* Rajan (Masons).
(c) Waqf, Mutawalli, people of the *Muhalla*.
(d) III.
(e) Late Mughal.
(f) None.
(g) Good.
(h) Unnecessary.
(j) The building is of no particular interest.

No. 195. (a) Gular Wali Mosque.
(c) Waqf, Mutawalli, Abdullah.
(d) III.
(e) Late Mughal.
(f) None.
(g) Good.
(h) Unnecessary.
(j) The mosque, a small building only, is two storeyed and is reached by 16 steps. The lower or basement storey consists of a few rooms used as

shops. It has been rebuilt and an inscription containing religious expressions and the date 1315 A. H. (1897—98 A. D.) has been placed on its central arch.

No. 196. (*a*) Gondni Wali Mosque II.
(*b*) Near Nagina Mahal.
(*c*) Waqf, Mutawalli, Sadr-ud-din.
(*d*) III.
(*e*) Late Mughal.
(*f*) None.
(*g*) Good.
(*h*) Unnecessary.
(*j*) A small building of no particular interest.

No. 197. (*a*) Mosque (unnamed).
(*b*) Chhatta Rajan.
(*c*) Waqf, Mutawalli, Ali Jan.
(*d*) III.
(*e*) Late Mughal.
(*f*) None.
(*g*) Good.
(*h*) Unnecessary.
(*j*) The mosque has been rebuilt. It is a small building of no particular interest.

No. 198. (*a*) Mosque (unnamed).
(*b*) Chhatta Chuhiya.
(*c*) Waqf, Mutawalli, Hajji Ghulam Muhammad.
(*d*) III.
(*e*) Late Mughal.
(*f*) None.
(*g*) Good.
(*h*) Unnecessary.
(*j*) A small building of no particular interest.

MUHALLA RODGARAN.

No. 199. (*a*) Gate (unnamed).
(*b*) Entrance to the school of Iradatullah.
(*c*) Waqf for the mosque inside the school, Mutawalli, Mir Arab.
(*d*) III.
(*e*) Muhammad Shah's reign.
(*f*) None.
(*g*) Ruinous.
(*h*) Unnecessary.

(*j*) The school, of which this is the gateway, no longer exists, its site being occupied by a Muhalla known as Madrasa-i-Iradatullah. Iradatullah refers to Iradatmand Khan, the title of Sharfu-d-Daula, a nobleman and general of Muhammad Shah. He was sent, at the end of the 5th year of the reign of Muhammad Shah, against Raja Ajit Singh, who had rebelled and taken possession of Ajmer and Sambhar, penetrating as far as Narnaul. Iradatmand Khan was accompanied by Raja Jai Singh Sawai, Muhammad Khan Bangash, and Gopal Singh, Raja of Bhadawar, at the head of an army of about one hundred thousand horse and more than two hundred elephants. Raja Ajit Singh on hearing the news, lost all courage, fled from Narnaul, and took refuge in the fort of Garh-patti. Here he held out for some time, and at last, mounting a camel, went off to Jodhpur. He then sued for peace, and made over his son Dhaukal Singh to be taken to court as a hostage.

(*k*) *Tarikhi Hindi*, Rustam Ali, *Elliot*, VIII, 43-4.

No. 200. (*a*) Grave of Nawwab Iradatmand Khan.

(*b*) In the centre of the ancient site of the school of Iradatmand Khan.

(*c*) Waqf, Mutawalli, Mir Arab.

(*d*) II *b*.

(*e*) Late Mughal.

(*f*) None.

(*g*) Good.

(*h*) Unnecessary.

(*j*) The grave stands on two platforms, one above the other. The first or the lower platform is of red stone paved with white marble slabs, while the upper platform and the Tawiz of the grave are totally of marble. There is no inscription on the grave, but on the lower platform there are two other graves said to be those of his relatives and one of them bears an inscribed headstone with the date 1188 A.H. (1774 A.D.)

(*l*) S. 78.

No. 201. (*a*) Grave of Nawwab Musa Yar Khan.

(*b*) To west of the grave of Iradatmand Khan, on its lower platform, in the school of Iradatmand Khan.

(*c*) Waqf, Mutawalli, Mir Arab.

(*d*) III.

(*e*) 6th Muharram, 1188 A. H. (19th March 1774 A.D.)

(*f*) On the headstone. Quotations from the Quran and—

(۱) چون سفر کرد از جهان نواب موسی یارخان * کرد ماتم هر یکے از دوستانش بیگمان

(۲) سال تاریخش چو جستم از خیال خویش گفت * باد یارب قصر و گلزار ابد در ان ان

بتاریخ ششم ماہ محرم سنه ۱۱۸۸ هجري از دار [ا] لفنا بدار بقا رحلت نمود

Translation.

(1) "When Nawwab Musa-yar-Khan set out on a journey from this world, every one of his friends, undoubtedly, lamented."

(2) "When I asked my mind the year of that, it said, 'O God! may the palace and garden of eternity be in his share'."

"On the 6th of the month of Muḥarram of the year 1188 Hijra (19th March 1774 A.D.) departed from the perishable abode to the everlasting one."

(*g*) Poor.

(*h*) Unnecessary.

No. 202. (*a*) Mosque (unnamed).

(*b*) In the school of Iradatmand Khan.

(*c*) Waqf, Mutawalli, Mir Arab.

(*d*) III.

(*e*) Late Mughal.

(*f*) None.

(*g*) Good.

(*h*) Unnecessary.

(*j*) The mosque which is a small building of no particular interest has been rebuilt.

No. 203. (*a*) Grave of Sayyid Mansur Ali.

(*b*) In front of mosque (No. 204).

(*c*) Waqf, Mutawalli, Ikramu-d-Din.

(*d*) III.

(*e*) Unknown.

(*f*) None.

(*g*) Good.

(*h*) Unnecessary.

(*j*) The grave is enclosed by wooden railings. There are two other graves within the enclosure on either side of that of Sayyid Mansur Ali. They are said to be those of a son and wife of the Sayyid.

No. 204. (*a*) Maidan wali Mosque.

(*b*) In the *Muhalla*.

(*c*) Waqf, Mutawalli, Miyan Abdu-s-Samad.

(*d*) III.

(*e*) Late Mughal.

(*f*) None.

(*g*) Good.

(*h*) Unnecessary.

(*j*) Within the mosque enclosure is the grave of one Sayyid Yaqut Shah on whose account the mosque, which is only a small building, was erected.

No. 205. (*a*) Imli wali mosque I.

(*b*) In the *Muhalla*.

(*c*) Waqf, Mutawalli, Abdur-r-Rahim.

d) III.

(*e*) Late Mughal.
(*f*) None.
(*g*) Good.
(*h*) Unnecessary.
(*i*) The mosque has been rebuilt and there is an inscription on its central arch referring to its reconstruction in the year 1313 A. H. (1895-96 A. D.).

KATRA SHAIKH CHAND.

No. 206. (*a*) Mosque (unnamed).
(*b*) In the *Muhalla*.
(*c*) Waqf, Mutawalli, Abdul Karim and Mirza Amir Beg.
(*d*) III.
(*e*) Late Mughal.
(*f*) None.
(*g*) Good.
(*h*) Unnecessary.
(*i*) A small building of no particular interest.

BAZAR LAL KUWAN.

No. 207. (*a*) Mir Afzal's Mosque.
(*b*) *Haveli* Mir Afzal.
(*c*) Waqf, Mutawalli, Sakhawat Husain.
(*d*) III.
(*e*) 1221 A. H. (1806 A.D.).
(*f*) On a loose piece of red sandstone housed in the mosque.

بعون الله تعالى

این مسجد نو اجداث بي بي صاحبه والدهٔ شیخ علي احمد مرحوم سجاده نشین فتحپور
و خانم صاحبه والده مرزا رحیم بیگ خان باهتمام مرزا مجهو در شهر رجب سنه ۱۲۲۱ هجري تیار شد .

Translation.

" With the help of the exalted God."

" This newly founded mosque of Bibi Sahiba, the mother of the late Ali Ahmad Sajjada Nashim of Fathpur, and of Khanam Sahiba, the mother of Mirza Rahim Beg Khan, was completed under Mirza Majjhu, in the month of Rajab of the year 1221 A. H. (1806 A. D.)."

(*g*) Good.
(*h*) Unnecessary.
(*i*) The mosque was built by two ladies under the supervision of one Mirza Majjhu. The inscription is on a loose piece of red sandstone housed within one of the apartments (Hujra) attached to the mosque.

No. 208. (*a*) Sabz Masjid (Green Mosque).
(*b*) Near Katra of Adina Beg.

(*c*) Waqf, Mutawalli, Sayyid Ali.

(*d*) III.

(*e*) 1196 A. H. (1781-82 A. D.).

f) On the central arch.

(۱) ادینه بیگ که هست خان عالیشان ❁ بکار نیک خدا بسکه داد توفیقش

(۲) بنا نمود چو باغ ارم یکے مسجد ❁ چنانکه کعبه نوشتن سزد بتعریفش

(۳) خط کتابه اورا به بین که میگوید ❁ بیا بخانه دین است سال تاریخش

سنه ۱۱۹۶

Translation.

(1) "Adina Beg, who is Khan of exalted rank, and whom God has given considerable resources to do good deeds,"

(2) "Built a mosque, like the garden of paradise, and such that it will be justifiable if it is called Kaba in praise."

(3) "See that the writing of its inscription says, the date of its erection is come to the house of religion."

"The year 1196."

(*g*) Good.

(*h*) Unnecessary.

(*j*) The mosque is a two storeyed building. The first storey which forms the floor of the mosque consists of four rooms used as shops. The upper storey contains the prayer chamber and a courtyard approached from the road by a flight of ten steps.

There is only one Adina Beg Khan known to History, who died in the year 1172 A. H. (1758-9 A. D.). If the same Adina Beg is meant here, the inscription on the central arch of the mosque must have been put up long after the actual erection of the mosque. Adina Beg Khan was an Arain by caste, and son of a man named Chunnu, an inhabitant of the village of Sharqpur, near Lahore. He was brought up in a Mughal family and was an accountant of considerable ability. He started his career as Collector of Revenue of the village of Kanak near Ludhiyana, from which humble position he advanced till he was made Governor of Sultanpur. Subsequently he received the Governorship of Doab (Jalandar) which he administered with great success. He was clever, diplomatic, and always successful in securing the favours of the Governors of Lahore. On finding his position weakened by the hostility of the Abdali Chiefs and the Sikhs, he invited the Marathas to his assistance, and with their help succeeded in conquering the whole district of Sirhind and Lahore. But he did not enjoy the fruits of this conquest, as he died soon afterwards on the 11th of Muharram in the 5th year of Alamgir II's reign. In the *Farhatu-n Nazirin* he is styled as "Bahram Jang."

(*k*) *Farhatu-n Nazirin*, *Elliot*, VIII, 167 *et seq.*
Latif, 214, 230 *et seq.*

No. 209. (*a*) Gate (unnamed).

(*b*) Entrance to the Katra of Adina Beg.

(*c*) Hakim Raziu-d-din Shifau-l Mulk.

(*d*) III.

(e) Late Mughal.
(f) None.
(g) Fair.
(h) Unnecessary.
(j) The Katra was, in all probability, the house of Adina Beg and this gate possibly an entrance to it.

No. 210. (a) Sannuji's Mosque.
(b) In the *Bazar*.
(c) Waqf, Mutawalli, Haidar Ali.
(d) III.
(e) Late Mughal period.
(f) None.
(g) Good.
(h) Unnecessary.
(j) The mosque was built by one Maulvi Sanaullah, *alias* Sannuji. It is a small building of no particular interest.

No. 211. (a) Well (Lal Kuwan).
(b) See above.
(c) Government.
(d) III.
(e) Pre-Mughal period.
(f) None.
(g) Good.
(h) Unnecessary.
(j) The well is built of red sandstone and hence is called the Lal Kuwan (red well).
(k) *Asar* (1847), chap. III, 67.

No. 212. (a) Lal Masjid (Red mosque) II.
(b) In the *Bazar*.
(c) Waqf, Mutawalli, Fasl-i Matin.
(d) III.
(e) Late Mughal.
(f) None.
(g) Good.
(h) Unnecessary.
(j) The mosque, which is a small building of no particular interest, is two storeyed, the lower storey consisting of rooms used as shops.

No. 213. (a) Gate (unnamed).
(b) Entrance to the Katra Sipihdar Khan.

(c) Patiala State.
(d) III.
(e) Late Mughal.
(f) None.
(g) Fair.
(h) Unnecessary.

No. 214. (a) Zinat Mahal.
(b) In the *Bazar*.
(c) Patiala State.
(d) III.
(e) 1262 A. H. (1846 A. D.).
(f) On the arch of the gate—

کرد اے ظفر زینت محل تعمیر قصر بے بدل * شد بر محل سال بنا این خانہ زینت محل

Translation.

"O Zafar! Zinat Mahal erected a matchless palace; the suitable date of erection became 'This house of Zinat Mahal.'"

(g) Good.
(h) Unnecessary.
(j) The house is large and spacious and possesses an imposing gateway. The verse is written on a piece of marble and contains the chronogram of the date of its erection, composed by Bahadur Shah II, the last Mughal Emperor of Delhi. His "*Nom-de-plume*" *Zafar* is contained in the verse. It was built by Zinat Mahal, the favourite wife of Bahadur Shah II.
(l) S. 77.

No. 215. (a) Mosque (unnamed).
(b) Gali Chabuk Sawaran.
(c) Waqf, Mutawalli, Badr-ud-din Khan.
(d) III.
(e) Late Mughal period.
(f) None.
(g) Good.
(h) Unnecessary.
(j) The mosque is of no particular interest and has been rebuilt.

MASJID TAHAWWUR KHAN.

No. 216. (a) Tahawwur Khan's Mosque.
(b) See above.
(c) Waqf, Mutawallis, Karamullah *alias* Nanne Khan and Abdurrahim Khan.
(d) III.
(e) 1140 A. H. (1727-8 A. D.).

(*f*) On the central arch—

(۱) بدوران محمد شاہ تہور شاہ تاشکندی * بنا فرمود مسجد را بتوفیق خداوندی

(۲) ہزار ویکصد وچہل بود دوتا این بناے خیر * بسعی خان عالیشان مرتب شد بخورسندی

Translation.

" In the reign of Muhammad Shah, Tahawwur Shah of Tashkand built the mosque with divine guidance."

" It was one thousand one hundred and forty when this good building was completed with happiness by the exertions of the Khan of exalted position."

on the lower entrance to the mosque

مسجد حنفیہ

ہر کہ آمد ز ارادت بیقین شام و سحر * خانہ از غیب ندا داد بیا فیض ببر

Translation.

" The mosque of the Hanafis.(1)"

" Whoever came with inclination and belief (to the mosque) evening and morning, he was accosted by the house from invisibility 'come and acquire grace.' "

(*g*) Good.

(*h*) Unnecessary.

(*j*) The mosque is on an upper storey, and is reached by 17 steps. The lower storey consists of 4 shops. The inscription on the lower entrance seems to have been put up at the time of the recent repairs. The verandah is of course modern.

Tahawwur Khan lived in the reign of Muhammad Shah and held the Zamindari of Shahjahanpur. His brother-in-law Muhammad Afzal Khan is said to have succeeded him as his heir, in the 11th year of the reign of Muhammad Shah.

(*k*) *Tarikh-i-Hindi*, Rustam Ali, *Elliot*, VIII, 47.

(*l*) S. 67.

No. 217. (*a*) Imliwali Mosque II.

(*b*) In the *Muhalla*.

(*c*) Waqf, Mutawalli, Zafarurrahman.

(*d*) III.

(*e*) Late Mughal period.

(*f*) None.

(*g*) Good.

(*h*) Unnecessary.

(*j*) The mosque is now under reconstruction. It is a small building of no particular interest.

BAZAR NAYABANS.

No. 218. (*a*) Sivalaya (unnamed).

(*b*) Kuncha Sanjogirama.

(1) Hanafi is a sect of Sunni Muhammadans who are the followers of Abu Hanifa, one of the four Imams or expounders of the Muslim law.

(c) Gutti.
(d) III.
(e) Late Mughal.
(f) None.
(g) Good.
(h) Unnecessary.
(j) Harjimal Khatri is said to have erected the temple. In it are images of Parvati, Ganapati and Kartikasvami. In front is a small temple of Thakuraji Kanhayaji or Krishna. To the right hand of the visitor is a temple of Ganga and to the left that of Hanumat. A small building of no particular interest.

MUHALLA NAYABANS.

No. 219. (a) Gendo's Temple.
(b) Kuncha Sanjogirama.
(c) Sri Rama.
(d) III.
(e) Late Mughal about 80 years old (?).
(f) None.
(g) Good.
(h) Unnecessary.
(j) The temple stands on an upper storey and is reached by 13 steps; the lower storey consists of 4 shops. It was built by a Hindu lady named Gendo. There is a shrine of Radha and Krishna. The image of the former is of black marble, and that of the latter of white. In the compound is a Sivalaya in which are enshrined the images of Parvati, Ganesa, Brahmadeva and Nandi. In niches to the visitor's right are the images of Bhairava and Hanumat besmeared with red lead. To his left in a niche is an image of Durga.

No. 220. (a) Sivalaya (unnamed).
(b) In the *Muhalla.*
(c) Prabhu (Parbhu).
(d) III.
(e) The temple is said to be of the time of the Emperor Shahjahan(?).
(f) None.
g) Good.
(h) Unnecessary.
(j) The temple appears to be of some importance as can be attested by the number of bells presented to it. The new *Mandap* was erected in 1883, which bears inscriptions in English and Devanagari, and in Urdu characters and the year.
In the temple are small images of Parvati, Ganapati, Brahma deva and Nandi and the ling of Siva.

No. 221. (a) Bhairava's Temple.

(*b*) Near No. 220.
(*c*) Prabhu Dayala.
(*d*) III.
(*e*) It is said to be about 100 years old. (?)
(*f*) None.
(*g*) Good.
(*h*) Unnecessary.
(*j*) There is no image of Bhairava, only a rude stone besmeared with red lead representing the god.

KHARI BAOLI.

No. 222. (*a*) Sivalaya (unnamed).
(*b*) *Gali* Batasan Khurd.
(*c*) Bholanatha.
(*e*) Phalguna Krishna, 5, Thursday (1850 A.D.).
(*f*) There is a Sanskrit inscription on a stone tablet over the gateway in five lines.

It runs :—

श्री शः पायात् ॥१ कपूरजातिराजन्यवंशे (वंशे) जातस्य धीमतः । श्रीमद्विजय-
रामस्य पत्नी कुर्य्या (कुर्य्यां) पतिव्रता ॥२॥ धर्मेहि भर्तुर्विधनादनन्तरम्वित्तं (वित्तं) तदीयम्विनि-
योजितं तथा । नूत्नालये श्रेष्ठतरे सुखप्रदे कार्याप्रतिष्ठामयकाय धूर्जटेः ॥३॥ चिन्तयन्त्यन-
पत्येत्थं स्वर्गता दैवयोगतः । पर्यायिष्ठेन रिक्थेन तस्यास्तु वचनादपि ॥४॥ सुन्याकामाङ्ग-
गोत्राभिर्मिते वैक्रमवायने फाल्गुनासितपञ्चम्या (म्यां) त्वष्टृभे गुरवासरे (गुरुवासरे) ॥६॥ सम्वत्
१९०७ फा० कृ० ५ गुरौ शुभम्

Translation.

May the Revered Siva protect. 'Being the devoted and virtuous wife of the illustrious and talented Vijayarama, born in the Kapura clan of the Kshatriyas, I should, after the death of my husband, spend his wealth on religious acts (or charity) and further (*atha*) should as well (*tatha*) install a ling of Siva in this comfortable and excellent new shrine.' Even while she was thinking thus she died (lit. went to heaven) unfortunately without issue. With that wealth of her, which remained, the wise Jethamalla, her youngest paternal uncle, acting on her oral direction, consecrated the ling of Siva of Vijayarama (named after Vijayarama) by the hands of the Brahmans in the year 1907 of the Vikrama era on Thursday, the 5th day of the dark fortnight of Phalguna, when the moon was in conjunction with the constellation presided over by tvashtri (Chitra) Samvat 1907 Pha. Kri. 5, on Thursday, welfare.

Another explanation is possible if we read Kurmya instead of Kuryam (In the above translation I have considered Kurya to be a mistake for Kuryam) and supposed it to be the name of the wife of Vijayarama, and read taya for tatha. The rendering then would be "Kurmya bestowed the wealth on charity." The first translation is preferable, for two reasons. (1) Nobody told me that the name of the lady was Kurmya (2) and it would mean a lady of Kurmachala (Kumaon), and can hardly be a proper name.

Explanation of certain words: Mayaka=maya=by me,

By Panini V. 3. 71 Avyayasarvanamnamakach prak teh.

Muni=7, Akasa=0, Anka=9 and Gotra=1. Hence 1907.

Panchamya may be a mistake for Panchamyam or the instrumental may have been used to show at the end of by Panini (Kaladhvanoh) Apavarge tritiya.

According to Taittiriya Brahmana, Tritiyashtaka Prapathaka, 1, Anuvaka 1-2, and Anuvaka 4-5, Tvashtri is the deity presiding over Chitra.

No. 223. (*a*) Mosque (unnamed). In Dr. Vogel's list given as Masjid-i-Khari Baoli.
(*b*) Kuncha-i-Nawab Mirza.
(*c*) Waqf, Mutawalli, Hafiz Asad Ali.
(*d*) III.
(*e*) Sher Shah's reign (?).
(*f*) None.
(*g*) Good.
(*h*) Unnecessary.
(*j*) The mosque which measures some 62′ 0″ north and south by 24″ 8″ east and west is built in the Afghan style of architecture and is said to have been built in the time of Sher Shah or his successor. The arches are low and massive and there are three large domes.

No. 224. (*a*) Serai Bangash.
(*b*) Near the Fathpuri Mosque.
(*c*) Lala Narain Das.
(*d*) III.
(*e*) Late Mughal period.
(*f*) None.
(*g*) Good.
(*h*) Unnecessary.
(*j*) The serai no more serves the purpose for which it was built, being now occupied by shops, etc. It possesses an imposing gateway which forms in itself a separate building with a central octagonal courtyard.

MASJID FATHPURI.

No. 225. (*a*) Fathpuri Mosque.
(*b*) Western extremity of the Chandni Chauk.
(*c*) Waqf, Mutawalli, a committee.
(*d*) II *b*.
(*e*) 1060 A. H. (1650 A.D.).
(*f*) None.
(*g*) Good.
(*h*) Unnecessary.
(*j*) The mosque was built by Fathpuri Begam, one of the wives of the Emperor Shah Jahan, in the year 1060 A. H. (1650 A. D.). It still bears her name and is one of the most important mosques in Delhi. It is built of red sandstone with a single dome and lofty flanking minarets. In the

centre of the mosque is its main and lofty arch, on either side of which are three wings with three scolloped arches. The courtyard is stone paved and has a large central tank. It is surrounded by a series of single and double storeyed apartments, used as shops and dwelling houses. The entrance to the enclosure is through three imposing gateways, which stand towards north, south and east. On the face of the mosque is an inscription recording repairs executed in the year 1289 A. H. (1872-3 A.D.) There are a few graves in the courtyard within a small masonry enclosure but none of them bears any inscription.

(*k*) *A.S.I. IV*, 70.
As. Res. IV, 70.
Carr Stephen, 257-9.
Cole (1st Report), XXVIII, CXCIX, CCIV.
Cooper, 37, 126.
Fanshawe, 53.
Hearn, 8.
Keene, 8.
Rodgers, 93.

(*l*) S. 76.

BAZAR FATHPURI.

No. 226. (*a*) Mosque (unnamed).
(*b*) Gondni ka Katra, near the Hammam of Bidu.
(*c*) Waqf, Mutawalli, Agha Hasan.
(*d*) III.
(*e*) Late Mughal period.
(*f*) None.
(*g*) Good.
(*h*) Unnecessary.
(*j*) The mosque stands at some height above the level of the ground. It possesses no particular interest.

No. 227. (*a*) Mosque (unnamed).
(*b*) Baryon ka Katra.
(*c*) Waqf, Mutawalli, Hafiz Ataurrahman.
(*d*) III.
(*e*) Late Mughal period.
(*f*) None.
(*g*) Good.
(*h*) Unnecessary.
(*j*) A small building of no particular interest, rebuilt after the mutiny.

MUHALLA BALLI MARAN.

No. 228. (*a*) Panjabiyan's Mosque.
(*b*) Haveli Husam-ud-din Haidar.

(c) Waqf, Mutawalli, Azizu-d-Din Churiwale.
(d) III.
(e) Late Mughal period.
(f) None.
(g) Good.
(h) Unnecessary.
(j) A small building of no particular interest.

No. 229. (a) Imliwali Mosque III.
(b) In the *Muhalla*.
(c) Waqf, Mutawalli, Maulvi Rafiu-d-Din.
(d) III.
(e) Late Mughal period.
(f) None.
(g) Good.
(h) Unnecessary.
(j) The mosque was built by one Maulvi Salim-ud-din. It measures 35′ 9″ north and south by 20′ 0″ east and west.

No. 230. (a) Kuppe Walan's Mosque.
(b) *Gali* Kuppe Walan.
(c) Waqf, Mutawalli, Maulvi Muhaiy-ud-din Khan, in Hyderabad State Service.
(d) III.
(e) Late Mughal period.
(f) None.
(g) Good.
(h) Unnecessary.
(j) The building is of no particular interest.

No. 231. (a) Gate (unnamed).
(b) Entrance to the Haveli of Husam-ud-din Haidar.
(c) Ataullah.
(d) III.
(e) Late Mughal period.
(f) None.
(g) Good.
(h) Unnecessary.
(j) Husamuddin Haidar was originally a resident of Lucknow. He lived in Delhi. He had two sons named Muzaffaru-d-Daula and Nawwab Husain Mirza, who held high posts in the service of Bahadur Shah II. The latter was *Nazir* in the fort.

No. 232. (a) Hakim Sharif Khan's Mosque.
(b) Near the house of Hakim Ajmal Khan.
(c) Hakim Ajmal Khan.

(*d*) III.
(*e*) 1261 A.H. (1845 A.D.).
(*f*) On the central arch—

(١) شکر خدا بسعي محمد شریف خان * شد طرح مسجدے که بود کعبه صفا
(٢) برخاست چون ندائے موذن خطیب عقل * گفتا بجوے سال وے از خانه خدا
١٢٦١ (?)

Translation.

(1) "Thanks to God that, by the efforts of Muhammad Sharif Khan, a mosque is erected which is the kaba of purity."

(2) "When the Muazzin's (one who calls the people to prayers by proclamation from a Mosque) call arose, the preacher of wisdom said, 'Seek the year of its foundation from the house of God. 1261(?).'"

(*g*) Good.
(*h*) Unnecessary.
(*j*) The mosque is of two storeys. The upper storey, which is the mosque proper, consists of a spacious courtyard and a domed prayer chamber with arched entrances. The lower storey comprises five shops. At the northern end of the courtyard there is a narrow staircase with 14 steps giving access to the mosque. The inscription, which is on the central arch, refers to the erection of the mosque by Sharif Khan, the great grandfather of Haziqul Mulk Hakim Ajmal Khan.

Hakim Sharif Khan, the son of Hakim Akmal Khan, was a famous Delhi physician, and was given a *jagir* and the title of *Ashraful Hukama* from the Mughal Emperors. He belonged to a family whose members have been renowned as physicians and who enjoyed the favour of the court as well as the public esteem. The original home of the founder of the family was in Central Asia, but he came from Kashgar into India with the Emperor Babar. During the reign of Akbar this family established itself at Agra, where its members were highly respected on account of their learning and piety. One of these, Hakim Muhammad Fazil Khan, greatly improved the position of the family by learning the art of medicine. During the time of Aurangzeb, Hakim Wasil Khan, then the head of the family, moved to Delhi. His sons Hakim Akmal Khan and Hakim Ajmal Khan were granted a *jagir* of two lakhs besides the rank of 3,000, Hakim Akmal Khan being given the title of Akmal-ul-Mahaqqaqin-ul-Mulk.

(*k*) *Imperial Coronation Durbar, Delhi*, 1911, I, 357.

No. 233. (*a*) Gate (unnamed).
(*b*) Entrance to the Kuncha-i-Raiman.
(*c*) Hakim Ajmal Khan.
(*d*) III.
(*e*) Late Mughal period.
(*f*) None.
(*g*) Good.
(*h*) Unnecessary.

No. 234. (*a*) Yek Burji (single domed) Mosque II.

(b) Kunchai Raiman.
(c) Waqf, Mutawalli, Hafiz Muhammad Umar.
(d) III.
(e) Late Afghan period.
(f) None.
(g) Excellent.
(h) Unnecessary.
(j) The mosque which measures 45′ 9″ north and south by 21′ 1″ east and west is so called from the single dome which covers its central apartment. The latter is entered through a low pointed arch. The general design and the thickness of walls point to the Afghan period of architecture. On either side of the central apartment is a room entered through an arch of the same style.

No. 235. (a) Unchi Mosque IV.
(b) Near the Kothi of Nawwab Luharu.
(c) Waqf, Mutawalli, Hafiz Muhummad Umar.
(d) III.
(e) 1227 A.H. (1812-3 A.D.).
(f) On the central arch—

(۱) چون مسجد دلفریب ودلچسپ و وسیع * تیار شد از فضل کریم مطلق
(۲) هاتف به نشاط سال تاریخش گفت * بنیاد نهاده اسکر خانه حق

Translation.

"When the charming, attractive and spacious mosque was completed by the grace of the supreme benevolent (God),"

"The invisible voice cheerfully said the year of its foundation 'Askar has laid the foundation of the house of God.'"

(g) Good.
(h) Unnecessary.
(j) The mosque, which is only a small structure, has triple domes and arched entrances. It is built on an upper storey reached by ten steps. The lower storey comprises five shops.

No. 236. (a) Pirji Wali Mosque.
(b) Barah Dari Sher Afgan Khan.
(c) Waqf, Mutawalli, Abdurrahman.
(d) III.
(e) Late Mughal period.
(f) None.
(g) Good.
(h) Unnecessary.
(j) The mosque was originally built by an ancestor of one Hakim Mahmud Khan (the father of Hakim Ajmal Khan), but it has been reconstructed.

The Barah Dari of Sher Afgan Khan after which the *Muhalla* is named is no longer in existence, having been demolished and occupied by private houses. There are several Sher Afgan Khans mentioned in history. This would appear to be Izzatu-d-daula Bahadur Safdar Jang who lived during the time of Muhammad Shah, and is buried some three miles outside Delhi.

(*k*) *Maasir*, II, 881-2.

No. 237. (*a*) Sivalaya of Hardev Das.

(*b*) Gali Pasiyan.

(*c*) Padmanarayana.

(*d*) III.

(*e*) Friday, the 6th day of the bright fortnight of Magha (Vikrama Samvat) 1907 (1850 A.D.)

(*f*) There is an inscribed stone tablet just over the door of the shrine. The inscription consists of 5 lines and is written in modern Devanagari characters. The language is Sanskrit. The two verses give the date, the fortnight, the month and the year when the image of Girija (Parvati) and the ling of Siva were placed in the sanctum as well as the name of the man who placed them there and who had two sons. In the 5th line the date is mentioned. The inscription runs :—

सम्मिते हायने स्वस्मिन्सप्तखाङ्कनिशाकरैः
माघे शुक्ले घटे सूर्ये दास्रेषष्ठ्यां भृगोर्दिने १
बलदेवसुतौ यस्य हरदेवस्तथापरः
श्रीमन्महेशदासेन स्थापितौ गिरिजाशिवौ २
सं० १९०७ मा० शु० ६ भृ

Translation.

"On Friday, the 6th day in the bright fortnight of (the month of) Magha in our year which is equal to 1907 (Vikrama Samvat 1907) when the sun is in the Kumbha Zodiac (Ghate) and on the conjunction of the moon with the constellation Asvini, this image of Girija (Parvati) and (this ling of) Siva are placed in this temple by wealthy Mahesadasa, whose one son is Baladeva and the other is Haradeva"

N.B.—Ghata=the sign Aquarius. Mahesadasa is a proper name. Dasra= pertaining to Asvini Kumars.

The temple was erected by the grandfather of Padmanarayana, the person who now looks after the affairs of the temple.

Two images are mentioned in the inscription noted (*vide f* above) and the temple has been therefore styled as a Sivalaya, *viz.*, a temple dedicated to the God Siva. As a matter of fact, it contains other images also. In front of the ling a small image of Nandi, to the visitor's right that of Ashtabhuja and to the left images of Ganapati and Brahmadeva, and facing the entrance that of Hanumat. Parvati is only Siva's better half. It may be urged that the bull is his attendant and Ganapati his son. Brahmadeva also may be connected with him. This does not account for the image of Hanumat which is perhaps a later addition.

No. 238. (*a*) Lala Fattesinga's Sivalaya.
(*b*) Kuncha-i Bibi Gauhar.
(*c*) Bhavani Prasada.
(*d*) III.
(*e*) Late Mughal.
(*f*) None.
(*g*) Good.
(*h*) Unnecessary.
(*j*) In the temple are enshrined a ling of Siva and images of Parvati, Ganapati, Nandi, Hanumat and Thakurji (Krishna). The temple was built by Lala Fatesinga.

No. 239. (*a*) Lakshmi Narayan's Sivalaya.
(*b*) Kuncha-i Bibi Gauhar.
(*c*) Ganga Prasada and Bholanatha.
(*d*) III.
(*e*) Late Mughal.
(*f*) None.
(*g*) Good.
(*h*) Unnecessary.
(*j*) In a temple are enshrined a ling of Siva and the images of Parvati, Ganapati, Nandi and Hanumat. The building is named after its builder.

No. 240. (*a*) Sivalaya (unnamed).
(*b*) Kuncha-i Bibi Gauhar.
(*c*) Lala Sitarama.
(*d*) III.
(*e*) Late Mughal.
(*f*) None.
(*g*) Good.
(*h*) Unnecessary.
(*j*) In the temple which is said to have been built by one Lala Munna Lal are enshrined a ling of Siva and the images of Parvati, Hanumat and Bhairava.

No. 241. (*a*) Mosque (unnamed).
(*b*) Kuncha-i Qutbi Begam.
(*c*) Waqf, Mutawalli, Muhammad Ismail.
(*d*) III.
(*e*) Late Mughal period.
(*f*) None.
(*g*) Good.
(*h*) Unnecessary.
(*j*) A small building of no particular interest.

No. 242. (a) The temple is generally called Pipal Mahadeva's Sivalaya.

(b) Pipal Mahadeva.

(c) Mulchanda.

(d) III.

(e) Magha Suddha, 5, Vikrama Samvat 1866 (1809 A. D.).

(f) There is an inscription on the outer wall of the temple. It is in three lines and is in modern Devanagari characters. It runs:

This inscription is evidently based on an older one which as far as decipherable reads.

(१) षंग . . हिमांशु संमितस . . यो विक्रमस्य

(२) प्रभो . . तिथौ स-

(३) मस्थापयत् ॥१॥ हशे (?)

(४) . . . पंचानन लछाराम हरहरेश्वर

(५) . . . सलम्बोदर: ॥ शुभमस्तु १८६६

It gives the name of the builder which is in the last line, and also the year Lachhirama can be made out in the 4th line. The 2nd and the 3rd lines give Samasthapayat (installed). The first line apparently gives the year.

(g) Good.

(h) Unnecessary.

(j) The temple was erected by Lambodara Lachhirama as can be seen from the two inscriptions mentioned above.

He was a Kasmiriyan Pandit.

In the temple are enshrined a ling of Siva and the images of Ganapati, Parvati, Nandi, Hanumat and Bhairava.

The image of Siva is a fine one and is said to have been brought from Jayapura (Jaipur).

No. 243. (a) Charandasis' temple.

(b) Gali Dasan.

(c) Basant Dasa.

(d) III.

(e) The temple is said to be built about 250 years ago. (?)

(f) None.

g) Good.

(h) Unnecessary.

(j) In the shrine are images of Radha and Krishna.

The founder of the Charandasi sect was Charandasa, who was a Bhargava by caste. The Charandasis, however, have done away with the caste system and all the Hindus except the Antyajas can be admitted into their sect. They are Vaishanava Sadhus. They respect the Vedas. It is laid down that they must not find fault with other sects.

To turn to Charandasa. He had an interview with Nadir Shah, the Persian Conqueror of India, who is said to have put Charandasa into prison. It is said that the latter was capable of performing miracles and that he left the prison one day at 2 A.M., though fettered, and repaired to Nadir Shaha's sleeping chamber unseen. The King apologised to Charandasa and thenceforward treated him very kindly. The story, though most probably fictitious, is nevertheless narrated with much enthusiasm. The Emperor Muhammad Shah respected Charandasa, and Shah Alam II granted four villages to the sect, 1 Musahidpura, District Gurgaon, 2 Gaodi, District Meerut, 3 Naugala, District Bulandshahr, and 4 Gangutana, Patiala State. They still possess these grants (?).

The Charandasis do not marry. They adopt *chelas*. Charandasa died in *Samvat* 1840 (1783 A.D.) at the age of 125.

No. 244. (*a*) Sivalaya (unnamed).

(*b*) Gali Dilsukharai.

(*c*) Srikisandasa.

(*d*) III.

(*e*) The temple is said to be 80 or 90 years old ?

(*f*) None.

(*g*) Good.

(*h*) Unnecessary.

(*j*) In the Sivalaya are enshrined a ling of Siva and the images of Parvati, Ganapati, Brahmadeva, Kartikasvami, Nandi and Hanumat and the charanapadukas of Vishnu.

In the same compound is a small temple of Thakurji (Krishna) in which are kept the images of Radha and Krishna as usual.

Lala Gumnirama erected the temple. He was the treasurer of Mr. Fraser, Resident of Delhi, and father of Dilsukharai.

No. 245. (*a*) Sivalaya (unnamed).

(*b*) Gali Dasan.

(*c*) Rai Bahadur Nanakchand.

(*d*) III.

(*e*) The temple was built 80 years ago.

(*f*) None.

(*g*) Good.

(*h*) Unnecessary.

(*j*) Rai Bahadur Nanakchand's father, Umidsing, built the temple. In it are enshrined a ling of Siva and the images of Parvati, Ganesa and Nandi.

No. 246. (*a*) Hanumanji's Temple.

(*b*) Pipal Mahadeva.

(*c*) Sadirama.

(*d*) III.

(*e*) Late Mughal.

(*f*) None.

(*g*) Good.

(*h*) Unnecessary.

(*j*) The temple, which is only a small building, has been recently rebuilt. It contains an image of Hanumat, a ling of Siva and a bull.

No. 247. (*a*) Rajaji's Temple.

(*b*) Pipal Mahadeva.
(*c*) Kunvar Manohar Lala.
(*d*) III.
(*e*) About 100 years old.
(*f*) None.
(*g*) Good.
(*h*) Unnecessary.
(*j*) The temple was built by Raja Ji Sukha Rai who is said to have held the post of *wazir* in the reign of Akbar II.

There is a small temple of Krishna attached in which the images of Radha and Krishna are enshrined.

There is also a Sivalaya in which is a ling of Siva and the images of Parvati, Ganesa, Brahmadeva and Hanumat.

No. 248. (*a*) Ragho Missar's Sivalaya.
(*b*) Pipal Mahadeva.
(*c*) Kallu.
(*d*) III.
(*e*) The temple is said to be 200 years old?
(*f*) None.
(*g*) Good.
(*h*) Unnecessary.
(*j*) Ragho Misra is said to have built the temple.

It contains a ling of Siva and the images of Parvati, Ganesa and Kartikasvami.

No. 249. (*a*) Mosque (unnamed).
(*b*) Chhatta Sufi, Pipal Mahadeo.
(*c*) None.
(*d*) III.
(*e*) Late Mughal period.
(*f*) None.
(*g*) Ruinous.
(*h*) Unnecessary.
(*j*) The mosque is now a heap of bricks and *debris*, and has been in this condition since the Mutiny, when the Muhammadan population of this *Muhalla*, who built it and looked after it, left the neighbourhood and took up their abode elsewhere.

No. 250. (*a*) Kaptan Wali Mosque.
(*b*) Barah Dari Sher Afgan Khan.
(*c*) Waqf, Mutawalli, Badru-d-Din and Iwaz Khan.
(*d*) III.
(*e*) Late Mughal period.
(*f*) None.
(*g*) Good.

(*h*) Unnecessary.
(*j*) A small building of no particular interest.

GALI QASIM JAN.

No. 251. (*a*) Mosque (unnamed).
(*b*) Madrasa Inayatullah.
(*c*) Waqf, Mutawalli, Shaikh Abdullah.
(*d*) III.
(*e*) Unknown.
(*f*) None.
(*g*) Good.
(*h*) Unnecessary.
(*j*) The mosque, which is small and of no particular interest, has been rebuilt.

No. 252. (*a*) Nawwab Ahmad Said Khan's Mosque.
(*b*) Near the Haveli of Kale Sahib.
(*c*) Waqf, Mutawalli, Nawwab Ahmad Said Khan.
(*d*) III.
(*e*) 1193 A.H. (1779 A.D.).
(*f*) On the northern arch—

(۱) مسجدے مثل روضہ رضوان * شد بنایش زدست قاسم خان
(۲) آب شیرین و چاہ چون زمزم * وقف او کرد چاہ و چار دوکان
(۳) از رفیع خواست چون ز تاریخش * گفت سہراب جنگ قاسم خان

۱۱۹۳

Translation.

(1) "The erection of this mosque which is like a garden of paradise was effected by the hands of Qasim Khan".
(2) "A well which is like Zamzam and has sweet water, he dedicated it as well as four shops."
(3) "When he asked Rafi its date, he replied, 'Suhrab Jang Qasim Khan.' 1193."

(*g*) Good.
(*h*) Unnecessary.
(*j*) The mosque stands on an upper storey, the lower storey consisting of four shops, which are referred to in the inscription to be found on the northern arch. It was built by Qasim Khan entitled Suhrab Jang, after whose name the street, in which it lies, is still known.

Qasim Khan was the son of Khuwaja Abdur-Rahman of Bukhara. He was Naib Wazir (Deputy Minister) in the reign of Shah Alam II, who, pleased with his services, granted him the *jagir* of Shamsabad, Oudh, and the title of Suhrab Jang.

No. 253. (*a*) Gate (unnamed).
(*b*) Entrance to the Haveli of Kale Sahib.

(*c*) Common property of the people of the Muhalla.
(*d*) III.
(*e*) Late Mughal period.
(*f*) None.
(*g*) Good.
(*h*) Unnecessary.
(*j*) The gate and the house which has now been occupied by a ***Muhalla***, was built by Sharafu-d-Daula Nawwab Faizullah Beg Khan, the son of Nawwab Qasim Khan (*see* No. 252). It afterwards came into the possession of Hajji Ghulam Nasiru-d-Din, commonly known as Miyan Kale Sahib, who lived during the reign of Akbar II and his successor. He was famed and esteemed for his piety.
(*k*) *Asar* (1847), chap. IV, 34-5.

No. 254. (*a*) Karora's Mosque.
(*b*) In the ***Muhalla***.
(*c*) Waqf, Mutawalli, Muin-ud-din.
(*d*) III.
(*e*) 1223 A.H. (1808-9 A.D.).
(*f*) On the central arch.

(۱) چون بتائید جناب کبریاے * خوش مرتب گشت این طاعت سراے
(۲) مصرع تاریخ ان هاتف بگفت * کرده کاین مسجد محمد خان بناے
سنه ۱۲۲۳

Translation.

(1) "When through the assistance of God this place of adoration was beautifully finished,"
(2) "An invisible voice said its chronogram 'This mosque was built by Muhammad Khan.'"

(*g*) Good.
(*h*) Unnecessary.
(*j*) The mosque, which is only a small building, is situated on a raised piece of ground. It has three arched entrances and is roofed by three domes. The mosque was erected by Muhammad Khan, who held the office of ***Karora*** or 'tax gatherer' in the reign of Akbar II.
(*l*) S. 75.

GALI HAKIM BAQA.

No. 255. (*a*) Sivalaya (unnamed).
(*b*) Near Qazi ka Hauz.
(*c*) Pandit Rama Kisan.
(*d*) III.
(*e*) About 150 or 200 years old (?)
(*f*) None.
(*g*) Good.
(*h*) Unnecessary.
(*j*) A ling of Siva and the images of Parvati, Ganapati, Nandi and Hanumat are enshrined in the temple, which consists of a pavilion on the roof of a house.

No. 256. (*a*) Mosque (unnamed).
(*b*) Near Qazi Ka Hauz.
(*c*) Waqf, Mutawlli, Munir-ud-din.
(*d*) III.
(*e*) Late Mughal.
(*f*) None.
(*g*) Good.
(*h*) Unnecessary.
(*j*) The mosque which is only a small building was built by one Hakim Baqaullah. It is double storeyed, the first storey forming the floor of the mosque consisting of two rooms which are now used as shops. The upper storey which is reached by 10 steps comprises the prayer chamber and a courtyard.

BAZAR CHAORI.

No. 257. (*a*) Sadirama's Temple.
(*b*) Kuncha Dayarama.
(*c*) Mattu Misra.
(*d*) III.
(*e*) Late Mughal.
(*f*) None.
(*g*) Good.
(*h*) Unnecessary.
(*j*) Sadirama built the temple.

To the visitor's left is a small temple of Thakurji or Krishna, in which are kept the images of Radha and Krishna as usual. To the right is a small temple of Hanumat. There is also a Sivalaya in which can be seen images of Parvati, Ganapati, Kartikasvami and Nandi.

In the enclosure there is a Dharmasala in which Brahmans are fed at times in large numbers.

No. 258. (*a*) Saddho Ghosan's (milkmaid's) Mosque.
(*b*) Muhalla Charkhe Walan.
(*c*) Waqf, Mutawalli, Fathpuri Committee.
(*d*) III.
(*e*) 1253 A. H. (1837-38 A.D.).
(*f*) On the central arch—

(۱) مسجد و مدرسه و چاه و مکان مسکن * همه ها وقف شد از عاجزه سدهو گدن
(۲) وارث هرسه مکان کس نشود غیر خدا * گر شود روز جزا دست من ازوے دامن
من الهجرة النبوي سنه ۱۲۵۳

Translation.

"(1) The mosque, the school, the well and the dwelling house have all been dedicated for charitable purposes by the humble Saddho, the milk maid."

"(2) No one except God should be heir to the three houses, and if there should be any, the skirt of his garment would be in my hand on the day of judgment."

"The year 1253 from the flight of the Prophet."

(g) Good.

(h) Unnecessary.

(j) The mosque is double storeyed, has three domes and three arches. The lower or basement storey which forms the floor of the mosque consists of four apartments used as shops.

EGERTON ROAD OR NAI SARAK.

No. 259. (a) Sarakwali Mosque.

(b) Raushan pura.

(c) Waqf, Mutawalli, Ilahi Bakhsh.

(d) III.

(e) Late Mughal period.

(f) None.

(g) Good.

(h) Unnecessary.

(j) A small building of no particular interest.

No. 260. (a) Rahim Ali Wakil's Mosque.

(b) Daiwara.

(c) Waqf, Mutawalli, Zamirul Haq.

(d) III.

(e) Late Mughal period.

(f) None.

(g) Good.

(h) Unnecessary.

(j) The mosque is known after the name of one Rahim Ali, *Wakil*. It is a small building of no particular interest.

No. 261. (a) Dargah Wali Mosque.

(b) Chira Khana, near Chhatta Tansukh Rai.

(c) Waqf, Mutawalli, Shah Faiyaz-ud-din.

(d) III.

(e) Late Mughal period.

(f) None.

(g) Good.

(h) Unnecessary.

(j) A small building of no particular interest.

No. 262. (a) Sadr Jahan's grave.

(b) Chira Khana, near Chhatta Tansukh Rai.

(c) Waqf, Mutawalli Faiyaz-ud-din.

(d) III.

(e) Unknown.

(*f*) None.

(*g*) Fair.

(*h*) Unnecessary.

(*j*) The tomb is of white marble, and stands within a masonry enclosure known as the Dargah. Sadr Jahan is a title generally given to a *Qazi* (judge). There is no inscription on the tomb which furnishes the name of the deceased or the date of death, nor does local tradition give any information regarding the tomb.

No. 263. (*a*) Sadanand Vaidya's Sivalaya.

(*b*) Mahalla Malivara, Patli Gali.

(*c*) Sadananda Vaidya.

(*d*) III.

(*e*) 13th day of the bright fortnight of Ashadha, Vikrama Samvat 1909 (1852 A.D.).

(*f*) A. There is an inscription on a stone built into a wall outside the temple in modern Devanagari characters and below it is the following Urdu inscription in one line.

شواله سري مهاراج پندت كنهيا لال جي كا سمت ۱۹۰۹ اساڑه سدي تيج

Translation.

" The Shivala (Sivalaya) of Sri Maharaj Pandit Kanhaiya Lal Ji, Sammat (Samvat) 1909. Third day of the bright fortnight of Asarh (Ashadha).

The former runs :—

श्री

शिवाला श्री महाराज पण्डित कन्हैया लालजीका ॥ सं ॥ १९०९ आषाढ़ शु० १३

Sri

(" This is ") the Sivalaya (temple of Siva) of the learned Maharaja Kanhayalala. 13th day of the bright fortnight of Ashadha Sam (Vikrama Samvat) 1909."

B. Inside the shrine is a long inscription which runs :—

(१) श्री ॥ व्यवस्था शिवाले

(२) ॥ श्रीमन्महाराज पंडित् कन्हैया लालजी पिता महाराज शालिग्रामजी वा कृपारामजीके की ॥

(३) संवत् १८८६ में बर्षासे मकान उनका गिर पड़ा था ॥ संवत् १८९८ में ईसी जगा की चौतर्फी दिवार कची

(४) खिचवाकर श्री महादेवजीको स्थापित किया और दिवानखाना अपने वास्ते बनवाया ॥ सं० १९०७

N.B.—Maharaja here is simply an honorific term and does not mean great king.

(५) तक उसी तौर रहा ॥ सं० १९०८ में शिवाला बनना शुरू हुवा बीच निगाहवानी महाराज ज्वाली-

(६) सिंहजीके ॥ सं० १९०९ में बनके तयार हो गया और प्रतिष्ठा मिति आषाढ़ शु० ३ को ब-

(७) ड़ी धूम से सालिग्रामजीने करी किस वास्ते पंडित्‌जी महाराज का शरीर बिमार था औ-

(८) र १ महीने १० दिन बाद प्रतिष्ठा के कैलासवासी हो गये ॥ सं० १९१४ में गदर हुआ सं० १९१५

(९) वा १६ में नै सड़क निकली. दिवानखाना सड़क में आगैया. दाम उस्के सरकार से सालिग्राम-

(१०) जी महाराज को मिले उन्होंने दिवार सड़क को तरफ बनवाई और जमीन बोबो सुजाने से मो-

(११) ल लेकर तखाना बनवाया और उसके ऊपर चार दिवार खड़ी करवाकर छोड़ दिया था

(१२) सं० १९२८ में दुकान की सूरत जीना वगैरा टीन मठन्‌ लाल नें बनवाया नवल मिस्तरी से ॥ सं० १९४०

(१३) मे दुसरा के बाजो नल फवारे का आला भैरव जोका वा छत तिदरी बनवाई वा मरम्मत शकिस्ता

(१४) रेख की येहीदास करवाता रहता है कुल नवीन असबाब इसी टीननें चढ़ाया है सं० १९१९

(१५) में महाराज सालिग्रामजी शिवलोकवासी हुये बाद उनके हरतौरकी सेवा येही चरणनुरागी कर रहा

(१६) है. यह व्यवस्था आज्ञा अनुकूल श्री शिवजी महाराजके टीन पंडित्‌ मिटन्‌लाल राय बहादुर पिन्‌शनर

(१७) ने खुदवाई है और जो किसी के नामको मिटाता है भगवत्‌ महाराज उस्के सात कुलके नामको मिटा देते हैं ॥

सं० १९४५ आषाढ़ शु० १३ शनिवार

As regards orthography it may be remarked that v is used for b as vanavaya for banavaya in line 12, vanavai for banavai in line 10 and vanake for banani in line 6. Again b is used for v as Sivalokabasi for Sivalokavasi; v and b are frequently interchanged in ancient Sanskrit inscriptions, especially those in Northern India.

Translation.

PROSPERITY.

A written declaration about the Sivalaya.

The house of the illustrious and learned Maharaja Kanhayalalji, whose father was (called) Maharaja Saligramaji or Kriparamji, had fallen down owing to the rains. In Samvat 1898 (the ling of) the illustrious (God) Siva was placed, after the walls of this place on the four sides were erected. And the hall was built for himself. Till Samvat 1908, (the building) remained in the same condition (taura). In Samvat 1908, the erection of the Sivalaya was begun under the supervision of Maharaja Jvalisimhaji. In Samvat 1909 (the Sivalaya) was ready and Maharaja Saligramaji consecrated it on the 3rd day of (the month of) Ashadha with great pomp. Why? Because the learned Maharaja was ill. And he died (lit. became an inhabitant of Kailasa) one month and ten days after the consecration. In Sam (that is Samvat) 1914, the Mutiny broke out. In Sam (Samvat) 1915 or 1916 the new road was made. The hall came in the street. Maharaja Saligramaji got compensation for it from the Government. He had built the wall on the side of the road, purchased the land from Sujana Bibi, made the cellar, erected the four walls and left out the work. In Samvat 1928 Mathanlala got made the shape of the shop (built the shop), staircase, etc., by (the hand of) Naval Mistry. In Sam (Samvat) 1940, on the other side, the pipe fountain, the niche of Bhairavji, roof, and the hall with three doors were made. The broken parts are repaired by this servant (of the God), all the materials are employed by this poor man. In Sam (Samvat) 1919 Maharaja Saligramaji died. After him this man who loves the feet (charananuragi) (of Siva) has been rendering all sorts of services. This written declaration (inscription) has been got engraved by poor learned Rai Bahadura Mitanlala, Pensioner, by order of the Favourable Sri Sivaji Maharaja. Whoever erases the name of another, Bhagavat Maharaja (God Siva) blots out his name with seven generations.

Sam (Samvat) 1945, Ashadha Su (Suddha) 13, Saturday.

(*g*) Good.

(*h*) Unnecessary.

(*j*) Rai Bahadur Mithanlala had the inscription engraved in Samvat 1945. He was the great uncle of Sadananda Vaidya, who now looks after the affairs of the temple.

Inside the shrine there is a ling and images of Parvati, Ganapati, Brahmadeva and Nandi. In a niche to the visitor's right is an image of Kala Bhairva and to the left images of Lala Bhairava, Hanumat and Kalidevi.

No. 264. (*a*) Diwan Singh's Temple.

(*b*) Chhatta Gosavi Makhanlala.

(*c*) Jugal Kisor.

(*d*) III.

(*e*) The temple is said to be about 100 years old.

(*f*) None.

(*g*) Good.

(*h*) Unnecessary.

(*j*) Divan Ahiluvali built the temple and it has been named after him.

To the visitor's right are the images of Radha and Krishna and to the left that of Hanumat. There is also a Sivalaya in which are images of Parvati, Ganapati, Kartikasvami, Nandi and Bhairava.

No. 265. (*a*) Goma's Sivalaya.

(*b*) Gali Bhairon, *Muhalla* Malivara.

(*c*) Jaggannatha.

(*d*) III.

(*e*) The temple is about 100 years old.

(*f*) None.

(*g*) Good.

(*h*) Unnecessary.

(*j*) A ling of Siva and images of Parvati, Ganapti, Brahmadeva and Nandi are enshrined in the temple. In a niche is an image of Hanumat.

A lady named Goma built the temple and it is named after her.

No. 266. (*a*) Hauzwali Mosque II.

(*b*) On the road.

(*c*) Waqf, Mutawalli, Hafiz Karam Ilahi.

(*d*) III.

(*e*) Late Mughal period.

(*f*) None.

(*g*) Good.

(*h*) Unnecessary.

(*j*) The mosque measures 40′ 9″ north and south by 23′ 6″ east and west. It has a spacious courtyard and tank.

KUNCHAI RAIMAN.

No. 267. (*a*) Pipalwali Mosque III.

(*b*) In the *Muhalla*.

(*c*) Waqf, Mutawalli, Hafiz, Fazl-i-Azim Chharrewale.

(*d*) III.

(*e*) Unknown.

(*f*) None.

(*g*) Good.

(*h*) Unnecessary.

(*j*) The mosque has been rebuilt. It is of two storeys. The lower one is the mosque, while the upper storey consists of rooms for Arabic students of the *Madrassa* on the roof of the mosque.

No. 268. (*a*) Baghichewali Mosque.

(*b*) In the *Muhalla*.

(*c*) Waqf, Mutawalli, Afzal Yar Khan.

(*d*) III.

(*e*) Late Mughal period.

(*f*) None.

(*g*) Good.

(*h*) Unnecessary.

(*j*) A small building of no particular interest.

No. 269. (*a*) Unchi Mosque V.

(*b*) In the *Muhalla*.

(*c*) Waqf, Mutawalli, Hakim Ajmal Khan.

(*d*) III.

(*e*) 1261 A. H. (1845 A. D.).

(*f*) On the central arch.

خانہ خدا ۱۲۶۱

Translation.

"House of God 1261."

(*g*) Good.

(*h*) Unnecessary.

(*j*) The mosque is a small building of two storeys, the lower of which serves as a shop. The chronogram and the date are written on the central arch.

No. 270. (*a*) Anarwali Mosque II.

(*b*) In the *Muhalla*.

(*c*) People of the *Muhalla*.

(*d*) III.

(*e*) Late Mughal period.

(*f*) None.

(*g*) Good.

(*h*) Unnecessary.

(*j*) A small building of no particular interest.

CHANDNI CHAUK.

No. 271. (*a*) Gate (unnamed).

(*b*) Entrance to the Haveli (house) of Haidar Quli Khan.

(*c*) Chaudhri Narain Singh.

(*d*) III.

(*e*) Late Mughal period.

(*f*) None.

(*g*) Good.

(*h*) Unnecessary.

(*j*) Haidar Quli Khan was appointed commander of artillery in the reign of Muhammad Shah by Sayyid Hussain Ali of Barha, the influential minister of Muhammad Shah and his two predecessors. The unlimited power and arrogance of Sayyid Husain Ali and his brother Sayyid Abdullah created a general discontent among the nobles of the court which was shared by Haidar Quli. He is believed to have been a participator in the murder of Husain Ali. He nevertheless strenuously opposed the Barha Sayyids when they took steps to take revenge for the murder of Husain Ali, and he completed their downfall by imprisoning Sayyid Abdullah, who died soon afterwards in prison. In reward for his loyalty he was raised to the rank of 7,000 and 6,000 horse, and was given the title of Muizzu-d-Daula Nasir Jang.

(*k*) *Muntakhab-ul Lubab, Elliot VII*, 483 *et seq.*

(*l*) S. 74.

No. 272. (*a*) Mosque (unnamed).
(*b*) Kuncha-i-Naicha Band.
(*c*) Waqf, Mutawalli, Muhammad Siddiq.
(*d*) III.
(*e*) Unknown.
(*f*) None.
(*g*) Good.
(*h*) Unnecessary.
(*j*) The mosque which is a small building of no particular interest has been rebuilt.

No. 273. (*a*) Khalifa Ji's Mosque.
(*b*) Kuncha-i Khan Chand.
(*c*) Hafiz Ahmad Husain Attar.
(*d*) II*b*.
(*e*) Unknown.
(*f*) None.
(*g*) Good.
(*h*) Unnecessary.
(*j*) The mosque which measures 37′ 3″ north and south by 16′ 9″ east and west has been recently reconstructed.

No. 274. (*a*) Sonehri Masjid (Golden Mosque) III.
(*b*) Near the Police Station.
(*c*) Waqf, Mutawalli, Zainul Abidin.
(*d*) II*b*.
(*e*) 1134 A. H. (1721-2 A. D.).
(*f*) On the central arch—

(۱) بعهد بادشاه هفت کشور * سلیمان فر محمد شاه دارر

(۲) به نذر شاه بهیکه آن قطب افاق * شد این مسجد به زینت در جهان طاق

(۳) خدا یا نیست لیک از روے احسان * بنام روشن الدوله ظفر خان

(۴) به تاریخش ز هجرت تا شمار است * هزار و یکصدوسی و چهار است

Translation.

"(1) In the reign of the king of seven climes, Muhammad Shah the sovereign who has Solomon-like splendour."

"(2) This mosque was made unrivalled in the world for its magnificence, for Shah Bhik the Polar Star of the age."

"(3) O God! it is not but for the sake of laying him under an obligation that it (the mosque) is named after Raushan-ud-daula Zafar Khan."

"(4) Its date, calculated from the flight (of the Prophet) is one thousand one hundred and thirty-four."

(*g*) Good.

(*h*) Unnecessary.

(*j*) The mosque stands on a masonry platform at some height above the level of the road. The top of the somewhat insignificant gateway is on a level with the court of the mosque, while the entrance itself is barely seven feet high. Ten narrow steps lead up to the court of the mosque which is paved with sandstone. There are three arched entrances to the mosque leading into three rooms covered by domes sheathed with gilded copper and with gilt finials.

The mosque is of considerable historical interest. It was here that Nadir Shah took his seat after ordering a general massacre of the inhabitants of Delhi on the morning of the 11th Zilhajjah of the year 1151 (22nd March 1739) and it was on this spot that he was solicited to desist from the massacre.

The inscription on the central arch records the erection of the mosque by Raushan-ud-Daulah Zafar Khan for Shah Bhik, for whose account *see* No. 39.

(*k*) *Asar* (1904), chap. II, 80-1.
A. S. I. IV, 70.
As. Res., IV, 70, 422-3.
Carr Stephen, 266-9.
Catalogue, 42, J. 50 (*a*).
Cooper, 24.
Elphinstone, 700.
Fanshawe, 50.
Hearn, 18, 234, 235.
Keene, 9.
Mundy, 37.
Oriental Annual, (1835), 71 ; (1838), 143.
Orlich, II, 6.
Rodgers, 94.
Wilson, 47.

(*l*) S. 73.

No. 275. (*a*) Kotwali or Police Station.

(*b*) *See* above.

(*c*) Government Police.

(*d*) III.

(*e*) Unknown.

(*f*) None.

(*g*) Good.

(*h*) Unnecessary.

(*j*) The old *kotwali* of Shahjahanabad. The front portion has always served its present function but the portion behind was once the residence of a well-known man, Maulana Fakhr-ud-din, who is buried near the mosque of Khuwaja Qutb-ud-din Bakhtiyar Kaki in Mahrauli.

(*k*) *Cooper*, 125.
Fanshawe, 50.
Hearn, 18.
Keene, 10.
(*l*) S. 72.

No. 276. (*a*) Gur Duwara Asis Ganj Siri Guru Tegh Bahadur Sahibji.
(*b*) Near the Police Station.
(*c*) Sikh Community.
(*d*) II *b*.
(*e*) The original temple is said to have been erected 267 years ago.
(*f*) There are three modern inscriptions in Gurumukhi of no special historical interest.
(*g*) Good.
(*h*) Unnecessary.
(*j*) The Gur Duwara was built in memory of Guru Tegh Bahadur who was beheaded by order of Aurangzeb in the year 1675 A.D. (on pausa suddha, 5, Vikrama samvat 1732 . . . . at about 11 A. M.). He had been kept in prison for 40 days during which he repeated constantly the hymns from the Adi Grantha. He was the son of Guru Har Gobind and the ninth Guru of the Sikhs. He was raised to the *Gaddi* amid considerable dissensions after the death of Guru Har Kishan. He surpassed in affluence and power even his renowned father. His rival for the *Gaddi* was his nephew Ram Rai who, after his discomfiture, found a means of avenging himself upon his successful competitor Tegh Bahadur, who now lived in splendour, by representing to the Emperor that the Guru's designs were not favourable to the State. Tegh Bahadur was accordingly brought to Delhi, but through the intercession of the Raja of Jaipur his life was saved, and he repaired to Patna, where he lived for five or six years. He then returned to the Punjab and is said to have abandoned his peaceful pursuits for a predatory career. He was consequently arrested and beheaded in Delhi by order of Aurangzeb. The banian tree, which marks the spot, is said to be dated from the time of the Guru. His picture hangs in the temple.
(*k*) *Latif*, 258-60.

No. 277. (*a*) Gate (Khuni [bloody] Darwaza).
(*b*) Leading to Dariba-i-Kalan.
(*c*) State.
(*d*) II*a*.
(*e*) Mughal period.
(*f*) None.
(*g*) Good.
(*h*) Should be declared a Protected Monument.

(*j*) Only the side piers of the gate now remain, the arch having fallen. The gate was so called as there was much bloodshed near it during Nadir Shah's massacre of the inhabitants of Delhi (*see* also No. 274).

(*k*) *Asar* (1847), chap. III, 51.
Cooper, 124.
Hearn, 17, 119, 235.
Heber, II, 305 (Coonia Darwaza).
Keene, 10.

No. 278. (*a*) Temple (unnamed).
(*b*) Kuncha-i Sukhananda.
(*c*) Hajarilala.
(*d*) III.
(*e*) About 125 years old?
(*f*) None.
(*g*) Good.
(*h*) Unnecessary.
(*j*) In the temple are the images of Chandprabhu and Parsvanatha (Parasnatha). The building which belongs to the Digambar sect of the Jains is said to have been built by one Sahib Singh. A peculiarity of the images of this sect is that they are naked.

No. 279. (*a*) Mohanlala Gosavi's Temple.
(*b*) Kuncha-i Sukhananda.
(*c*) Sivasankara.
(*d*) III.
(*e*) The temple is about 90 years old.
(*f*) None.
(*g*) Good.
(*h*) Unnecessary.
(*j*) In the temple are the images of Radha and Krishna, the former of white marble and the latter of black marble.
Mohanlala Gosavi built the temple, and it has been named after him. He was a well-known singer and poet. The present is the 4th generation from him.

No. 280. (*a*) Gulab Rai Mihr Chand's Temple.
(*b*) Kuncha-i Sukhananda.
(*c*) Lala Ishri Parshad, Government Treasurer.
(*d*) III.
(*e*) Mughal period.
(*f*) None.
(*g*) Good.
(*h*) Unnecessary.

(*j*) The temple was built by Lala Gulab Rai. It is a double storeyed building, the upper storey being occupied by the temple, while the lower one is used as a dwelling house by a relative of the owner.

Gulab Rai, the founder of the temple, was the son of Saharanbir Singh, who founded the town of Saharanpur, for which he was given a *jagir* by Emperor Akbar. Gulab Rai was the first of the family to come to Delhi, where he started a banking business. During his lifetime the bank acquired great fame and after his death it was styled Gulab Rai Mihr Chand by his son Mihr Chand. The old firm still exists. Saligram, the 6th in succession of Lala Gulab Rai, having resigned service under Muhammadan Emperors of Delhi was appointed Government treasurer by the English in 1825, and gave satisfaction. He rendered considerable services to the Government during the Mutiny.

There are about 30 images in the temple including that of Chandra Prabhu, the 8th tirthankara, that of Parsvanatha, 23rd tirthankara, and that of Mahavira, the 24th tirthankara.

(*k*) *Imperial Coronation Durbar, Delhi*, 1911, I, 375-6.

MALIWARA.

No. 281. (*a*) Savalji's Sivalaya.

(*b*) Bhojapura.

(*c*) Chhuttan Misra. (Sanwal Das ?)

(*d*) III.

(*e*) Late Mughal.

(*f*) None.

(*g*) Good.

(*h*) Unnecessary.

(*j*) The building contains a ling of Siva, two images of Ganapati, one of Parvati, one of Kartikasvami and one of Nandi.

No. 282. (*a*) Temple (unnamed).

(*b*) Baidwara.

(*c*) Lakshmichanda and Umraosing.

(*d*) III.

(*e*) The temple is about 175 years old ?

(*f*) None.

(*g*) Good.

(*h*) Unnecessary.

(*j*) The temple is on the first floor and is a fine building, belonging to the Jains or Sraogis.

In the middle is an image of Chandraprabhu and above him that of Mahavira. To its left and to the visitor's right is an image of Bahubala and there are about 200 or 250 images more. The building is *panchaiti* or belonging to the whole community.

No. 283. (*a*) Khunbaha (*Khunbaha*=The fine paid for murder or the shedding of blood) Mosque.

(*b*) In the *Muhalla.*

(*c*) Waqf, Mutawalli Ahmad Husain (dentist).

(*d*) III.

(*e*) Late Mughal period (time of Muhammad Shah).

(*f*) None.

(*g*) Good.

(*h*) Unnecessary.

(*j*) The mosque which is only a small building has three domes and three arched entrances. Its courtyard, at the south-east corner of which is an octagonal tank, is paved with red sandstone. It is entered through a small gateway towards the north, beyond which there is a long covered passage giving access to the courtyard of the mosque. At the inner entrance of this passage there is a recess, on the west side in which are to be found two graves. One of these graves has a headstone on which there are inscribed the names of twelve *Imams* and the words

تحریر شعبان سنه ۱۵ مقدس ما ...

(written in Shaban of the year 15 of holy......). The names of the twelve *Imams* show that the man who is buried in the grave professed the Shia faith. After the years which is given as "15" in figures, there is a word meaning "holy," and after that again there are several words which are undecipherable and leave the date uncertain. In all probability the "year 15" represents the year of the reign of some Emperor, possibly of Muhammad Shah.

The following story told by the owner Ahmad Husain explains the origin of its name, '*Khunbaha.*' On the foundation of Shahjahanabad, pieces of land were granted by the Emperor to the nobles, courtiers, officials and servants of the State as sites for their houses. Among the recipients were two brothers Anwar and Munawwar, blacksmiths in the service of Shahjahan, who had acquired land near the Jami mosque, hard by the house of the *Ustad* Hamid, Shahjahan's famous master-builder (see No. 325) the site of which can still be traced by the quarter which still bears his name (Kuncha-i Ustad Hamid). During the reign of Muhammad Shah a descendant of the blacksmith named Muhammad Ali, *alias* Nazar Muhammad, was murdered by Shibkaran Das, a jeweller, in a quarrel which arose because the latter or one of his companions threw coloured water on to him during the Holi festival. The jeweller's house was therefore confiscated and given to the family of the deceased. A portion of the house was transformed into this mosque and hence it has been given the name '*Khunbaha,*' *i.e.*, "received as a fine paid for murder." Another portion of the house was converted into an *Imambara*, but this is no longer in existence.

The tomb with the headstone is said to be that of Muhammad Ali, but this story must be accepted with care. Was Muhammad Ali actually killed in the affray? The confiscation of the house and its transference could not be effected so soon as to enable his descendants to bury him there. He was possibly wounded, and lingering for some time died after the court had decided that the jeweller's house be given to him, and during this period the mosque was built or was under construction.

No. 284. (*a*) Hakim Ajitsing and Jivansing's Temple.
(*b*) Chhatta Madan Gopala.
(*c*) Lachhu.
(*d*) III.
(*e*) It is about 100 years old.
(*f*) None.
(*g*) Good.
(*h*) Unnecessary.
(*j*) Thani, daughter of Hakim Ajitsing, built the temple which measures 49 feet 6 inches by 31 feet 9 inches. Jivansing was his son-in-law. The present is the 4th generation from Hakim Ajitsing.
The building is twofold. Facing the visitor is a temple of Radha and Krishna and to the right is a Sivalaya in which are placed images of Parvati, Ganapati, Kartikasvami and Nandi.

No. 285. (*a*) *Jauhris'* (Jewellers') Temple.
(*b*) Naughara *Muhalla.*
(*c*) Chhajjumala Bahori.
(*d*) III.
(*e*) About 200 years old (see also paragraph *j*).
(*f*) None.
(*g*) Good.
(*h*) Unnecessary.
(*j*) To the visitor's right is an image of Bhairava. In the sanctum and in the centre is an image of Sambhava, the 3rd tirthankara. To the visitor's right and Sambhava's left is an image of Neminatha, the 22nd tirthankara, and to its left and visitor's right is an image of Vimalnatha, the 13th tirthankara. To the visitor's left and Sambhava's right is an image of Neminatha, the 21st tirthankara, and to its right and the visitor's left is an image of Parsvanatha, the 23rd tirthankara.
The temple which occupies the upper storey of the building measures 52 feet 9 inches by 25 feet 4 inches and is said to have been founded during the time of the Emperor Shahjahan by the Jain community. It was rebuilt some 50 years ago. The interior of the temple proper which occupies the upper storey of the building is decorated with gilt painting. It was repaired about 38 years back.

CHIRAKHANA.

No. 286. (*a*) Mosque (unnamed).
(*b*) Near Chhatta Madan Gopal.
(*c*) Waqf, Mutawalli, Khubi, Qadir Bakhsh, etc., water carriers.
(*d*) III.
(*e*) Late Mughal period.
(*f*) None.
(*g*) Good.
(*h*) Unnecessary.
(*j*) A small building of no particular interest.

No. 287. (*a*) Jauhris' (Jewellers') temple.
(*b*) In the ***Muhalla***.
(*c*) Lala Matthumala.
(*d*) III.
(*e*) Late Mughal.
(*f*) None.
(*g*) Good.
(*h*) Unnecessary.
(*j*) There are about 20 or 25 images in the temple. Those worth noticing are: To the visitor's left an image of Bhairava besmeared with red lead, in front an image of Parsvanatha, the 23rd tirthankara, to the right an image of Sreyamsa, the 11th tirthankara, and to the left an image of Rishabha, the 1st tirthankara.

The temple, which measures 18 feet × 15 feet, is a Jain one of the Svetambara sect. The images of this sect are clad in white clothes and decorated.

No. 288. (*a*) Mosque (unnamed).
(*b*) In the ***Muhalla***.
(*c*) Waqf, Mutawalli, Abdurrazzaq.
(*d*) III.
(*e*) Late Mughal period.
(*f*) None.
(*g*) Good.
(*h*) Unnecessary.
(*j*) The building is of no particular interest.

No. 289. (*a*) Mosque (unnamed).
(*b*) In the ***Muhalla***.
(*c*) Waqf, Mutawalli, Abdurrazzaq.
(*d*) III.
(*e*) Late Mughal period.
(*f*) None.
(*g*) Good.
(*h*) Unnecessary.
(*j*) The mosque occupies the upper storey, the lower storey consisting of two shops.

No 290. (*a*) Shahtutwali Mosque. (*Shahtut*=mulberry).
(*b*) *Gali* Matawali.
(*c*) Waqf, Mutawalli, Qamruddin.
(*d*) III.
(*e*) Late Mughal period.
(*f*) None.
(*g*) Good.
(*h*) Unnecessary.
(*j*) A small building of no particular interest.

MUHALLA KHAJUR KI MASJID.

No. 291. (*a*) Sivalaya (unnamed).
(*b*) Chelpuri.
(*c*) Raja Narayanalala, Barrister-at-law.
(*d*) III.
(*e*) The temple is more than 112 years old.
(*f*) None.
(*g*) Good.
(*h*) Unnecessary.
(*j*) Munshi Jivanlala, grandfather of the present barrister, purchased the temple which is a domed pavilion some 6 feet 9 inches square, along with some other property some 112 years ago. The latter is unable to give the exact date when it was erected by its previous owner or his ancestors.
A ling of Siva and the images of Parvati, Ganapati and Nandi are enshrined in the temple.

No. 292. (*a*) Mosque (unnamed).
(*b*) In the *Muhalla*.
(*c*) Waqf, Mutawalli, Abdul Rashid.
(*d*) III.
(*e*) Late Mughal period.
(*f*) None.
(*g*) Good.
(*h*) Unnecessary.
(*j*) The mosque is a small building of no particular interest. It stands on a raised piece of ground and is reached by nine steps.

No. 293. (*a*) Lala Bansidharalal's Sivalaya.
(*b*) In the *Muhalla*.
(*c*) Lala Bansidhara.
(*d*) III.
(*e*) Late Mughal.
(*f*) None.
(*g*) Good.
(*h*) Unnecessary.
(*j*) A small Sivalaya only in which are enshrined a ling of Siva and the images of Parvati, Ganesa Kartikasvami and Nandi.

No. 294. (*a*) Chaudhari Himmat-sing's Sivalaya.
(*b*) In the *Muhalla*.
(*c*) Lala Motirama.
(*d*) III.
(*e*) Late Mughal.
(*f*) None.

(g) Good.
(h) Unnecessary.
(j) Himmatsing's father, Motilala, built the temple which is some 5 feet 6 inches square. In it are enshrined the images of Parvati, Ganapati, Brahmadeva, Nandi and Hanumat and a ling of Siva.

No. 295. (a) Mosque, Khajurwali (of palm tree) II.
(b) In the *Muhalla.*
(c) Waqf, Mutawalli, Abdul Wahhab.
(d) III.
(e) Late Mughal period.
(f) None.
(g) Good.
(h) Unnecessary.
(j) The mosque has received its name from the palm tree standing in the courtyard. It is a small building of no particular interest.

No. 296. (a) Jain Temple.
(b) In the *Muhalla.*
(c) Jankidasa.
(d) III.
(e) It is said to be 173 years old?
(f) None.
(g) Good.
(h) Unnecessary.
(j) One Ayamal, an officer in the Commissariat Department of Muhammadshah, who incurred the displeasure of his master was afraid that his house would be confiscated. To avoid this mishap, Ayamal kept an image in his house and declared the place to be a temple dedicating, it is said, all his property thereto. It is the third Jain temple in Shahjahanabad of the Digambara sect.

There are about 200 images of the tirthankaras in the temple.

DHARAMPURA.

No. 297. (a) Tophakhanevala's Sivalaya.
(b) Near *Gali* Bhutwali.
(c) Chunilala and Sankar Dayala.
(d) III.
(e) Late Mughal.
(f) None.
(g) Good.
(h) Unnecessary.
(j) Chunilala says that probably it was his grandfather who built the Sivalaya. He was a contractor who served under the late Mughal Emperors as an officer for providing materials for the artillery. Lala Devakinandana rendered good services to the British Government during the disturbances at the time of the Indian Mutiny of 1857, in furnishing

Military Stores to Magazines as certified by H. Lewis, President, Committee of Ordnance, on February 10, 1858. His firm supplied all petty stores during the siege of Delhi.

No. 298. (*a*) Chandi Misra's Sivalaya.
(*b*) In the *Muhalla.*
(*c*) Chandi Misra.
(*d*) III.
(*e*) About 200 years old.
(*f*) None.
(*g*) Good.
(*h*) Unnecessary.
(*j*) Phulanji Kayastha built the temple.

In the temple are enshrined a ling of Siva and the images of Parvati Ganapati, Kartikasvami and Nandi. In the niches facing the visitor can be seen images of Hanumat and Bhairava.

It is said that some unnatural phenomena occur here. But this is an idle tale and does not throw any light on archæology.

In the compound of the temple is a carved stone probably belonging to some older building.

No. 299. (*a*) Tephakhanevala's temple. (Srilala Gosavi's temple.)
(*b*) At the entrance to the *Gali* Pahar Wali.
(*c*) Madanlala and Singanatha.
(*d*) III.
(*e*) Late Mughal.
(*f*) There is a modern inscription in one line above the gate. It runs:

श्री किशोरी रमणजीको मंद्र

Translation.

"a temple of Revered Kisori (Radha) and her lover (Krishna)."

(*g*) Good.
(*h*) Unnecessary.
(*j*) The temple is on the ground floor of a building, the remainder being used as a residence by the owner.

No. 300. (*a*) Sivalaya (unnamed).
(*b*) Gali Pahar Wali Khurd.
(*c*) Sukhadeva.
(*d*) III.
(*e*) Late Mughal.
(*f*) None.
(*g*) Good.
(*h*) Unnecessary.
(*j*) One Bahadur Singh's sister, Javardevi, built the temple some years before the Mutiny.

It stands on a raised piece of ground and is domed. The entrance to the temple is through three arched entrances in front of which is a red sandstone courtyard approached from the road by 13 steps.

In it are enshrined a ling of Siva and the images of Parvati, Ganesa and Kartikasvami. That of Parvati is a fine one. In a niche is placed another image of Ganesa.

No. 301. (*a*) Jain Temple generally called 'Navamandir' by the Jains.

(*b*) Chelpuri.

(*c*) Lala Isriprasada and Amarsinga.

(*d*) III.

(*e*) A. D. 1807, Samvat 1864.

(*f*) None.

(*g*) Good.

(*h*) Unnecessary.

(*j*) The temple was built by Lala Harsukharai at a cost, it is said, of 5 lacs of rupees. It took 7 years to build. It is a common tendency to exaggerate the sums spent, but undoubtedly the temple cost Harsukharai a good deal. He was a councillor of the Raja of Bharatpur.

The centre of the raised platform is crowned by an image of Adinatha, the first tirthankara. Below him are two dvarapalas or doorkeepers. There are two niches, one to the visitor's right and the other to the left in which are enshrined many images. To the visitor's left there is another small temple containing more than 300 images.

This Jain temple is a fine one, and the three marble pillared halls, shrine and porch are worth examination from an artistic standpoint. The marble work and the small pillars wreathed with flowers are worth observing.

The temple is upstairs and reached by 13 steps. The entrance doors are of brass.

The temple is one of the Digambara sect.

(*k*) *Asar*, (1847), chap. III, 47.
Fanshawe, 67.
Fergusson, 66-7.

CHATTA SHAHJI.

No. 302. (*a*) Mosque (unnamed).

(*b*) Near Shah Bula Ka Barh.

(*c*) Waqf, Mutawalli Chhote.

(*d*) III.

(*e*) Late Mughal period.

(*f*) None.

(*g*) Good.

(*h*) Unnecessary.

(*j*) A small building of no particular interest.

No. 303. (*a*) House of Shahji.

(*b*) In the *Muhalla*.

(*c*) Muhammad Hasan Khan, Abul Hasan Khan and Shaikh Abdul Qadir.
(*d*) III.
(*e*) Late Mughal period.
(*f*) None.
(*g*) Fair.
(*h*) Unnecessary.
(*j*) The whole *chhatta* with its gate is said to have been the house of Shah-ji whose real name is mentioned as Nawwab Shadi Khan. He cameto India from Balkh, during the time of Shah Alam II. He conspired with the Marahatas during their occupation of Delhi and the allowance granted to the Emperor by the Marahatas was paid through him. He with two or three others, one of whom was Munshi Bhavani Shankar, were the agents of the Marahatas in Delhi. It is recorded that Nawwab Shadi Khan was also the Superintendent of *Teh Bazari* (weights and measures) in Delhi and when a considerable quantity of shells (*Kauris*) had accumulated he with the Emperor's permission built of them a bridge called Kauriya Pul, now no longer in existence.

NAIWARA.

No. 304. (*a*) Ghasiram's Sivalaya.
(*b*) In the *Muhalla*.
(*c*) Lallu Gosavi.
(*d*) III.
(*e*) About 66 years old.
(*f*) None.
(*g*) Good.
(*h*) Unnecessary.
(*j*) Ghasirama, a Khatri, built the temple. His descendant, Jatthamala, was a servant of the Emperor Muhammad Shah and the property was afterwards confiscated as he took part in the Mutiny.
In the niches are the images of Parvati and Ganapati.
There is also a ling of Siva and an image of Nandi.

MUHALLA CHHIPIWARA KALAN.

No. 305. (*a*) Babaji's Sivalaya.
(*b*) In the *Muhalla*.
(*c*) People of the *Muhalla*.
(*d*) III.
(*e*) Late Mughal.
(*f*) None.
(*g*) Good.
(*h*) Unnecessary.
(*j*) There was an old temple on the site of the present one. The new one was rebuilt about 25 years ago, by Lala Lalitaprasada Khatri, of Calcutta..
There are two lings of Siva, both of them Achala (lit. those that cannot be removed). Near both of them are images of Parvati, Ganapati,

Kartikasvami and Nandi. To the visitor's right are the images of Durga, Bhairava, Ganga and Hanumat.

An annual ceremony called Sanji is performed in the month of Asvina The images are decorated and taken out daily for three or four days to the accompaniment of singing.

No. 306. (a) Balavala Sivalaya.

(b) In the *Muhalla.*

(c) Local residents.

(d) III.

(e) About 200 years old?

(f) None.

(g) Good.

(h) Unnecessary.

(j) There are two small temples of Siva, in each of which is a ling of Siva and images of Parvati, Ganapati and Nandi. In the larger one is an image of Kartikasvami also. To the visitor's right in a niche is an image Hanumat besmeared with red lead.

Kanjimal, jeweller, repaired a part of the temple about 6 years ago.

There is a *bala* (*barh*=banian) tree in the temple and hence it is called Balavala Sivalaya.

No. 307. (a) Jhajjarvala's temple.

(b) In the *Muhalla.*

(c) Local residents.

(d) III.

(e) Late Mughal.

(f) None.

(g) Good.

(h) Unnecessary.

(j) There are two small temples, (1) one of Radha and Krishna and (2) the other of Siva. In the former can be seen the images of Radha and Krishna and in the latter those of Parvati, Ganapati, Kartikasvami and Nandi. In two niches to the visitor's right are the images of Ganga and Hanumat.

A Brahmana of Jhajjar built the temple; hence it is called Jhajaravala's Mandir.

No. 308. (a) Sahib Sing's temple.

(b) In the *Muhalla.*

(c) Indra Narayana.

(d) III.

(e) Late Mughal.

(f) None.

(g) Good.

(h) Unnecessary.

(*j*) Indra Narayan's father, Rai Bahadur Sahib Sing, repaired the temple, which measures 29 feet 3 inches by 27 feet 3 inches about 40 years ago. He was a Khatri.

There are two small temples, (1) one of Radha and Krishna and (2) the other of Siva. In the former are the images of Parvati, Ganapati, Kartikasvami and Nandi, and in a niche are two images of Hanumat.

REHAT KA KUWAN.

No. 309. (*a*) Chandi Walan's Mosque.
(*b*) In the *Muhalla.*
(*c*) Waqf, Mutawalli, Zahir-ud-Din.
(*d*) III.
(*e*) Late Mughal period.
(*f*) None.
(*g*) Good.
(*h*) Unnecessary.
(*j*) A small building of no particular interest.

CHHATTA PARTAB SINGH OR GALI PIPAL WALI.

No. 310. (*a*) Naika (barber's) Sivalaya.
(*b*) *Gali* Pipalvali.
(*c*) Local residents.
(*d*) III.
(*e*) The temple is about 125 years old?
(*f*) None.
(*g*) Good.
(*h*) Unnecessary.
(*j*) The temple was repaired about 25 years back by a barber; (some say by 'Gendo *nayan*', *i.e.*, the wife of a barber), hence, it is called Naika Sivalaya.

In the temple are enshrined a ling of Siva and images of Parvati, Ganapati and Nandi. In a niche is an image of Hanumat.

No. 311. (*a*) Baba Jairam's temple.
(*b*) Close to No. 312.
(*c*) Lala Hajarilala.
(*d*) III.
(*e*) The temple is about 200 years old?
(*f*) None.
(*g*) Good.
(*h*) Unnecessary.
(*j*) There are two temples, (1) one of Siva in which are kept the images of Parvati, Ganapati, Kartikasvami and Nandi besides the ling of Siva, and the other (2) of Radha and Krishna.

No. 312. (*a*) Sitalpuri Temple.

(*b*) In the ***Muhalla.***

(*c*) Local Residents.

(*d*) III.

(*e*) It is about 150 years old.

(*f*) There is an inscription in 5 lines just above the staircase, which leads to the temple upstairs. It runs: Sri Sitalpuri Darbara purana isake malika pancha hai ge Biramana aura Baniya Mahamiyoka thoka charane naya banava diya panchati Baniyokine Samvat 1940.

(१) श्री सीतलपुरी दरबार पुराना ईस (sic)
(२) के मालिक पंच हैगी बीरामण और
(३) बनीया महमीयोका थोक चारने
नया बनवा दीया पंचाती बनीयो—
कीने संमत् १९४०

Translation.

Sacred. Sitalpuri is an old Darbara. Panchas are the owners (of this temple). A group of Brahmanas and Banias of Mahamiya erected it (the temple) at the expense of the panchas, in Samat 1940.

(*g*) Good.

(*h*) Unnecessary.

(*j*) The temple which measures some 13 feet square is the upper storey of the building, of which the lower storey, consisting of one room, is occupied by the *Pujari* (priest). It also serves as a hall for the *Panchayat* or meeting of the Hindu community. On the doorway which leads up to the temple there is the *Nagari* inscription quoted above, dated *Samvat* 1940 (1883 A. D.)

No. 313. (*a*) Barhwali (Banyan tree) Mosque I.

(*b*) In the ***Muhalla.***

(*c*) Waqf, Mutawalli, Muhammad Yusuf.

(*d*) III.

(*e*) 1060 A. H. (1650 A. D.).

(*f*) On the doorway. A pious ejaculation, then.

هوالغني سنه ١٠٦٠ هجري

Translation.

"He is rich. The year 1060 Hijra."

(*g*) Good.

(*h*) Unnecessary.

(*j*) The mosque is but a small one, and has on its doorway an inscription containing a pious ejaculation and the year 1060 A. H. which is probably the date of its erection.

No. 314. (*a*) Rajan's (masons') Mosque.

(*b*) In the ***Muhalla.***

(*c*) Waqf, Mutawalli, Muhammad Yusuf.

(*d*) III.

(*e*) 1061 A. H. (1651 A. D.).

(*f*) On the doorway of a room at the south-east corner of the mosque, there is inscribed the *Kalima* (Muhammadan creed) and the year 1061 A. H.

(*g*) Good.

(*h*) Unnecessary.

(*j*) The mosque has nothing particular to commend it to notice. On the entrance to a room at its south-east corner, there is an inscription containing the Muhammadan creed and the year 1061 A. H. This in all probability refers to the date of the erection of the mosque. There is another inscription on the gateway of the mosque that opens towards the Gali Pipal Wali. This inscription refers to the well that is in front of the gate and runs as follows :—

چاه مسجد راجان سنه ۱۰٦۰ هجري

Translation.

" The well of the mosque of masons ; the year 1060 Hijra. "

KINARI BAZAR.

No. 315. (*a*) Lala Sham Lal's Sivalaya.

(*b*) Chelpuri.

(*c*) Prabhu Dayala.

(*d*) III.

(*e*) About 70 years old.

(*f*) None.

(*g*) Good.

(*h*) Unnecessary.

(*j*) Rai Sham Lal built the temple and it is called after him.

In the temple are enshrined a ling of Siva and the images of Parvati, Durga, Ganapati Kartikasvami and Nandi.

N.B.—Parvati and Durga mean the same thing. But Durga is represented as having killed the demon महिषासुर while Parvati is shown simply as the wife of Siva in her womanly charm. Hence there are two images.

No. 316. (*a*) Jauhris' (Jewellers') Temple.

(*b*) Chelpuri.

(*c*) Lala Chchhajjumala.

(*d*) III.

(*e*) About 100 years old.

(*f*) None.

(*g*) Good.

(*h*) Unnecessary.

(*j*) The middle image in the sanctum is that of Sumati, the 5th tirthankara. The two on either side of it are of Adinatha. To the visitor's right and its left is an image of Ajitnatha, the second tirthankara. To the visitor's left and to the right of Adinatha is an image of Nemi, the 21st tirthankara. To the visitor's right in a niche is an image of Bhairava.

The pillars and pavement are of white marble and like No. 285 is decorated with gilt painting.

N.B.—Jauhri means a jeweller, and the temple is called Jauhrika Mandir as many of the Jains frequenting the temple are jewellers. It occupies the upper storey and measures 29′ 4″ by 24′ 12.″ It was reconstructed in 1877.

DARIBA-KALAN.

No. 317. (*a*) Nawwab Sahib's Mosque.

(*b*) In the ***Muhalla***.

(*c*) Waqf, Mutawallis, Nawwab Ahmad Said Khan and Nawwab Ahmad Rashid Khan.

(*d*) III.

(*e*) 1135 A. H. (1722—3 A. D.)

(*f*) On the Central Arch.

(۱) در زمان شه خورشید سریر * ظل حق ماه زمین شاه زمان

(۲) ناصر الدین که محمد شاه است * تیغ او کفر شکن در دوران

(۳) شرف الدوله بنا فرموده * مسجد و مدرسه عالیشان

(۴) این دو بیت الشرف علم و عمل * همچو سعدین فلک کرده قران

(۵) سال تاریخ بنا گفت خرد * قبلهٔ حج ارادت کیشان

۱۱۳۵

Translation.

(1) "In the time of the king who has the sun for his throne, and who is the shadow of God, the moon of the earth, and the king of the age;"

(2) "Nasiruddin who is (called) Muhammad Shah and whose sword annihilates incredulity (*kufr*) of the age;"

(3) "Sharafud-Daula has built a grand mosque and school."

(4) "These two glorious houses of knowledge and practice were brought in conjunction like two beneficent stars (Jupiter and Venus) by heaven."

(5) "Wisdom said the chronogram of the date of its foundation '(It is) The Qibla of the pilgrimage (Haj) of the believers', 1135."

(*g*) Good.

(*h*) Unnecessary.

(*j*) The mosque is double storeyed. The lower storey consists of a series of shops; the mosque is on the upper storey and consists of three apartments roofed with three large domes with gilt finials. Fifteen narrow steps lead to the courtyard of the mosque, which is paved with sandstone. The inscription refers to the erection of a mosque and a school by Nawwab Sharafud-Daula during the time of Muhammad Shah.

(*k*) *Asar*, (1847), chap. III, 49.

(*l*) S 71.

No. 318. (*a*) Mandir Hatksevara Mahadeva, also known as Gujrati's Temple.
(*b*) Lattu shah ka *Kuncha.*
(*c*) Pandit Sankarlala.
(*d*) III.
(*e*) C. 1173 A. H. (1759—60 A. D.).
(*f*) None.
(*g*) Good.
(*h*) Unnecessary.
(*j*) In the temple are enshrined a ling of Siva and the images of Parvati and Nandi. In a niche is another image of Ganapati.

The sale deeds in possession of the supervisor of the temple show that the land for building the temple was purchased by one Mittha Lal Nagar in the year 1173 A. H. It is a small building and has been rebuilt.

No. 319. (*a*) Mosque (unnamed).
(*b*) Mashru ka Katra.
(*c*) Unknown.
(*d*) III.
(*e*) Mughal period.
(*f*) None.
(*g*) Good.
(*h*) Unnecessary.
(*j*) The mosque consists of three apartments which are roofed by domes. It has three arched entrances.

No. 320. (*a*) Mosque (unnamed).
(*b*) *Gali* Kanjas.
(*c*) *See* below.
(*d*) III.
(*e*) Late Mughal period.
(*f*) None.
(*g*) Ruinous.
(*h*) Unnecessary.
(*j*) The mosque stands on a raised piece of ground. It had originally two halls, one behind the other, the inner hall extending as far as the road, built on the roof of some shops in the *Bazar* of the *Dariba.* The shops and the inner hall have been taken from the Mosque and sold by the descendants of its founder The remaining portion of the mosque has also ceased to serve its real purpose, and is now rented as a godown. It is a mosque of the Shias and is possessed by a family professing that faith.

No. 321. (*a*) Badru-d-Din Mohrkan's Mosque.
(*b*) In the *Muhalla.*
(*c*) Waqf, Mutawalli, Zahiru-d-Din.
(*d*) III.
(*e*) 1254 A.H. (1838-9 A.D.).

(*f*) On the outer surface of the western wall.

(۱) چون افتاب روشن توحید ذوالجلال * بنمود رخ ز مطلع این غرا کمال

(۲) ای عابدان دهر چو این سجده گاه نور * بینید در رکوع درآئید چون هلال

—o—

(۱) بندۂ مسکین بدرالدین علیخان از نیاز * کرد این تعمیر بهر خالق رب العلا

(۲) از سر برکات هاتف سال تاریخش بگفت * مهبط فیض الهي مسجد نیکو بنا

Translation.

(1) "When the luminous sun of the unity of the Majestic (God) showed its face from the rising place of this perfection of brightness (*i.e.*, mosque)."

(2) "O religious persons of the world! when you see this serene place of worship bend yourself down like crescent."

—o—

(1) "The humble slave Badru-d-Dīn Ali Khan, through supplication, erected this building for the Creator who is the exalted maintainer."

(2) "With a view of blessings an invisible crier said the date of its foundation, '(It is) the place where the Divine grace descends, (and it is) the mosque of auspicious foundation.'"

(*g*) Good.

(*h*) Unnecessary.

(*j*) The mosque which is double storeyed is but a small building, and is reached by 10 steps from the road. The inscription on the outer surface of its western wall, written in white letters on black ground, states that it was built by Badru-d-Din Ali Khan, the well-known seal engraver of Delhi.

No. 322. (*a*) Jain Temple.

(*b*) Kuncha-i Seth.

(*c*) Lala Isriprasada.

(*d*) III.

(*e*) 1834 A.D.?

(*f*) On the pedestal of the image of Santinatha is inscribed Sam 1923 and that of Adinatha Su Sam 1929 Vaisa Su 3.

(*g*) Good.

(*h*) Unnecessary.

(*j*) The temple, which is a first-floor, has doors of brass; it was erected by the Jain community of Delhi, six years being spent in building.

In the sanctum on a raised platform or column is an image of Adinatha.

To the visitor's left are two images of Chandraprabhu. On three sides are three halls and the pillars of the shrine and those of the halls are of marble. To the visitor's right is a niche which is inlaid with mosaic work and lead.

(*k*) *Asar* (1847), chap. III, 48.

No. 323. (*a*) Jain Temple
(*b*) Kuncha-i Seth.
(*c*) Lala Isriprasada.
(*d*) III.
(*e*) 1840 A.D. ?
(*f*) (1) On one image of marble of Chandraprabhu the date inscribed is :
Sam 1935 Ma Su
(2) On the second is inscribed the date :
Samvat 1549 varshe vaisakha sudi 5.
(3) And on the third the date : 1893, Phâlguna Suddha 11.
(*g*) Good.
(*h*) Unnecessary.
(*j*) There are three images of Chandraprabhu two of marble and one of brass. The last is seated on a silver throne.

Indraji, a *shroff*, bought one image from a *Durrani* (a man from Kabul). The latter had demanded Rs. 500 as the price of the image. The former was a poor man and unable to pay the price. He sold his own property as well as the shop of which he was not the owner. He kept the idol in his house and gave it to the *panchas* that they might erect a temple.

The image purchased from the *Durrani* is the largest one in the centre. It is dated Samvat 1549.

No. 324. (*a*) Phulwalan's mosque.
(*b*) In the *Muhalla*.
(*c*) Waqf, Mutawalli, Yatim Khana.
(*d*) III.
(*e*) Late Mughal period.
(*f*) None.
(*g*) Good.
(*h*) Unnecessary.
(*j*) The mosque is double-storeyed, the lower storey consisting of three shops.

No. 325. (*a*) Gate (unnamed).
(*b*) Entrance to the Kuncha-i-Ustad Hamid.
(*c*) Waqf, Mutawalli, Muhammad Akbar.
(*d*) III.
(*e*) Mughal period.
(*f*) None.
(*g*) Fair.
(*h*) Unnecessary.
(*j*) The gateway is an entrance to the *Kuncha* (street) which once composed the house of Ustad Hamid, the famous master-builder of Shah Jahan (see Nos. 1 and 283).

No. 326. (*a*) Mosque (unnamed).

(*b*) Kuncha-i-Ustad Hamid.
(*c*) Waqf, Mutawalli, Muhammad Akbar.
(*d*) III.
(*e*) Mughal period.
(*f*) None.
(*g*) Good.
(*h*) Unnecessary.
(*j*) The mosque is built on the gateway which forms an entrance to the *Kuncha* (street) of Ustad Hamid.

JAMI MASJID.

No. 327. (*a*) Jami Masjid.
(*b*) *See* above.
(*c*) Waqf, Mutawalli, a Committee.
(*d*) I *b*.
(*e*) Begun on the 10th Shawwal 1060 A.H. (6th October 1650 A.D.).
(*f*) On the central arch in Tughra characters

يا هادي

"O Guide" (one of the 99 names of God).
On the remaining ten arches beginning from north

Arch I.

بفرمان شهنشاه جهان پادشاه زمين و زمان كيهان خديو كشورستان گيتي خداوند گردون توان موسس قوانين عدل و سياست مشيد اركان ملك و دولت بسيار دان عالي فطرت قضا فرمان قدر قدرت فرخنده راے خجسته منظر فرخ طالع بلند اختر اسمان حشمت انجم سپاه خورشيد عظمت فلك بارگاه

Arch II.

مظهر قدرت الهي مورد كرامت نامتناهي مظهر كلمة الله العليا مروج الملة الحنيفية البيضا ملجاء الملوك والسلاطين خليفة الله في الارضين الخاقان الا عدل الاعظم والقا ان الاجل الاكرم ابو مظفر شهاب الدين محمد صاحبقران ثاني شاهجهان پادشاه غازي لا زالت رايات دولته منصورة و اعداء حضرته مقهورة كه ديده بصيرت حق بينش از شعشه انوار هدايت انما يعمر مساجد الله

Arch III.

من آمن بالله واليوم الاخر مستنير است و آئينهٔ ضمير صدق گزينش از اشعه مشكات روايت احب البلاد الى الله مساجدها فروغ پذير اين مسجد كوه اساس گردون مماس كه كريمهٔ لمسجد اسس على التقوى بيان بنيان پائدار اوست و بينه و القى فى الارض رواسى ان تميد بكم كتابهٔ ايوان استوار او قمهٔ و قبهٔ فلك شانش از طبقات آسمان گذشته و شرفه طاق سپهر نشانش بارج كيوان پيوسته

Arch IV.

(۱) گرز طاق و قبه مقصوره اش جوئے نشان
هيچ نتوان گفت غير از كهكشان و آسمان
(۲) فرد بودے قبه گر گردون نبودے ثانيش
طاق بودے طاق گر جفتش نبودے كهكشان

فروغ شمسه پيش طاق جهان نمايش روشني بخش مصابيح سموات پرتو كلس گنبد عالم آرايش نور افزائے قناديل جنات منبر سنگ مرمرش چون صخره مسجد اقصى مرقات

Jama Masjid

Jama Masjid.

Arch V.

مقام قاب قوسین او ادنی محراب فیض گسترش مانند صبح صادق کشاده پیشانی بشارت رسان ولقد جاء هم من ربهم الهدی ابواب رحمت ایابش صلاے و الله یدعو الی دارالسلام بمسامع خاص و عام رسانیده منار سپهر مدارش نداے و یجزی الذین احسنوا بالحسنی از نه رواق گنبد فیروزه‌فام گذرانیده سقف رفیع باصفایش تماشا گاه روحانیان کرهٔ افلاک

Arch VII.

صحن وسیع دلکشایش سجده‌گاه پاک نژادان معمورهٔ خاک روح فضائی فیض التما و طیب هوائی روح افزایش از روضهٔ رضوان حکایت کرده و عذوبت ماء معین حوض دلنشین نظافت امایش از چشمهٔ سلسبیل خبر داده در روز جمعه دهم شهر شوال ۱۰۶۰ سال هزار و شصت هجری موافق سال چهارم از دور سیوم جلوس میمنت مانوس بساعت خجسته

Arch VIII.

و طالع شایسته سرمایه ابتنا و پیرایه تاسیس یافت و در عرض مدت شش سال بحسن سعی کار پردازان کاردان کارگذار و فرط اعتنا و اهتمام کار فرمایان صاحب اقتدار و بذل جد و جهد استادان ماهر دانشور و وفور کوشش پیشه‌کاران چابک دست صاحب هنر و انفاق مبلغ ده لک زرینهٔ صورت انجام و طراز اختتام پذیرفت و مقارن اتمام در روز عید فطر

Arch IX.

بفر قدوم اقدس پادشاه ظل الله صافي نیت خدا اگاه زیب و زینت گرفت و باقامت نماز عید و اداے وظایف اسلام چون مسجدالحرام در روز عید اضحي مرجع طوایف انام گردید و مباني اسلام و ایمان را متانت و اصانت کرامت فرمود سیاحان ربع مسکون و مسالک نوردان کوه و هامون را اراسته عمارتے باین رفعت و حصانت در آئینهٔ بصر

Arch X.

و مرات خیال مرتسم نگشته و حقایق گذاران وقایع دهر و فکرت پردازان نظم و نثر را که سوانح نگاران بدایع ارباب ملک و دولت و صنایع شناسان اصحاب مکنت و قدرتند افراخته بناے باین شکوه و عظمت بر زبان قلم و قلم زبان نگذشته فرازندهٔ کاخ هستي و طرازندهٔ بلندي و پستي این بنیان رفیع را که قرةالعین بینش و زینت بخش کارخانهٔ آفرینش است

Arch XI.

پائدار داشته صدائے تسبیح مسبحانش را هنگامه آراے ذاکران مجامع ملکوت و زمزمهٔ تهلیل مهللانش را نشاط افزاے معتکفان جوامع جبروت داراد و روس منابر معمورهٔ جهانرا بخطبهٔ دولت جاوید طراز این پادشاه دادگر دین پرور که بمیا من ذات مقدس مبارکش ابواب امن و امان بر روے روزگار کشاده است آراسته داراد بحق الحق و اهله - کتبه نور الله احمد -

Translation.

Arch I.—" By the order of the Emperor of the world; king of the earth and the age; Lord of the world; conqueror of kingdoms; master of the world; powerful as the sky; founder of the laws of justice and administration; strengthener of the pillars of state and wealth; well-knowing; of exalted nature; whose commands are like the decree of fate, and position like that of Providence; of happy intellect, and auspicious appearance; fortunate and lucky; having grandeur like the firmament, soldiers (as numerous) as stars; glory like the sun, and the court (as spacious) as the sky;

Arch II.—the manifestation of the Almighty's power; the recipient of unlimited blessings; the proclaimer of the great word of God; the promulgator of the bright faith of Hanifa [1]; the asylum of princes and kings; the deputy of God on earth; the just and great king; the great and glorious Lord (named) Abu-l-Muzaffar Shihab-ud-Din Muhammad Sahibqiran-i sani (the second Lord of happy conjunction) Shahjahan Badshah Ghazi (the king and champion of faith), may the flags of his kingdom ever remain victorious, and the enemies of his Majesty subdued, whose eye of God seeing perception is lighted up by the radiance of the lights of guidance of "Verily, he populates mosques of God

Arch III.—who believes in God and the last day", and the mirror of whose truth adopting conscience has received light from the flame of the lamp of the tradition "The places most loved by God are mosques"; this mosque with its foundation (as firm) as a mountain, and as lofty as the firmament, which has for the description of its strong foundation the noble (verse) "Verily the mosque founded on piety", and the clear (verse) "The mountains were cast into the earth in order to make it firm" for the inscription of its strong hall; whose sky-like pinnacle and dome have gone beyond the folds of the firmament, and the cornice of whose sky-like vaults has reached the height of Saturn;

Arch IV.—(1) If you want to know what the vault and cupola of its prayer chamber are like, nothing can be said except (that they resemble) the milky way and sky.

(2) The dome would have been matchless had the firmament not been its equal, the vault would have been unique had the milky way not been its pair.

The brilliancy of the Shamsa [2] of whose world showing arch gives light to the lamps of heavens (*i.e.*, stars); the reflection of the pinnacle of whose world adorning dome increases the light of the chandelier of Paradise; whose marble pulpit, like the rock of Solomon's temple, is a ladder to

Arch V.—the point *Qaba Qausain au adna* [3]; whose grace-spreading Mihrab, like the true and broad foreheaded dawn gives the good news "Verily there has come to them from their God the right path"; whose doors, which are the resort of mercy, have brought to the hearing of great and small the announcement "And God invites to the abode of peace"; whose minars, which are the orbits of heavens, have sent the call "(God) will compensate those, who do good, with goodness" beyond the nine folds of the blue-coloured dome (sky); whose lofty and polished roof is the pleasure ground of the spirits of the celestial sphere;

Arch VII.—whose spacious and pleasant courtyard is the place of worship of the pure-born of this terrestrial and populated world, and the favourable refreshing good and soul-strengthening air thereof resembles (the breeze of) the garden of Paradise; the sweetness of the pure water of whose pleasing and purifying tank represents the spring of Salsabil, [4] on Friday, the tenth of the month of Shawwal of the year one thousand and sixty Hijra, corresponding to the fourth year of the third cycle of the auspicious reign, at the propitious moment

Arch VIII.—and the fortunate time obtained the wealth of foundation and ornament of stability; and during the period of six years, with the efficient exertions of expert and skilful workmen, with the great application and devotion of respectable superintendents, with the hearty efforts of sagacious and wise

(1) Abu Hanifa Numan, the son of Sabit of Kufa, was one of the four great expounders of Muslim law and religion.
(2) Literally a figure resembling the sun. The secondary meaning is an ornament. Here it means a figure put up as a decoration on the keystone of an arch.
(3) Literally meaning the place of two bows length or nearer than that. This is a reference to the close proximity of the Prophet to God when he ascended the heavens from *Sakhra* (a rock) which is on *Mirqat* (a staircase) in Masjid-i Aqsa (Solomon's temple).
(4) Name of a spring in Paradise.

masters; and with the great exertions of apt-handed and skilled artificers at a cost of ten lacs of rupees, obtained the form of completion and the feature of finish. Soon after its completion, on the day of Id-i-Fitr[1];

Arch IX.—It was adorned and embellished by the magnificence of the holiest steps of the king, the shadow of God, pure-intentioned, and God-knowing; and on the day of Id-i-uzha[2] it became the resort of the crowds of people, by his (the King's) saying the Id prayers and discharging the exercises of Islam as (is done) in Masjidu-l-Haram (Kaba), and blessed the foundations of Islam and faith with firmness and strength. To those who have made the tour of the inhabited fourth portion (of the globe) and travellers (traversing) mountains and woods, an adorned building of such loftiness and strength have never been reflected in the mirror of their sight,

Arch X.—and the looking-glass of their imagination, nor to the relaters of the events of the age and the careful students of prose and poetry, who are the biographers of the important personages of the country and kingdom, and are the connoisseurs of the persons of might and power, has a lofty edifice of such grandeur and magnificence been brought on the tongue of their pen and the pen of their tongue. May the builder of the mansion of life and the designer of high and low places keeping this exalted building firm, which is like the pupil of the eye of sight, and the embellisher of the workhouse of creation,

Arch XI.—continue the sound of the repeaters of the praises of God on a rosary, in it, giving grace to the noise of the assembly of God praising angels, and the melodious voice of the readers of the Muhammadan creed and the name of God, in it, increasing joy of the congregations of recluse angels of the highest order; and decorate the heads of the pulpits of the inhabited world with the Khutba[3] of the eternity adorning reign of this king who is an administrator of justice and a cherisher of faith, and by the blessings of whose august and holy person the doors of peace and security have been opened for the world, for the sake of God and His people. Written by Nurullah Ahmad."

(*g*) Excellent.

(*h*) Unnecessary.

(*i*) The Jami Masjid is also styled ***Masjid-i-Jahan Numa*** (world-showing mosque). It was built by Shahjahan, and is one of the largest mosques in India. Its foundation was laid on Friday, the 10th *Shawwal* 1060 (6th October 1650 A.D.) under the superintendence of Sadullah Khan, the Prime Minister, and Fazil Khan Mir-i-Saman, and 5,000 men working daily, it was finished in 6 years at the cost of 10 lacs of rupees. The mosque stands on rocky ground commonly known as ***Bhojla Pahari.*** The red sandstone terrace is some 30 feet above the level of the ground. The courtyard of the mosque is reached on three sides, east, north and south, by three broad flights of steps, all built of red sandstone. The main eastern gate is considered the "royal entrance" and is reached by a flight of thirty-five steps. The mosque is surmounted by three domes ornamented with alternate stripes of black and white marble, and gilt pinnacles. The façade is flanked by two lofty minarets, longitudinally striped with white marble and red stone, about 130 feet

---

(1) The festival celebrated at the end of Ramazan.
(2) The festival of sacrifices celebrated two months and ten days after Id-i-Fitr.
(3) Address or sermon delivered by the Imam on the occasion of Id and Friday prayers. It contains the name of the reigning monarch.

high, and containing 130 steps. The minarets are divided by three projecting galleries and are surmounted by open twelve-sided domed pavilions. On the back of the mosque are four small minarets treated like those in front. The prayer chamber or western aisle has seven arched entrances, the internal walls of the mosque, waist high, being faced with marble. Another aisle of eleven arches fronts the court-yard; the centre arch is higher than the flanking arches and is emphasised by minarets surmounted by the usual octagonal cupolas. Over these arched entrances are tablets of white marble inlaid with inscriptions in black marble. The floor of the mosque is of black and white marble ornamented in imitation of the *Mosalla* (the prayer carpet); a thin black marble border marks off eight hundred and ninety-nine divisions, each 3 feet long and $1\frac{1}{2}$ feet broad. Close to this stands the pulpit which, reached by four balustraded steps, is supposed to have been cut out of one block of marble. The court of the mosque is enclosed by open arched colonnades, at the angles of which are twelve-sided open pavilions surmounted by marble domes with gilt pinnacles. In a room in the north-eastern corner of the court, the relics of the Prophet are piously preserved. These relics were formerly kept in the rooms at the north-western corner of the courtyard. The place was enclosed with a red stone screen, built in the reign of Alamgir II, by Ilmas Khan, a nobleman and a eunuch attached to the imperial household. He also put up the following inscription on the screen :—

(۱) پیش آثار مبارک سرور آخر زمان
در زمان شاه عالمگیر خاقان جهان

(۲) با سیادت ساخت دیوار حجر از سنگ سرخ
بندهٔ با اعتقاد از صدق دل الماس خان

(۳) سال تاریخ بنا چون میر جست از عقل و هوش
گفت هاتف بهر خود را کردهٔ ابواب جنان

Translation.

(1) "In front of the blessed relics of the chief of the last age (the Prophet Muhammad) during the time of Shah Alamgir, the king of the world,"

(2) "With greatness a wall of red stone was built, with a true heart, by the faithful slave Ilmas Khan."

(3). "When Mir asked Thought and Intelligence the year of its erection, an invisible voice said, 'He has opened for himself the doors of Paradise'."

The inscription is not *in situ* but kept elsewhere in the mosque.

The courtyard, in the centre of which is a marble tank, is paved with red sandstone. The western portion of the tank was railed off by a low marble balustrade by Muhammad Tahsin Khan, a eunuch, to secure from defilement the spot where the Prophet had appeared to him in a dream in the year 1180 A. H. (1766 A.D.). The following inscription records the auspicious event :—

کوثر محمد رسول الله

۱۱۸۰

(۱) رسول دیده اند اینجا ولی و اهل الله بجاست گر شود این سنگ هم زیارتگاه

(۲) بنای سال به تحسین و آفرین هاتف بگفت احاطه جای نشست رسول الله

۱۱۸۰

باني جای ادب داعي محمد تحسین محلی بادشاهي

Translation.

" Kausar (name of a spring in Paradise) of Muhammad, the messenger of God. 1180."

(1) " Saints and the people of God have seen the Prophet here; it is proper if this stone also should become a place of pilgrimage."

(2) " The year of its construction, the invisible voice said with praise and applause, ' The enclosure of the seat of the messenger of God '."

" The founder of the place of respect Muhammad Tahsim, the Royal eunuch, who prays for blessings. 1180."

The mosque has been considerably repaired since its construction.

In the year 1829 A.D. Mirza Salim, son of Akbar II, erected a sandstone pulpit under the central entrance of the mosque as a seat for the *Mukabbir*, he who assists the *Imam* by giving the time by which the various motions in the prayer are regulated.

(*k*) *Archer*, I, 106 *et seq.*
A. S. I., I, 225; IV, 69, 421.
As. Res., IV, 308, 420; V (1807), 190.
Auckland, 7, 8, 16.
Banister Fletcher, 677.
Baxter, 29.
Bernier, 278.
Cavenagh, 30.
C. S. Range, 258 *et seq.*
Carr Stephen, 250—6.
Catalogue, 42, J, 50.
Cities, 141.
Cooper, 19, 38.
Crane, 151.
Daniell, I and II, Plates I, XXIII.
Fanshawe, 44—8.
Fergusson, II, 318.
Gardens, 92.
Historical, I, 311.
Heber, II, 285, 295.
Havell, 2, 130, 209—10.
Hodges, 118.
Impressions, 171
Low, 163, *et seq.*

Matheson, 362.
Mintura, 228.
Mundy, 37.
Oriental Annual (1840), 29.
Orlich, II, 4, 5, 26 *et seq.*
Pennell, 159.
Prinsep, 22—3, 48.
Roberts, II, 233.
Rodgers, 92.
Russell, 73.
Sleeman, II, 272.
Matheson, 362.
Memoirs, 19.
Tavernier, I, 101 (grand mosque).
Thevenot, III, 42.
Tour, 172.
Turks in India, 140.
Wilson, 42.
Asar (1847), chap. III, 1—16.

PARADE GROUND.

No. 328. (*a*) Hare Bhare Sahib's grave.
(*b*) Before the eastern gate of the Jami Masjid.
(*c*) Waqf, Mutawalli, Sayyid Abul Hasan.
(*d*) III.
(*e*) 1065 A.H. (1654-5 A.D.).
(*f*) None.
(*g*) Good.
(*h*) Unnecessary.
(*j*) The grave stands on a raised platform enclosed by wooden railings. In the middle of the platform a tree divides the enclosure, the northern half with green painted railings, containing the tomb of Hare Bhare Sahib. At the head of the grave is a masonry pillar with lamp niches.
The history of this saint is obscure. The *Mujawir* of the Dargah says that he was the spiritual leader of Sarmad Sahib, and came from his native place Sabzwar into Delhi during the time of Shahjahan.
(*k*) *Mazarat*, Part II, 29.
Keene, 15.
(*l*) S. 70.

No. 329. (*a*) Sarmad Sahib's grave.
(*b*) Before the eastern gate of the Jami Masjid.
(*c*) Waqf, Mutawalli, Sayyid Abul Hasan.
(*d*) III.
(*e*) 1070 A.H. (1659-60 A.D.).
(*f*) On a stone slab built into the pillar at the head of the grave.

الله اکبر

(۱) شاه سرمد در عهد عالمگیر　　چو سفر ساخته بخلد برین

(۲) گفت تاریخ اکبر مسکین　　لحد مرقد شهید سرمد این

Translation.

God is great.

(1) "When Shah Sarmad in the reign of Alamgir set out on a journey to Paradise,

(2) Poor Akbar said the date, 'This is the grave of Sarmad the Martyr'."

(*g*) Good.

(*h*) Unnecessary.

(*j*) The grave lies within the southern half of the enclosure mentioned in No. 328. It is distinguished from the northern half by the colour of its railings which are painted red. This grave has a similar masonry pillar with lamp niches, and on it has been fixed an incised slab of stone containing the above inscription in Persian.

Sarmad was originally a Jew, but he embraced Islam and became a trader. He subsequently became *Sufi* and was so deeply immersed in mysticism that he became oblivious of himself and the world. In this state he came to Delhi in the time of Shahjahan and moved about the city naked. Dara Shikoh, who showed marked leanings to the *Sufi* sect, was wont to visit the mystic and induced the Emperor to do the same. The Emperor appointed one Inayat Khan to make inquiries about the saint, but these failed to satisfy the Emperor and confirm his belief in Sarmad. At the beginning of the reign of Aurangzeb, he began to call himself by the name of the Deity in a loud voice. This could not be tolerated by the orthodox Aurangzeb and consequently, with the advice of the Maulvis, the execution of the saint was ordered. *Sufis* hold that the execution of Sarmad, for which Aurangzeb's fanaticism was responsible, was the chief cause of the downfall of the Mughal rule in India.

(*k*) *Mazarat.* Part II, 27—9.
Keene, 15.

(*l*) S. 69.

No. 330. (*a*) Grave of Sayyid Shah Muhammad *alias* Hinga Madani (of Medina).

(*b*) In front of the eastern gate of the Jami Masjid, near the graves of Sarmad and Hare Bhare.

(*c*) Waqf, Mutawalli, Sayyid Abul Hasan.

(*d*) III.

(*e*) 1085 A.H. (1674-5 A.D.).

(*f*) None.

(*g*) Fair.

(*h*) Unnecessary.

(*j*) The tomb is some few inches below the level of the ground and lies towards south of the platform containing the graves of Sarmad and Hare Bhare. He is said to have been the *Khalifa* or successor of Sarmad.

(*k*) *Mazarat*, Part II, 29.

No. 331. (*a*) Shah Kalimullah Jahanabadi's grave.

(*b*) Between the Fort and Jami Masjid.

(*c*) Waqf, Mutawalli, Muhammad Ali.

(*d*) III.

(*e*) 1142 A.H. (1729 A.D.).

(*f*) On the head stone of the grave.

(۱) فضل و کمال خویش بود   مرهم قلب ریش بود

(۲) سال وصالش گفته هاتف   قطب زمانه خویش بود

Translation.

(1) "He was eminence and perfection of self; he was an ointment to a wounded heart."

(2) "The invisible voice said the year of his death, 'He was a Qutb of his time.'"

(*g*) Good.

(*h*) Unnecessary.

(*j*) The grave stands on a double platform inclosed by wooden railings. The first or lower platform contains two more tombs besides that of Jahanabadi. They are said to be those of his sons. The tomb of Kalimullah Jahanabadi stands on the upper platform which is of stone. The *tawiz* of the grave is of white marble, hollow in the middle and filled in with earth. The inscription is on the second platform towards north. Behind the inscription there is a masonry pillar for lamps.

Shaikh Kalimullah was a pious and learned man of his time, well known for his literary attainments and saintly attributes. He was author of several works, both religious and secular, and had a large number of disciples. He was contented with his lot and invariably refused the allowance repeatedly offered to him by the Emperor Farrukhsiyar. He died in the reign of Muhammad Shah, on the 24th Rabi-u-l Awwal of the year 1142 A.H. (17th October 1729 A.D.).

(*k*) *Mazarat*, Part II, 26—7.

No. 332. (*a*) Sayyid Bhure Shah's grave.

(*b*) Below the fort wall on the other side of the ditch, midway between the Lahore and Delhi gates.

(*c*) Waqf, Mutawalli, Zahur Husain.

(*d*) III.

(*e*) Unknown.

(*f*) None.

(*g*) Good.

(*h*) Unnecessary.

(*j*) The grave stands on a double platform. The lower or the first platform, paved with brick, appears to be modern. The upper platform and the *tawiz* of the grave over it, together with the masonry pillar with lamp niches, are all built of plastered masonry. No account of this saint is to hand nor is it known when he died.

(*k*) *Mazarat*. Part II, 17 *n*.

No. 333. (*a*) Urdu Temple.

(*b*) Near the Lahore Gate of the Fort.

(*c*) Lala Ramchanda.

(*d*) II *b*.

(*e*) 1656 A.D. ?

(*f*) None.

(*g*) Good.

(*h*) Unnecessary.

(*j*) The temple is said to be as old as the time of the Emperor Sahajahan, and to be the oldest Jain temple of Sahajahanabad.

It was called Urdu Mandir as it was erected for the Jains in the army of the Emperor.

There is a legend that Aurangzeb once issued orders that the temple drums should not be beaten, but his orders were not obeyed. Nobody, however, could be seen beating them. The Emperor himself came to the temple and satisfying himself that there was no one there, thereupon issued orders that the drums might be struck without molestation in future. The tradition regarding its foundation is that it was originally a 'camp' temple, consisting of a small tent wherein a Jain soldier placed an image for his private worship and that on this spot the temple was afterwards erected. It is held in considerable importance locally.

The large new temple to the visitor's left was erected in Samvat 1935, and is of white marble. All the images are modern.

Facing the visitor is an older temple, in the main sanctum of which are three images, the middle one being of Parsavanatha, all bearing the Samvat 1548. They are therefore 422 years old.

No. 334. (*a*) Appa Gangadhara's Temple.

(*b*) Near the Lahori Gate of the Fort.

(*c*) Lala Bholumala.

(*d*) II *b*.

(*e*) Late Mughal, probably about 1761. ?

(*f*) On the gate to the visitor's right and left hand:

जीना दरवाजा
माधोराम
खन्ना

In Sarafi

To the visitor's right:

STAIRS AND GATE
BUILT BY
MADHO RAM
KHANNA.

येह जीना और दरवाजा
लाला सरबूमलजीके पोते
लाला किशनचन्द्रजीके बेटे
माधोराम खन्नाने बनवाया

There is also an Urdu inscription in one line.

On the 11th step: १ जीना और दरवाजा बिशम्बर दयाल की
यादमे बनवागया स्वर्गवास हुवे श्रावण
शुक्ला ७ सं० १९६४

On the 9th step:

(1) STAIRS AND GATE BUILT IN MEMORY OF BISHAMBHAR DIAL.

(2) DIED ON 16TH AUGUST 1907.

On a step leading to the Mandap the name of—

(1) MADAN MOHANLAL KHATRI
and the year 1903.

Below it in one line the same name in Sarafi.

On the four brass doors the name बिशम्बर दयाल is written.

(*g*) Good.

(*h*) Unnecessary.

(*j*) The original temple was built by Appa Gangadhara, a Maratha Brahman in the service of Sindia.

The temple is one of Gaurisankara (that is, of Parvati and Siva). There are two images, one of Gauri and the other of Siva, while below them is a ling of Siva, and the images of Parvati, Ganapati, Nandi and Garuda. In a niche is an image of Hanumat. On three sides is ornate work in glass of various colours.

To the visitor's right is a small temple of Radha and Krishna.

To the left is a temple of Jamnaji, an image of Ganapati being kept in a neighbouring niche.

This temple is of interest since it was erected during the Maratha supremacy, and is the only temple in Delhi which was erected by a Maratha in the period covered by this list.

The temple is of considerable importance on account of its position. It lies on the road from the city to the Jamna bathing *ghats*. It is continually visited throughout the day by Hindu worshippers of both sexes. Marble is freely used in this building which consists of three separate enclosed apartments all used for worship, internally decorated with gilt painting. The temple has been considerably added to and improved.

CITY (North of the Chandni Chauk.)

BAGHICHA MADHO DAS.

No. 335. (*a*) Rama Rama Temple.

(*b*) In front of the *Baghicha* of Madhavadasa.

(*c*) Ramasvarupa.

(*d*) III.

(*e*) It is said to be about 200 years old. ?

(*f*) None.

(*g*) Good.

(*h*) Unnecessary.

(*j*) There are two stories current regarding this building. One is that there a Sadhu, who always used to utter "Rama Rama," was wont to stay in the temple and it was, therefore, so called. The other story is that a number of Marwaris erected the temple at their common expense and as it could not be named after any person in particular, it was decided that it should be called Rama Rama Mandir after the God enshrined in it. It is noteworthy that the temple is called, not "Rama Mandir," but "Rama Rama Mandir." The repetition of the name of Rama and the existence of the Sadhu would indicate that the first story is most probably correct. In the sanctum are three images. That of Rama is of black marble and is in the centre, that of Lakshmana is to Rama's right and that of Sita to the left. The two last are of white marble. In front is a small temple of Hanumat.

No. 336. (*a*) Madhavadasa's Temple.

(*b*) In the *Muhalla.*

(*c*) Jayaramdasa.

(*d*) III.

(*e*) The temple is said to be about 350 years old. ?

(*f*) A. In the temple are the charanapadukas of Raghavadasa, the inscription on which runs :—

(१) यह चरनुपादका श्री महंत राघोदासजीके है

Yaha charanupadaka (*sic*) sri Mahanta Raghodasajike hai.

(२) संवत् १८४५ सावन वदी ३० मावस मंगलवार

Samvat 1945 Sâvana (*sic*) vadi 30 mavasa (*sic*) mangalavara.

Translation.

These foot-prints are of the illustrious Mahanta Raghodasa. Samvat 1945, Tuesday, Amavasya, 30th day, the dark fortnight of Sravana.

N. B.—Lit Charana = a foot, and paduka = Sandal. Hence charanapaduka = a foot-print.

B. There are also the charanapadukas of Baladevadasa, the inscription on which runs :—

श्री संवत १९५३ मीती (*sic*) जेठ (*sic*)

वदी २ बुधवार को

महंत बलदेवदासजीकी

चरणपादुका पधराई

Translation.

On Wednesday, the second day of the dark fortnight Jyeshtha, Samvat 1953, the charanapadukas of Mahanta Baladevadasaji were placed (lit. were seated) here.

C. On slab of the mandap are the following inscriptions :—

Urdu inscription in 3 lines.

BAGHICHEE
OF MADHODASS
THE FOUNDER OF
THIS MONASTERY.

माधवदासकी बगीची

परम रम्य सुंदर यह धरनी
महिमा अमित जाय नहि बरनी
संवत् १९१३

Translation.

Garden of Madhavadasa. This land is very lovely and charming. Greatness cannot be measured (is unequalled). It is indescribable.

D. On a large white marble slab presented to the temple is written :

दास नंदराम पत्थरवाला देाल्ली
संवत् १९२९

Dasa Nandarama Pattharvala Dilli
Sabatta (*sic*) 1929.

E. On a slab of the temple of Satyanarayana is an inscription of no interest and written by the present Mahant and therefore need not be copied.

(*g*) Good.

(*h*) Unnecessary.

(*j*) The temple is named after Madhavadasa. He was a Vaishnava Sadhu. Akbar is traditionally connected with him. The Emperor once came to Madhavadasa, who is supposed to have worked a miracle to convince him of his capabilities. Several *chakkis* were moving, but nobody could be seen working at them. The Emperor, struck at the miracle, enquired if the Sadhu would care to be presented with gifts. Madhavadasa, however, asked for nothing except his good-will. In India every Sadhu is credited with miraculous powers and Madhavadasa was evidently no exception.

There are several temples in the courtyard.

One is of Rama in which are enshrined three images : that of Rama in the centro, that of Lakshmana to its right and that of Sita to its left. The first is of black marble, the last two of white marble. The latter are well executed.

There is a temple of Ramesvara Mahadeva in front of it, in which are enshrined images of Parvati, Ganapati and Nandi besides a ling of Siva.

Next comes the *gadi* (seat) of Mahant Madhavadasa followed by the temple of Davaji, *i.e.*, Balarama, in which are kept images of Balarama and Revati. That of Revati is worthy of notice and perhaps the best of its kind in Delhi.

Next comes the temple of Jamnaji.

There is also a temple dedicated to Satyanarayana, the white marble image in which is well cut, and bears the modern and unimportant inscription to which reference has been made above.

This is followed by the temple of Ganga, and the temple of Radha and Krishna; the image of the former being of white marble and that of the latter of black marble. The walls of the temple are inlaid with lead.

There is also a temple of Lakshmi and Narayana, the images in both being of white marble and the temple walls inlaid with lead.

The temple of Badri Narayana is of no interest.

There is also an image of Kedarnatha and three images of Ganapati and one of Parvati.

KAURIYA PUL.

No. 337. (*a*) Sivalaya (unnamed).

(*b*) Chah Indara.

(*c*) Mahanta Ramajidasa.

(*d*) III.

(*e*) The temple is said to be more than 200 years old. ?

(*f*) None.

(*g*) Good.

(*h*) Unnecessary.

(*j*) The temple was repaired by Mahanta Ramanujadasa. In the Sivalaya are enshrined a ling of Siva and the images of Parvati, Ganapati and Nandi. In a niche is an image of Hanumat.

In another small temple can be seen an image of Hanumat and brass images of Vyankatesa and Krishna.

Near the temple there is a well named "*Chah-i Indara*" after which the Muhalla is known. The well is said to be of considerable antiquity, built by *Banjaras* in the pre-Mughal period.

For the origin of the name '*Kauriya Pul*' see No. 303.

No. 338. (*a*) Mosque (unnamed).

(*b*) Sarai Topkhana.

(*c*) Hafiz Zainul Abidin.

(*d*) III.

(*e*) Late Mughal period.

(*f*) None.

(*g*) Good.

(*h*) Unnecessary.

(*j*) The place on which the *Serai* stands was once occupied by the *Topkhana* after which the *Serai* is known. The mosque was built before the removal of the *Topkhana*, and the *Serai* was erected in its place.

CHANDNI CHAUK.

No. 339. (*a*) Jhajjaravalas' Temple.
(*b*) In the Chauk.
(*c*) Jagadisaji.
(*d*) III.
(*e*) The temple is more than 125 years old.
(*f*) None.
(*g*) Good.
(*h*) Unnecessary.
(*j*) Hardevaji built the temple. He was an inhabitant of Jhajjar and hence the temple is called Jhajjaravalas' Mandir. The present generation is the 6th from Hardevaji.

In one temple are images of Radha and Krishna, the former being of white marble, the latter of black marble.

There is also a Sivalaya in which are enshrined a ling of Siva and the images of Parvati, Ganapati, Kartikasvami and Nandi. In a niche is an image of Hanumat.

No. 340. (*a*) The Begam's Bagh, or the Queen's garden.
(*b*) See above.
(*c*) Government.
(*d*) II*a*.
(*e*) 1060 A.H. (1650 A.D.).
(*f*) None.
(*g*) Good.
(*h*) Unnecessary.
(*j*) The garden was laid out in the year 1060 A.H. by Jahan Ara Begam, the favourite and eldest daughter of Shahjahan; it is now known as the Queen's garden. The original size and the shape of the garden has been considerably altered, and its enclosure walls and pavilions have nearly all disappeared. One or two of the latter and a four arched room, now occupied by a public library, give some idea of the old buildings. The Delhi canal, known as *Faiz Nahr*, recently blocked and filled up, ran through it; traces of the canal are still extant in the garden.

The "*Faiz Nahr*" is commonly known as *Nahr-i Sa'dat Khan.* The origin of this name is unknown. It would appear that Saadat Khan, to whom the canal is attributed, may have been connected in some way with it; but there is nothing to show that any one of the name of Saadat Khan participated in its construction. The canal was cut in the year 691 A.H. (1291-2 A.D.), by Jalāluddin Firoz Shah Khalji from the village Khizrabad to Sufaidon where Firozshah had a "*Shikargah.*" In the year 969 A. H. (1561-2 A.D.) it was repaired by Shihabu-d-Din Ahmad Khan, the Governor of Delhi, who gave it the name of *Nahr-i Shihab.* Possibly

"*Nahr-i Saadat Khan*" should have originally been *Nahr-i Shahabu-d-Din Khan*, and the lapse of years have resulted in the change of name. In the year 1048 A. H. (1638-9 A. D.) Shahjahan ordered its repair and extended the canal from Sufaidon to the Fort. These repairs were carried out in 1820 A. D. under English supervision. The canal, where it passes through the city, has, recently been covered on sanitary grounds.

(*k*) *Auckland*, 96.
Carr Stephen, 56.
Fanshawe, 20, 52, 53.
Gardens, 113.
Hearn, 6, 19.
Keene, 8.
Wilson, 46.
Asar (1847), chap. III, 2—5, 55—56 ; (1904), chap. II, 53—54, chap. III, 69—70.

No. 341. (*a*) Mosque of the *Phiranchas*.
(*b*) Kuncha-i Qabil Attar, near Queen's gardens.
(*c*) Waqf, Mutawalli, Hajji Abdul Qaiyum.
(*d*) III.
(*e*) Late Mughal period.
(*f*) None.
(*g*) Good.
(*h*) Unnecessary.
(*j*) The *Phiranchas* are Panjabi *Khattris* who have embraced Islam. They are so called because they have renounced their old Hindu religion. They observe caste rules and generally intermarry among themselves.

No. 342. (*a*) Mosque (unnamed).
(*b*) *Gali* Saidani.
(*c*) Waqf, Mutawalli, Muhammad Ahmad.
(*d*) III.
(*e*) Late Mughal period.
(*f*) None.
(*g*) Good.
(*h*) Unnecessary.
(*j*) The mosque was built by one Amani Begam, a *Sayyid* by caste and wife of Rahim Bakhsh. It is a small building of no particular interest.

No. 343. (*a*) Gate (unnamed).
(*b*) Entrance to Kuncha-i Ghasi Ram.
(*c*) Durgi, daughter of Kalyan Singh.
(*d*) III.
(*e*) Mughal.
(*f*) None.
(*g*) Fair.

(*h*) Unnecessary.

(*j*) The gate has been recently repaired. A very interesting anecdote is told of Ghasi Ram, who is said to have been a Royal Astrologer or *Pandit* of the Mughal Emperors. One day one of the Emperors, whose name is not known, asked him the name of the gate of the city through which he was to pass that day. The astute astrologer knew that if he named one gate the Emperor would probably use another and accordingly suggested that he might write his prediction on a piece of paper which might be examined after the Emperor had issued from the city. He also thought that the Emperor would consider the astrologer obliged to name one of the gates and that he might checkmate him by opening a new one. The *Pandit* accordingly wrote his prediction "that the Emperor would pass that day through a new gate" He was right. The Emperor, after receiving the prediction from the *Pandit,* ordered a new door to be opened in the city wall, which is now called *khirki* (postern) Farashkhana, and passed through it, a measure which quite concurred with the foretelling of the astrologer. On reading the written prediction the Emperor was much pleased and conferred upon Ghasi Ram the piece of land now occupied by the *Kuncha* known after him. The astrologer built a house, now transformed into a *Muhalla,* this gateway, in all probability, being the entrance thereto. If the story is founded on fact, the Emperor mentioned must have been Shahjahan, as the *khirki* Farashkhana is of the same date as the other city gates and made when Shahjahanabad was built.

MUHALLA KACHCHA BAGH.

No. 344. (*a*) Hakim Mehr Ali Shah's Mosque.

(*b*) In the *Muhalla.*

(*c*) Waqf, Mutawalli, Abdul Ghafur.

(*d*) III.

(*e*) Late Mughal period.

(*f*) None.

(*g*) Good.

(*h*) Unnecessary.

(*j*) The mosque was built by one Mihr Ali Shah. In the courtyard are several graves, said to be those of the family of Mihr Ali. One of these graves, which contains an inscription bearing the date and the name of the deceased, deserves special attention and is treated of separately under the next number.

No. 345 (*a*) Shah Abdullatif's Tomb.

(*b*) Within the compound of the mosque of Mihr Ali (No. 344).

(*c*) Waqf, Mutawalli, Abdul Ghafur.

III.

(*e*) 1237 A.H. (1821-2 A.D.).

(*f*) On a loose piece of stone placed in the compound of the mosque.

هو اللطيف الخبير

(۱) چورفت از جهان شاه عبداللطیف   ازیں واقعه خسته دل شد امیر

(۲) بتاریخ ان گفت هاتف ز آه   علیم سلیم لطیف خبیر

۱۲۳۷

Translation.

"He is Benign and Omniscient."

(1) "When Shah Abdul Latif repaired from the world, at this event Amir became sick at heart."

(2) "For its date an invisible voice said mournfully, 'All-knowing, perfect, benign and omniscient.' 1237 (1821-2 A. D.)."

(*g*) Fair.

(*h*) Unnecessary.

(*j*) The inscription is incised on a loose piece of stone, formerly fixed, in all probability, at the head of the grave. The latter lies within a small masonry enclosure. It is said to be that of the *Pir* (spiritual guide) of Mihr Ali, who built the mosque in the compound of which the grave lies.

No. 346. (*a*) Amarasinga's Sivalaya.

(*b*) Kuncha-i Mahajani.

(*c*) Bahadursing Sultan Gokal.

(*d*) III.

(*e*) About 80 years old.

(*f*) None.

(*g*) Good.

(*h*) Unnecessary.

(*j*) Amarasing, great-grandfather of Bahadursing (above) built the temple. In it are enshrined a ling of Siva, two images of Parvati, one of Ganapati, one of Kartikasvami and one of Nandi. To the visitor's right is a small temple of Hanumat.

NATWON KA KUNCHA.

No. 347. (*a*) Sivalaya (unnamed).

(*b*) In the *Muhalla.*

(*c*) Gangajivana.

(*d*) III.

(*e*) Late Mughal.

(*f*) None.

(*g*) Good.

(*h*) Unnecessary.

(*j*) The temple was built at public expense. (1)
In it is a ling of Siva with images of Parvati, Ganapati, Kartikasvami, Nandi and Hanumat.

(1) Some say it was built by one Hasa Mal.

No. 348. (*a*) Imambara.

(*b*) In the *Muhalla.*

(*c*) Waqf, Mutawalli, Muhammad Askari.

(*d*) III.

(*e*) Late Mughal period.

(*f*) None.

(*g*) Good.

(*h*) Unnecessary.

(*j*) The building is three arches deep, and has 3 arched entrances. It has a large enclosure, but the walls enclosing the whole are ruinous. The *Imambara* is used as a residence by the *Mutawalli,* by whose ancestors it was erected.

No. 349. (*a*) Mosque (unnamed).

(*b*) Near Imambara.

(*c*) Waqf, Mutawalli, Chaudhri Zainul Abidin.

(*d*) III.

(*e*) 1166 A.H. (1752-3 A.D.).

(*f*) On the central arch. Quotations from the Quran and then the following inscription.

(۱) زفیض قدس مالوب لطف احمد　　بنائے قبله عالم نماشد

(۲) بعهد سعد احمد شاه غازي　　سعید الله راسعي بجاشد

(۳) سروش غیب گفت ازروے انصاف　　مثني كعبه عالي بناشد

Translation.

(1) "By the grace of the holy . . . . and the favour of Ahmad (the Prophet) the foundation (of this building), which shows the *Qibla* to the whole world, was laid down."

(2) "In the auspicious reign of Ahmad Shah, the champion of the faith, the efforts of Saidullah were brought to perfection."

(3) "The invisible angel justly said, 'a duplicate of the exalted *kaba*' is constructed."

(*g*) Good.

(*h*) Unnecessary.

(*j*) The mosque, which is a small building of no particular interest, has been rebuilt.

KATRA NIL.

No. 350. (*a*) Mosque (unnamed).

(*b*) In the *Muhalla.*

(*c*) Waqf, Mutawalli, Fasih-ud-din.

(*d*) III.

(*e*) Late Mughal period.

(*f*) None.

(*g*) Good.

(*h*) Unnecessary.

(*j*) The mosque consists of three domed apartments with arched entrance

It stands on raised ground. Under the courtyard, which is approached by a flight of steps, are three shops possessed by the family of Rai Bahadur Lala Chhunna Mal. The mosque together with the shops were confiscated and sold by the Government after the Mutiny.

No. 351. (*a*) Gorakhanatha Misra's Sivalaya.
(*b*) *Gali* Dhobian.
(*c*) Sukhadeva Misra.
(*d*) III.
(*e*) Mutiny period. (?) Enquiries made subsequently seem to point to this building having been erected *after* the Mutiny.
(*f*) None.
(*g*) Good.
(*h*) Unnecessary.
(*j*) Lalita Bibi and Dhauti built the temple. Gorakhanatha was the husband of Dhauti and Lalita was the daughter-in-law of Gorakhanatha.

In it are enshrined a ling of Siva and the images of Parvati, Ganapati, Kartikasvami and Nandi. To the visitor's right and left are images of Hanumat.

No. 352. (*a*) Sivalaya (unnamed).
(*b*) *Gali* Dhobian.
(*c*) Gokalchanda.
(*d*) III.
(*e*) About 130 years old.
(Some say it was built a few years before the Mutiny.)
(*f*) None.
(*g*) Good.
(*h*) Unnecessary.
(*j*) The temple was built by Ganga Misra (Bhanta Misra). The present generation is the sixth from his.

In the temple are enshrined a ling of Siva and the images of Parvati, Ganapati, Kartikasvami and Nandi. To the visitor's right in a niche is an image of Hanumat, and to the left are images of Siva, Parvati and Ganapati.

No. 353. (*a*) Jhabba Misra's Temple.
(*b*) Ballubhai's *Gali*.
(*c*) Jamnadasa.
(*d*) III.
(*e*) Samvat 1904 (A.D. 1847).
(*f*) There is a stone tablet over the gate of the temple, on which is the following inscription in 10 lines. It runs :

(1) श्री गणेशाय नम: उपकारी (*sic*) परम
Sri Ganesaya namh Upakari parama

(2) सरो मोतोसुता(ता) सुभमान मंदर षत (ति)
Saro Motisuta Subhamana (‖) Manadar ata (ti)

(3) सुंदर रचे सेट षत्री जात सदा लिये
Sundara rache Set Kshatri jata ‖ 1 ‖ sada liye

(4) वस वस (वास) वसो सुखी रहो महाराज ॥
vasa vasa vaso sukhi raho maharaja ‖

(5) धन संपतसे रेहे भरे जगदंबा र-
dhana sampata sai rehe bhare Jagadamba ra—

(6) खे लाज मोष सुफल दरसन मी-
khe laja 2 Moksha suphala darasana mi-

(7) ले जो पूजे चीत लगाय ॥ चौरासीके
le jo puje chita lagaya‖ chaurasike

(8) फंद सब छीन मे जाय वीलाय ॥ ३ ॥
phanda sava chhina mai jaya vilaya ‖ 3 ‖

(9) संवत् १९०४ था प्रघट भट जगदेव ॥
Samvata 1904 tha praghata Bhata Jagadeva‖

(10) सवारायसुत वीप्रकी लज्या रखी अंब
Savarayasuta Vipra (vipra) ki lajya rakhi Amba.

Translation.

Adoration to the illustrious Ganesa. The Great Benevolent Saro (Saro), daughter of Moti, by caste a Seta Kshatriya, has built this very beautiful and auspicious (*subhamana*) temple. Always trust in the goddess. Maharaja, may you live happily with wealth and progeny. May Jagadamba (Kali, lit. Mother of the World) preserve honour. He who worships with intent the goddess, shall get the fruit, final beatitude. The 84 wanderings (of the births) will all be over in a moment. (When this temple was erected) the (Vikrama) Samvat year was 1904. May (Goddess) Amba (that is, Kali) preserve credit (lit. cover shame) of the well-known Bhatta Jagadeva, a Brahmana, son of Savaraya (Sivaraya).

The inscription was whitewashed. Letters are not well cut. The grammar is poor. The metre is Doha and this is of help in deciphering the inscription.

(*g*) Good.

(*h*) Unnecessary.

(*j*) Saro Misrani built the temple. Jhabba Misra was the son of her sister.
It is dedicated to Kali Devi and the image is of black marble. In a niche is another image of black marble.

No. 354. (*a*) Bada Sivalaya.

(*b*) In the *Muhalla.*

(*c*) Rai Bahadura Lala Siva Prasada.

(*d*) III.

(*e*) About 100 years old.

(*f*) None.

(*g*) Good.

(*h*) Unnecessary.

(*j*) Lala Sivaprasad's great-grandfather built the temple which measures 46′ 6″ by 33′ 3″. This is the fourth generation from his.
In the Sivalaya are enshrined a ling of Siva and the images of Parvati, Ganapati, Kartikasvami and Nandi. In a niche to the visitor's left is an image of Hanumat.

There are two other images, one of Radha and the other of Krishna, but these were enshrined 5 years ago. So it is evident that these are of minor importance and later additions, and hence the building has been styled a Sivalaya (that is a temple mainly dedicated to God Siva).

No. 355. (*a*) Mosque (unnamed).

(*b*) In front of the *Gali* Talaiya.

(*c*) Waqf, Mutawalli, Yatimkhana.

(*d*) III.

(*e*) Late Mughal period.

(*f*) None.

(*g*) Good.

(*h*) Unnecessary.

(*j*) The mosque is on the upper storey. The courtyard, which serves as a roof for some three shops, is reached by a narrow staircase of thirteen steps and overlooks the road.

No. 356. (*a*) Chota Temple, also called Bhanukumarji's Temple.

(*b*) *Gali* Ghantesvara Mahadeva.

(*c*) Chakla Mala.

(*d*) III.

(*e*) About Vikrama Samvat 1800.

(*f*) None.

(*g*) Good.

(*h*) Unnecessary.

(*j*) There are two images, one of Radha and the other of Krishna, both of them of mixed metals, the latter being blacker than the former. Raja Murlidhara Gosvami built the temple, which measures 21′ 3″ by 17′ 3″. His son was Bhanukumarji, after whom the temple has been named. (?)

The temple seems originally to have been the house of some well-to-do person. It is entered through a small doorway, beyond which is the courtyard of the house. Nearly half of this is occupied by a raised platform, which, together with the temple proper, consisting of three five-arched halls, one behind the other, is paved with slabs of black and white marble. The halls of the temple are decorated with glasswork.

No. 357. (*a*) Bada Temple or Ladliji's Temple.

(*b*) *Gali* Ghantesvara Mahadeva.

(*c*) Lala Ganpatrao.

(*d*) III.
(*e*) About Vikrama year 1700.
(*f*) None.
(*g*) Good.
(*h*) Unnecessary.
(*j*) The temple was built by Naval Gosvami Pradyumnaji. He also placed the images of Radha and Krishna. Naval Gosvami laid stress on the worship of Ladliji (Radha) and, therefore, the temple is called Mandir Ladliji.

Bansidhara is referred to in "The History of the Punjab Chiefs," page 262. He was a pious man, and Surajmal Jat, Raja of Bharatpur, was one of his disciples.

There are two images, one of Radha and the other of Krishna; that of the former is of brass and that of the latter of black marble. To the visitor's right is an image of Tulsi, of silver, in a small temple.

No. 358. (*a*) Sivalaya Ghantesvara Mahadeva.
(*b*) *Gali* Ghantesvara Mahadeva.
(*c*) Dayasankara and Bansidhara.
(*d*) III.
(*e*) Late Mughal.
(*f*) None.
(*g*) Good.
(*h*) Unnecessary.
(*j*) The ling of Siva is supposed to be as old as the compilation of the Saubhari Samhita and the Padmapurana. This question may be discussed at some length. It is argued by Mahamahopadyaya Banke Rai and others that the name Kasi occurring in Saubhari Samhita and Padmapurana must be Katra Nila since Kasi is called Vidyapura, and Ghantesvara Mahadeva was called Visvesvara. That Katra Nila was called Vidyapura is proved by the title-deed of the house in which the Mahamahopadyaya lives. It is referred to in the "Coronation Durbar Ancient History of Indra Prastha" on page 7. It is by no means certain if Katra Nila is the same Vidyapura, *viz.*, a synonym for Kasi, simply because Kasi (Benares) is also called Vidyapura. There may have been two Vidyapuras. The name Visvesvara, said to have been given to the ling in Katra Nila, is not in itself a convincing proof. Instances can be quoted where the same story and names are repeated in different localities. We have for instance the tale of the seven tiger cubs. Visvesvara means "Lord of the Universe" and is applied to other lings of Siva also. We must, therefore, wait before deciding the question. If any inscription is found in Delhi bearing the name of Kasi, then in all probability Katra Nila may be said to be the place referred to in Saubhari Samhita and Padmapurana. Even in that case it may simply be likened to Kasi (Benares). The building is furnished with many bells.

No. 359. (*a*) Dhumimal Khanna's Sivalaya.
(*b*) *Gali* Ghantesvara Mahadeva.

(c) Lala Jangliprasada.
(d) III.
(e) About 70 years old.
(f) None.
(g) Good.
(h) Unnecessary.
(j) Dhumimal built the temple.
In the Sivalaya are enshrined a ling of Siva and images of Parvati, Ganapati, Suryanarayana, Kartikasvami and Nandi.

No. 360. (a) Manakchanda and Visvesvaranath's Sivalaya.
(b) In the *Muhalla*.
(c) Madhavarava Balakrama.
(d) III.
(e) Vikrama Samvat 1902, Sake 1769, Magha Sukla Panchami, Saturday.
(f) There is an inscription on a stone tablet over the shrine in one line. It is :

(१) श्री गणेशाय नम(:) ॥ संवत १९०२ शाके (*sic*) १७६९ माघ शुक्ल पंचमी शनि दिने विश्वेश्वरनाथ माणकचंदने शिवस्थापन कीया

In a hall to the visitor's right is another inscription, which runs :

(१) यह चित्र लाला माणकचंदजी का
(२) सम्बत १९०२ में
(३) लाला विश्वेश्वरनाथ माणकचंदने शिवस्थापन किया

Translation of (A) :—Adoration to the illustrious Ganesa (lit. Lord of multitude or collection). On Saturday, the 5th day of the bright fortnight of Magha, Saka year 1769, Samvat 1902, Visvesvaranatha and Manakchanda placed (the ling) of Siva.
Translation of (B) :—This is the picture of Lala Manakchanda. In Samvat (year) 1902 (1845 A.D.) Lala Visvesvaranatha and Manikchanda placed (the ling of) Siva.
(g) Good.
(h) Unnecessary.
(j) The temple was erected by Visvesvaranatha and Manakchanda. The latter was a Khatri.
In the temple are enshrined a ling of Siva and images of Parvati, Ganapati, Kartikasvami and Nandi. To the visitor's right in a niche is an image of Hanumat and to the left that of Annapurna.

No. 361. (a) Rangi Misra's Sivalaya.
(b) Nai Basti.
(c) Pandit Attan Misra.
(d) III.
(e) Samvat 1891.
(f) None.
(g) Good.
(h) Unnecessary.

The temple was built by Chhanga Misra, great-grandfather of Attan Misra. Rangi Misra repaired it.

In the temple are enshrined a ling of Siva and images of Parvati, Ganapati and Nandi. In the niches are images of Hanumat and Durga.

MUHALLA KUNCHA GHASIRAMA.

No. 362. (*a*) Bhairavji's Temple.

(*b*) In the *Muhalla.*

(*c*) Sadinatha.

(*d*) III.

(*e*) Late Mughal.

(*f*) None.

(*g*) Good.

(*h*) Unnecessary.

(*j*) There is a stone besmeared with red lead which can be seen from outside and which represents Bhairava.

In the temple are also enshrined the images of Mahadeva and Parvati, seated on a bull. They are of white marble.

The original old temple was a small one, the new one built in dressed stone being erected in Samvat 1969.

Annexed to it is a double-storeyed room for the use of *pujaris.*

No. 363. (*a*) Sarvan's Sivalaya.

(*b*) In the *Muhalla.*

(*c*) Mahadevaji.

(*d*) III.

(*e*) Late Mughal.

(*f*) None.

(*g*) Good.

(*h*) Unnecessary.

(*j*) Sarvan built the temple, and it is called after her. The lower storey is used by *pujaris.*

In it are enshrined a ling of Siva and images of Parvati, Ganapati, Kartikasvami and Nandi. In the niches facing the visitor are the images of Parvati and Siva, Parvati (single) and Hanumat.

No. 364. (*a*) House of Munshi Bhawani Shankar, also called *Namak-haram-ki Haveli.*

(*b*) In the *Muhalla.*

(*c*) Lala Madan Lal.

(*d*) III.

(*e*) Late Mughal period.

(*f*) None.

(*g*) Fair.

(*h*) Unnecessary.

(*j*) The house is large and imposing, and has two gateways, on the east and west. That towards the east is lofty and furnished with projecting stone windows.

Munshi Bhawani Shankar was a *Khatri* who rose to power and wealth during the occupation of Delhi by the Marathas. Originally *Bakhshi* in Gwalior State, he was, when the Marathas took Delhi, transferred there to a responsible position. However, he conspired with the English against his employers and was dismissed. The English gave him a pension which was enjoyed by his descendants. On account of his dealings with the English he was nicknamed by the Marāṭhas *Namak Haram*, (False to his salt) and this house was called *Namak-haram-ki Haveli* (the house of one who is not true to his salt). Munshi Bhawani Shankar was greatly incensed at this, and complained against it to his new patrons the English, who were then in possession of Delhi. Orders were given in a general proclamation that no one should call him *Namak Haram* or his house *Namak-haram-ki Haveli*, a measure which caused the use of his nickname still more.

(*k*) S. 83.

No. 365. (*a*) Manakchanda Khatri's Temple.
(*b*) In the *Muhalla*.
(*c*) Nand Lal.
(*d*) III.
(*e*) About 60 years old.
(*f*) None.
(*g*) Good.
(*h*) Unnecessary.
(*j*) The temple was repaired by Lala Laksmanadasa 9 months back.

In it are enshrined a ling of Siva and the images of Parvati, Ganapati, Brahmadeva and Nandi.

BAZAR FATHPURI.

No. 366. (*a*) *Kachahri* (court) of Bhawani Shankar.
(*b*) Chhatta Bhawani Shankar.
(*c*) Ram Chand Munshi Ram.
(*d*) III.
(*e*) Late Mughal period.
(*f*) None.
(*g*) Good.
(*h*) Unnecessary.
(*j*) The building is said to have been the court of Bhawani Shankar. It is imposing in design, double-storied, and consisting of numerous apartments and halls. On the upper storey over-looking the main road is a long parapeted balcony, in the middle of which is a small pavilion of stone adorned with inlaid work. It is furnished with two gateways, one opening towards the west, and the other towards tho south into the Chandni Chauk. The former is of some size, and seems to have been

the principal entrance to the whole *Chhatta* (the collection of houses) of Bhawani Shankar.

(*k*) S. 82.

No. 367. (*a*) Jotiprasada's Temple.
(*b*) Gali Lahorian.
(*c*) Jotiprasada.
(*d*) III.
(*e*) It is about 200 years old ?
(*f*) None.
(*g*) Good.
(*h*) Unnecessary.
(*j*) Jotiprasada repaired the temple about 12 years ago.

In it are enshrined a ling of Siva and the images of Parvati, Ganapati, Kartikasvami and Nandi.

GANDI GALI.

No. 368. (*a*) Visvesvaranath's Sivalaya.
(*b*) Bambe-ki *Gali.*
(*c*) Ramkisandasa.
(*d*) III.
(*e*) Late Moghal.
(*f*) None.
(*g*) Good.
(*h*) Unnecessary.
(*j*) Of no particular interest. It consists of a pavilion in a masonry enclosure and was built by one Visvesvaranath.

No. 369. (*a*) Kaliprasada's Sivalaya.
(*b*) In the *Muhalla.*
(*c*) Purvo.
(*d*) III.
(*e*) The temple is more than 100 years old ?
(*f*) None.
(*g*) Good.
(*h*) Unnecessary.
(*j*) Chhunna Misra, great-grandfather of Kaliprasada erected the temple (some say it was erected by one Gosain Manack Chand). Purvo is the daughter of Kaliprasada.

In the temple are enshrined a ling of Siva and images of Parvati, Ganapati and Nandi of white marble. In a niche is an image of Hanumat.

BAZAR KHARI BAOLI.

No. 370. (*a*) Gauri Sankar's Sivalaya.

(*b*) Katra Maidagaran.

(*c*) Harphula.

(*d*) III.

(*e*) Late Mughal.

(*f*) On a stone tablet above the staircase is the following modern inscription :—

श्री गणेशाय नम:

Sri Ganesayanamh.

यह शीवाला पनडत गोरी संकर का है

Yaha Sivala Panadata (sic) Gori (sic) Sankara ka hai

मिती बैसाख सुदी १३ सं० १९५६

Miti baisakha sudi 13 sam : 1956.

खुखीने बनवाया

Khukhine banavaya.

Translation.

Adoration to Ganesa.

This Sivalaya is of Pandita Gauri Sankara.

Date, the 13th day of the bright fortnight of Vaisakha Sam (Samvat) 1956.

It was built by Khukhi.

(*g*) Good.

(*h*) Unnecessary.

(*j*) The temple is an old one but repaired on the above date.
In it are enshrined a ling of Siva and the images of Parvati, Ganapati and Nandi. In a niche is an image of Hanumat.

PHATAK HABSH KHAN.

No. 371. (*a*) Gate of Habsh Khan.

(*b*) See above.

(*c*) Lala Kunj Lal.

(*d*) II *b*.

(*e*) Period of Shahjahan.

(*f*) None.

(*g*) Fair.

(*h*) Unnecessary.

(*j*) The gate is composed of three arches covered with a flat roof. Its design has little to commend it.

Tradition records, that the gate was built by Habsh Khan, whose real name was Sidi Miftah. He lived in the reigns of Shahjahan and Aurangzeb. It was afterwards repaired by Faulad Khan, a descendant of Habsh Khan who was *Kotwal* of Delhi at the time of its invasion by Nadir Shah. Sidi Miftah was a *Habshi* (Abyssinian) by extract, and originally a slave of the Nizam Shahi Kings of Ahmad Nagar. He enjoyed the trust and confidence of his masters and was appointed by them as Governor of the Udgir fort. He held this fort for Nizam Shahi Kings against the approach of Shahjahan. Ultimately he yielded, and having made over the fort to the Emperor entered his service in 1046 A. H. He was given the title of Habsh Khan, and was raised to the rank of 3,000 and 1,500 *Sawars.*

(*k*) *Maasir*, I, 579—583.

No. 372. (*a*) Yak Burji Mosque III.

(*b*) Near Piron kā Kaṭra.

(*c*) Waqf Mutawalli, Hajji Latif Bakhsh.

(*d*) II *b*.

(*e*) Tug͟hlaq period.

(*f*) None.

(*g*) Excellent.

(*h*) Unnecessary.

(*j*) The mosque, though not a large one, is of interest on account of its age and style of architecture. It consists of three compartments of which the central one being domed, the remaining two apartments being provided with vaulted roofs. The entrance of these apartments is through low pointed arches.

No. 373. (*a*) Miyan Sahib's Mosque.

(*b*) Dhobi Katra.

(*c*) Waqf, Mutawalli, Muhammad Zikriya.

(*d*) III.

(*e*) Aurangzeb's reign.

(*f*) None.

(*g*) Good.

(*h*) Unnecessary.

(*j*) The mosque was originally built of red sandstone, during the time of Aurangzeb, by his wife Aurangabadi Begam. It has been reconstructed.

(*k*) *Asar* (1847), chap. III, 58.

No. 374. (*a*) Gate (unnamed).

(*b*) Entrance to Gali Teliyan.

(*c*) Rai Bahadur Sheo Parshad, C.I.E.

(*d*) III.

(*e*) Late Mughal.

(*f*) None.

(*g*) Fair.

(*h*) Unnecessary.

(*j*) The *Phatak* or gateway is of imposing design. In the side walls are double storied apartments for the use of porters.

The gateway is one of the few original entrances to a spacious house locally known as the *Haveli* of the Nawwab Wazir. The tradition does not give the name of the builder, but mentions that it was bestowed upon a musician by a Nawwab of Oudh. It is not unlikely that Abul Mansur Safdar Jang the Nawwāb Wazir of Oudh was the builder of the house. The reasons for the supposition being that Safdarjang was the first Governor of Oudh to receive the title of Nawwab Wazir, and to reside permanently at Delhi in the capacity of a minister. His successor, no doubt, continued to enjoy the same title, but never resided in Delhi. The size of the house would seem to indicate its having been built by a person of importance, such as Safdar Jang. The Nawwabs of Oudh who succeeded him never visited Delhi and did not require it, this may have led to its being conferred upon a favourite musician.

No. 375. (*a*) Ramzān Shah's mosque.
(*b*) Kuncha-i Maulvi Qāsim.
(*c*) Waqf, Mutawalli, Hajji Ismail.
(*d*) III.
(*e*) 1216 A. H. (1801-02 A. D.).
(*f*) On a loose piece of stone placed in the mosque. Quotation from the Quran, and then the following inscription :—

بانیه امیر النسا زوجه نواب یعقوب علیخان مرحوم خوشدامن نواب منصور خان سنه ۱۲۱۶

Translation.

"The founder is Amir-un-Nisa, the wife of the late Nawwab Yaqub Ali Khan and mother-in-law of Nawwab Mansur Khan,, the year 1216.

(*g*) Good.
(*h*) Unnecessary.
(*j*) The mosque is situated at some height above the road. It is flat roofed and has five arched entrances. An inscription written on a loose piece of stone and housed in the mosque refers to Amir-un-Nisa, who built the mosque, as the wife of Yaqub Ali Khan and the mother-in-law of Nawwab Mansur Khan. Nothing is known of Yaqub Khan, but a traditional account is given about Mansur, who is said to have been a courtier of Shāh Alam II. His real name was Safdar Khan and he came from the east as a youth with Shah Alam. He amassed great wealth, and strenuously supported Shāh Alam when blinded by Ghulam Qadir.

No. 376. (*a*) Muhtasib's Mosque.
(*b*) Kuncha-i Maulvi Qasim.
(*c*) Waqf, Mutawalli, Siraju-din, and Rahim Bakhsh.
(*d*) II*b*.
(*e*) 1136 A. H. (1723-4 A. D.)
(*f*) On the central arch.

(۱) در زمان داور عالم پناه دادرس * پادشاه دین محمد شاه غازي جم حشم
(۲) مسند آرای شریعت میر عدل احتساب * ناصب اعلام دین و هادم دیر و صنم
(۳) کرده در دلي بنائی مسجد گردون شکوه * کز تماشایش نگه شد ناظر بیت الحرم
(۴) چون فضای خاطر صاحبدلان صحنش وسیع * گنبدش چون گنبد گردون منقش یکقلم
(۵) از پئے تاریخ اتمامش سروش غیب گفت * کعبه ثاني بنائے بو سعید با کرم
۱۱۳۶

(1) "In the reign of the monarch who is a protection to the world, a dispenser of justice and the king of the religion (named) Muhammad Shah the champion of the faith and having pomp like Jamshid,"

(2) "The Chief of inquisitorial justice, who adorns the seat of Muhammadan law, raises the standards of religion and demolishes temples and idols,"

(3) "Built in Delhi a mosque grand like heaven, the beholding of which affords to sight the pleasure of seeing the *kaba*."

(4) "Its courtyard is as spacious as the prospect of saintly persons and its dome is all painted like the dome of heavens."

(5) "For the date of its completion the invisible angel said 'A second *kaba* erected by Bu-Said the generous'."

"1136 (1723-4 A. D.)"

(*g*) Good.

(*h*) Unnecessary.

(*j*) The mosque is a large one with a spacious courtyard bounded on the east by several apartments now used as a *maktab* (school). Close to the latter in the courtyard, is a large tank for purpose of ablution. Towards the west is the prayer chamber which consists of three domed rooms with arched entrances. The inscription on the central arch records that the mosque was built by Abu Said the *Muhtasib* (the inquisitor) in the year 1136 A. H. (1723-4 A. D.)

Abu Said was the hereditary inquisitor of Delhi. The head of his family Muhammad Taqi Chalpi, came to India from Persia during the reign of Shahjahan and at once received Royal favour. His son was appointed as the first grand inquisitor of Delhi. The *farman* which conferred the post upon him made it hereditary so long as the family could produce a capable man.

(*k*) *Tazkirat-ul-Maasirin*, in possession of Muhammad Zikriya of Delhi, p. 98.

MUHALLA PATTE WALAN.

No. 377. (*a*) Yek Burji Mosque IV.

(*b*) Near the city wall.

(*c*) Wazir Beg.

(*d*) III.

(*e*) Tughlaq Period.

(*f*) None.

(*g*) Good.

(*h*) Unnecessary.

(*j*) The mosque consists of three apartments, the central being roofed with a large dome. The side rooms of either wing have vaulted roofs. The soffits of the dome and vaults are decorated with ornamental plaster work. The arches are all low and pointed.

NAHR SAADAT KHAN.

No. 378. (*a*) Mosque (unnamed).

(*b*) Near Kabul Gate and close to the Police Station.

(*c*) Ḥajji Abdul Ghani.

(*d*) III.

(*e*) Late Mughal.

(*f*) None.
(*g*) Good.
(*h*) Unnecessary.
(*j*) A small building of no particular interest.

No. 379. (*a*) Mosque of the *Sarban* (a camel driver).
(*b*) In front of katra of Lala Narain Das.
(*c*) Waqf, Mutawalli, Abdul Ghaffar and Muhammad Umar.
(*d*) III.
(*e*) Late Mughal.
(*f*) None.
(*g*) Good.
(*h*) Unnecessary.
(*j*) The mosque was built on the right bank of the canal. The prayer chamber consists of two halls each with 3 arched entrances and covered with a flat roof. At the eastern side of the courtyard is an apartment, near which, and facing the doorway of the mosque is an arched opening which once led through a narrow underground passage to the canal so that worshippers might conveniently perform their ablutions.

No. 380. (*a*) Narayanadasa's Temple.
(*b*) Near Dufferin Bridge.
(*c*) Lala Ramanatha.
(*d*) III.
(*e*) About 70 years old.
(*f*) None.
(*g*) Good.
(*h*) Unnecessary.
(*j*) The temple was built by Narayanadasa. He was Ramanatha's grandfather;

Narayanadasa.
Jaggannatha.
Ramanatha.

To the visitor's left is a temple of Hanumat, to its left is an image of Ganesa, with images of brass of Radha and Krishna; beneath the niche set apart for Ganesa, is a ling of Siva. Near the latter small images of Parvati, Ganesa and Nandi.

In front of the shrines is another Sivalaya, the apartment connecting them serving as a *Dharamshala*. The ling is called Narmadesvara.

No. 381. (*a*) *Phatak* (gate) Nahr Saadat Khan.
(*b*) Entrance to the *Haveli* of Nawwab Wazir.
(*c*) Rai Bahadur Sheo Parshad, C.I.E.
(*d*) II *b*.
(*e*) Late Mughal.
(*f*) None.
(*g*) Good.

(*h*) Unnecessary.

(*j*) Another entrance to the *Haveli* of the Nawwab Wazir. It has been recently repaired, but the roof which was in a ruined condition has been removed like the other gateways of the *Haveli.* It had double storeyed apartments which have been repaired, and considerably changed in form.

No. 382. (*a*) *Barah Dari* of the Nawwab Wazir.

(*b*) Phatak Nahr Saadat Khan.

(*c*) Rai Bahadur Sheo Prashad, C.I.E.

(*d*) III.

(*e*) Late Mughal.

(*f*) None.

(*g*) Good.

(*h*) Unnecessary.

(*j*) The *Barah Dari* was one of the various houses of the *Haveli* of the Nawwab Wazir. A portion of its central hall, the arched gateways and a few other adjoining apartments are still extant. It has been recently repaired and to a great extent reconstructed.

No. 383. (*a*) Gate (unnamed).

(*b*) Phatak Nahr Saadat Khan, northern entrance to the Rang Mahal.

(*c*) Lala Amir Singh, etc.

(*d*) III.

(*e*) Late Mughal.

(*f*) None.

(*g*) Fair.

(*h*) Unnecessary.

(*j*) The gateway consists of two arches. It was an entrance to the Rang Mahal, a house probably used as a *Zenana* in the *Haveli* of the Nawwab Wazir. The Rang Mahal has now disappeared, its site being appropriated for private dwellings. Its only remains are two gates and a portion of wall.

No. 384. (*a*) Gate (unnamed).

(*b*) Phatak Nahr Saadat Khan, western entrance to the Rang Mahal.

(*c*) Lala Amir Singh.

(*d*) III.

(*e*) Late Mughal.

(*f*) None.

(*g*) Fair.

(*h*) Unnecessary.

(*j*) Another entrance to the Rang Mahal of the Nawwab Wazir.

No. 385 (*a*) Gate (unnamed).

(*b*) Entrance to Gali Teliyan from Katra Ghee.

(c) Lala Ramchand.
(d) II *b*.
(e) Late Mughal.
(f) None.
(g) Ruinous.
(h) Unnecessary.
(j) Another entrance to the *Haveli* of the Nawwab Wazir. It consists of three arches of which the roof has gone. In the side walls of the gate are rooms intended for porters.
(l) S. 68.

No. 386. (a) Gate (unnamed).
(b) Entrance to the Katra Ghee.
(c) Lala Ram Chand.
(d) III.
(e) Late Mughal.
(f) None.
(g) Ruinous.
(h) Unnecessary.
(j) The gate serves as an entrance to an enclosure, which probably belonged to the *Haveli* of the Nawwab Wazir. It was once used as a mart for *ghee* and hence its name.

No. 387. (a) Ghaziu-d-Din's mosque known as Maulvi Hafizulla Khan's Mosque.
(b) Over the canal in front of Phatak Nahr Saadat Khan.
(c) Waqf, Mutawalli, Waliullah Khan.
(d) II *b*.
(e) 1140 A. H. (1727—28 A. D.)
(f) On the central arch.

(۱) از فیوضات خدا و مصطفیٰ و پادشاه
غازي‌الدین خان بهادر پیر و دین متین
(۲) کرد احیا مسجدے بر روے نهر از بهر خلق
هرستون پایه‌اش چون سد اسکندر متین
(۳) اب نهر از خاک روبی هوآے درگهش
روح پرور شد چو آب خضر در روے زمین
(۴) هر رواقش همچو چشم مست خوبان دلفریب
هرستون و پایه اش چون سد اسکندر متین
(۵) بیشك و بے شبهه میگردد دعائش مستجاب
هرکه مالد بر زمین و طاق محرابش جبین
(۶) سال تاریخش بنظم از فضل حق گفتا که شد
مسجدے احمد بنا از رحمت للعالمین
۱۱۴۰

Translation.

(1) "By the grace of God, Mustufa (the Prophet) and the king, Ghaziuddin Khan Bahadur, the follower of the strong religion."

(2) "Brought into being a mosque on the canal for the people, everv pillar of which is as strong as Alexander's wall."

(3) "The water of the canal, on account of cleaning the wind of its court of the dust, became soul nourisher on the earth, like the water of *Khizr*[1] (*i.e.*, fountain of life.)"

(4) "Each of its eaves is attractive like the eye of the intoxicated beauties, every pillar and pier is firm like the wall of Alexander."

(5) "Surely and certainly, his prayer is accepted, who rubs his forehead with its floor, niche and *Mihrab.*"

(6) "The date of its foundation was said in poetry by the favour of God 'The mosque of Ahmad was founded through compassion for worlds'."

"1140 (1727-8 A.D.)"

(*g*) Good.

(*h*) Unnecessary.

(*j*) The mosque was built over the Nahr Saadat Khan. (See No. 340). It is entered through three small doorways, in the northern wall of the courtyard. Towards the south and east of the courtyard are apartments, those on the east being double storied, and now occupied by the *Mutawalli* of the mosque. On the west is the mosque proper or prayer chamber roofed by three domes and with arched entrances. The inscription on the central arch records that the mosque was built by Ghazi-ud-Din Khan. His real name was Ahmad Beg, *alias* Kosa. He was the foster brother of Muizzu-d-Din Jahandar Shah (Mughal Emperor, 1712—13 A.D.) with whom he first took service. Later owing to a difference with the Emperor he entered the service of Prince Azimush-shan who sent him to Bengal with his son Farrukhsiyar. On the death of Bahadur Shah, Farrukhsiyar put forward his claims to the throne and having conferred the title of Ghazi-ud-Din Khan on Ahmad Beg asked him to make preparations for war. When Farrukhsiyar gained victory over his uncle Jahandar Shah he bestowed upon him the title of Ghalib Jang and the rank of 6,000 and 5,000 *Sawars*. At first he was not favoured by Sayyid Husain Ali and Sayyid Abdullah of Barah who caused him to be imprisoned with the Emperor Farrukhsiyar ; subsequently during the reign of Muhammad Shah Qutbul Mulk Sayyid Abdullah contracted a friendship with him and he sided with the latter against the Emperor. He was, however, pardoned by Muhammad Shah and restored to his former rank.

(*k*) *Maasir*. II, 879—82.

MORI GATE ROAD.

No. 388. (*a*) Rai Bel's Mosque.

(*b*) Kuncha-i Muattar Khan.

(*c*) Waqf, Mutawalli, Munshi Muhammad Ali Khan.

(*d*) III.

(1) *Khizr* is the name of a prophet, who is believed to have discovered and drunk the fountain of life, wherefore he will not die till the last trumpet.

(*e*) Mughal.
(*f*) None.
(*g*) Good.
(*h*) Unnecessary.
(*j*) The mosque is entered through a low doorway and consists of three domed apartments entered by low pointed arches.

No. 389. (*a*) Shias' Mosque.
(*b*) In the *Muhalla.*
(*c*) Nawwab Sayyid Ahmad Mirza.
(*d*) III.
(*e*) Late Mughal.
(*f*) None.
(*g*) Fair.
(*h*) Unnecessary.
(*j*) The mosque stands on raised ground, and is approached from the road by 5 steps, through a small doorway. Its prayer chamber is domed and has the same number of arched entrances. At the south-east corner of the courtyard there is a small tank called *Qullatain*, of which the water is considered by the Shias to be exceptionally pure. (*Qullatain*=The dual of *Qullatun*, a large bucket of water carried on a camel.)

MORI GATE.

No. 390. (*a*) *Imambara* of Nawwab Sayyid Ahmad Mirza.
(*b*) Dhobi Wara.
(*c*) Waqf, Mutawalli, Nawwab Sayyid Ahmad Mirza.
(*d*) III.
(*e*) Late Mughal.
(*f*) None.
(*g*) Fair.
(*h*) Unnecessary.
(*j*) The *Imambara* consists of a large enclosure, with attendant halls, each having three arched entrances and a flat roof. In the inner hall there are three graves, the central one being that of the founder of the *Imambara* and the remaining two those of his wives. Besides these there are various other graves in the outer hall and enclosure, said to be those of relatives of the founder. Among the latter there is one with a small head-pillar which is said to mark the last resting place of the thumb of Muhammad Hussain Khan, the grand-father of the founder. The thumb was cut off in battle and Muhammad Hussain Khan having preserved it, brought it back to Delhi where he interred it, and thus marked the spot.

The *Imambara* was built by Saifu-d-Daula Sayyid Razi Khan Bahadur Salabat Jang, a *Vakil* of the East India Company at the court of Shah 'Alam II. The titles of Sayyid Razi Khan as "Saifu-d-Daula" and "Salabat Jang" have been confirmed by a seal which is in possession of Nawwab Sayyid Ahmad Mirza and is dated 1206 A. H. (1791—2 A. D.).

No. 391. (*a*) Ghulam Nabi's Mosque.
(*b*) Muhalla Dor walan.
(*c*) Waqf, Mutawalli, Ilahi Bakhsh.
(*d*) III.
(*e*) Unknown.
(*f*) None.
(*g*) Good.
(*h*) Unnecessary.
(*j*) The mosque has been rebuilt and enlarged. It is of no special interest.

No. 392. (*a*) Burhya's (old woman's) Mosque II.
(*b*) Muhalla Dor walan.
(*c*) Waqf, Mutawalli, Ahmad Hussain.
(*d*) III.
(*e*) Late Mughal.
(*f*) None.
(*g*) Good.
(*h*) Unnecessary.
(*j*) The mosque is said to have been built by an old woman, whose name is not known. It has a flat roof and three arched entrances, the middle one of which is divided into three smaller arches.

GANDA NALA.

No. 393. (*a*) Barhwali (Banyan tree) Mosque II.
(*b*) In the ***Muhalla***.
(*c*) Waqf, Mutawalli, Alimu-d-Din.
(*d*) III.
(*e*) Late Mughal.
(*f*) None.
(*g*) Good.
(*h*) Unnecessary.
(*j*) The mosque has received its name from the ***banyan*** tree which stands close to the doorway. At the foot of the tree there is a small ruined pavilion, known as a ***than*** (seat or tomb) of a ***Sayyid***, and respected and worshipped principally by Hindus.

No. 394. (*a*) Takyawali Mosque (*Takya*=abode or resting place of the Muhammadan mendicants.)
(*b*) In the ***Muhalla***.
(*c*) Waqf, Mutawalli, Mirza Talib Zafar Beg.
(*d*) III.
(*e*) Unknown.
(*f*) None.

(*g*) Good.
(*h*) Unnecessary.
(*j*) The mosque has been rebuilt. It is of no special interest.

KASHMIR GATE.

No. 395. (*a*) Maulvi Muhammad Baqar's Mosque.
(*b*) *Gali* Panja.
(*c*) Waqf, Mutawalli, Muhammad Ibrahim.
(*d*) III.
(*e*) 1271 A. H. (1854-5 A. D.).
(*f*) On the doorway.

هوالعلی الاعلی

مسجد شیعیان اهلبیت طاهرین سنه ۱۲۷۱

Translation.

He is Ali, the most exalted.

The mosque of the Shias (followers) of pure Ahl-i-Bait (members of the house of the Prophet), the year 1271.

(*g*) Good.
(*h*) Unnecessary.
(*j*) The mosque is entered through a doorway, on which the inscription, recorded above, is to be found. The prayer chamber consists of two halls, the inner one having five arched entrances, and the outer one only three. Beyond the outer hall, is the courtyard close to which, towards the east, is a small tank called by the Shias, *Qullatain.*

No. 396. (*a*) Dargah Panja Sharif.
(*b*) *Gali* Panja.
(*c*) Waqf, Mutawalli, Parwarish Husain.
(*d*) III.
(*e*) Late Mughal.
(*f*) None.
(*g*) Good.
(*h*) Unnecessary.
(*j*) The *Dargah* consists of a large enclosure, a mosque and a pavilion, where the hand mark of Ali, the son-in-law of the Prophet, along with some other relics, is preserved. Hence the whole enclosure is called the *Dargah Panja Sharif* (the court of the holy hand or hand mark). In the courtyard lie a considerable number of graves, among which two that are inscribed, deserve special attention, and are dealt with separately below.

No. 397. (*a*) Grave of Mirza Muhammad.
(*b*) *Gali* Panja, in the Dargah of Panja Sharif, close to the pavilion of the Dargah towards east.

(*c*) Waqf, Mutawalli, Parwarish Hussain.
(*d*) III.
(*e*) 1235 A. H. (1819-20 A.D.).
(*f*) On the *tawiz* of the grave.

یا غفار

بسم الله الرحمن الرحیم

(۱) آن مرزا محمد وان حاوي علوم حامي دين و شيعيه اولاد مصطفى
(۲) جان مے دمید در تن دین محمدي از نطق روح پرور انفاس و جانفزا
(۳) شد جان دین برون و خرد گفت سال او در شیونش بگریه بگو وا محمدا
(۴) شید این مصرع تاریخ نوشت از سر افسوس
واے افسوس محمد سفر از دار فنا کرد

Translation.

O Forgiver !

"In the name of God the merciful and compassionate."

(1) "That Mirza Muhammad and that master of learning who was defender of the faith and adherent of the children of Mustafa (the Prophet)."
(2) "He blew life into the body of the Muhammadan religion by his soul sustaining speech and life increasing breaths."
(3) "The life of the religion departed, and wisdom said the year of his death 'Bewailing him say weeping, alas ! O Muhammad.'"
(4) "Shaid wrote this chronogram with sorrow 'Ah ! alas ! Muhammad set out on a journey from the perishable world.'"

(*g*) Good.
(*h*) Unnecessary.
(*j*) The inscription is written on the *tawiz* of the grave which is of stone.

No. 398. (*a*) Grave of Abul Qasim.
(*b*) *Gali* Panja, in the Dargah of Panja Sharif, before the pavilion of the Dargah.
(*c*) Waqf, Mutawalli, Parwarish Hussain.
(*d*) III.
(*e*) 1227 A.H. (1812-3 A.D.).
(*f*) On the *tawiz* of the grave.

ابوالقاسم محمد شفیع یوم حسابش باد سنه ۱۲۲۷

"May Abul Qasim Muhammad (the Prophet) be his intercessor on the day of judgment. The year 1227.

(*g*) Fair.
(*h*) Unnecessary.
(*j*) The *tawiz* of the grave is level with the ground and contains the above quoted inscription written on it.

No. 399. (*a*) Maulvi Ataullah's Mosque.
(*b*) *Khirki* Ibrahim Ali Khan.

(c) Waqf, Mutawalli, Hajji Ashraf.
(d) III.
(e) Mughal.
(f) None.
(g) Good.
(h) Unnecessary.
(j) The mosque, and the tomb (No. 400), with a few other small apartments stand in a masonry inclosure. It is built of red sandstone and over the prayer chamber is a room erected for the accommodation of Arabic students. It was erected by Maulvi Ataullah who held some post during the Mughal period.

No. 400. (a) Tomb (unknown).
(b) Khirki Ibrahim Ali Khan.
(c) Waqf, Mutawalli, Ayub Beg.
(d) III.
(e) Mughal.
(f) None.
(g) Good.
(h) Unnecessary.
(j) The tomb consists of four ornamental stone walls. It has no roof. The *Tawiz* of the grave is of white marble, containing the "throne verse" written round it.

No. 401. (a) Mosque (unnamed).
(b) Chabi ganj.
(c) Waqf, Mutawalli, Umrao Mirza.
(d) III.
(e) Late Mughal.
(f) None.
(g) Ruinous.
(h) Unnecessary.
(j) The mosque was built by one Ashuri Khanam, a Muhammadan lady. It is double storeyed, the lower storey consisting of 3 shops. A narrow staircase leads to the courtyard of the mosque which is in a very ruined condition. The prayer chamber is roofed by three domes and has the same number of arched entrances.

No. 402. (a) Sufi Ji's mosque.
(b) *Gali* Kanchni.
(c) Waqf, Mutawalli, Abdullah Shah.
(d) III.
(e) 1229 A.H. (1814 A. D.).
(f) Quotation from the Quran and date.
(g) Good.

(*h*) Unnecessary.
(*j*) Nothing is known of this building.

No. 403. (*a*) Sivalaya (unnamed).
(*b*) *Gali* Kanchani.
(*c*) Khatri Umravsing.
(*d*) III.
(*e*) About 90 years old.
(*f*) None.
(*g*) Good.
(*h*) Unnecessary.
(*j*) Ajjudyaprasada and Thakuradasa built the temple. The former was a Khatri and the latter a Bania.
The present is the fourth generation from the former.
There are two small temples, one of Siva and the other of Hanumat.
In the former are enshrined images of Siva with Parvati on his lap, Parvati, Ganesa, Kartikasvami and Nandi. In the latter is an image of Hanumat besmeared with red lead along with several small images of brass. In the temple and outside it are hung about 30 bells.

No. 404. (*a*) Mosque (unnamed).
(*b*) *Gali* Kanchani.
(*c*) Waqf, Mutawalli, Chote Jamadar in Railway.
(*d*) II *b*.
(*e*) 1015 A.H. (1606-07 A.D.).
(*f*) On the central *Mihrab*.

الله اكبر

(۱) بعهد شاه نورالدين جهانگير ابن شاه اكبر بحمد الله على احمد شده اين بقعه راباني

(۲) همان باني شده درفكر تاريخ بناے او ز فيض حق ندا امد بنا شد كعبه ثاني

سنه ۱۰۱۵ هجري ...

Translation.

"God is great."

(1) "In the reign of the King Nuruddin Jahangir, the son of the King Akbar, Ali Ahmad, with the praise of God, became the founder of this building."
(2) "The same founder mused on the date of its foundation; a voice came by the grace of God, 'A second *Kaba* is built.'"
"Year 1015 Hijra...."
(*g*) Good.
(*h*) Unnecessary.
(*j*) The mosque is small, and covered with a flat roof. An inscription written in a line on the *Mihrab* shows that it was built by one Ali Ahmad Shah in 1015 A.H. (1606-07 A. D.).

MASJID PANIPATYAN.

No. 405. (*a*) Mosque of Panipatyan. In Dr. Vogel's list given as Mosque of Lutfullah Khan Sadiq of Panipat.

(*b*) In the *Muhalla*.

(*c*) Waqf, Mutawalli, Saidu-d-Din.

(*d*) II*b*.

(*e*) 1138 A.H. (1725-26 A. D.).

(*f*) On the central arch.

مسجد لطف الله خان صادق
۱۱۳۸

Translation.

"Mosque of Lutfullah Khan Sadiq 1138."

(*g*) Good.

(*h*) Unnecessary.

(*j*) The mosque stands in an enclosure containing a few *kachcha* houses which are part of the same property. It consists of three apartments with arched entrances and vaulted roofs. The arcades to the north and south of the court of the mosque are rented out.

No. 406. (*a*) Fakhru-l Masajid.

(*b*) Near the Kashmir gate.

(*c*) Waqf, Mutawalli, Committee Fathpuri.

(*d*) II*b*.

(*e*) 1141 A. H. (1728-29 A. D.).

(*f*) On the central arch.

(۱) خان دین پرور شجاعت خان بجنت یافت جا
با رضاے حق تعالی از طفیل مرتضے
(۲) صدر خاتو نان کنیز فاطمه فخر جهان
یادگارش ساخت این مسجد بفضل مصطفی
۱۱۴۱

Translation.

(1) "The Khan, the cherisher of religion (named) Shujaat Khan got a place in paradise, by the will of the exalted God and for the sake of Murtaza (Ali)."

(2) "The chief of ladies, (named) Kaniz Fatima, the pride of the world, built this mosque in his memory by the grace of Mustafa (the Prophet)" "1141 A. H. (1728-29 A. D.)."

(*g*) Good.

(*h*) Unnecessary.

(*j*) The mosque stands on a platform about 8 feet above the ground. The court of the mosque is enclosed on three sides, on the west by the mosque, and on the north and the south by two arcades.

The mosque stands on a sandstone plinth two feet in height. It consists of three rooms each entered through engrailed arches and surmounted by a dome banded longitudinally with black and white marble, and topped with gilded finials. The mosque is flanked by minarets which are banded like the domes with marble and red sandstone, and surmounted by small octagonal open cupolas with gilded domes and pinnacles. On either sides of the central arch is a small minaret banded with marble and red sandstone and surmounted by four pillared open pavilions. The floor of the mosque is paved with white marble, and from the floor to the height of about 4½ feet the inner walls are faced with the same material, the rest of the walls being of sandstone. The left wall of the mosque, and the colonnade on the same side were damaged during the seige of Delhi in 1857, and a cannon ball dismantled the pavilion of the minaret on its north-eastern corner. The inscription on its central arch refers to Sahujaat Khan and his wife, Kaniz-i Fatima entitled Fakhr-i Jahan who built the mosque in memory of her husband. She called it Fakhru-l Masajid after herself.

Shujaat Khan was a noble in the court of Aurangzeb. He began as a commander of Akbarabad (Agra) fort and rose to the post of Commander of artillery and the rank of 4,000 and 2,500 *Sawars*. His real name was Rad Andaz Beg, Shujaat Khan being the title given to him in the year 1083 A. H. (1672-73 A. D.). He was killed a year later fighting against the Afghans.

(*k*) *Carr Stephen*, 270-71.
Fanshawe, 68.
Keene, 25.
Asar (1847), chap. III 60—68, (1904), chap. IV, 88—9.
Maasir. II, 679—81.
(*l*) S. 81.

No. 407. (*a*) Kashmir gate.
(*b*) Northern entrance to the city.
(*c*) Government.
(*d*) I*a*.
(*e*) Period of Shahjahan.
(*f*) On a stone tablet, fixed at the foot of the central wall, between the two arched opening of the Kashmiri gate.

"On the 14th September 1857 the British force stormed Delhi. It was after sunrise on that day that this undermentioned party advancing from Ludlow castle in the face of a heavy fire and crossing the bridge which had been almost totally destroyed lodged powder bags against and blew in the right leaf of this gate thus opening a way for the assaulting column.

Lieutenant Duncan Home „ Philip Salkeld	Bengal Engineers „ „ . . .	mortally wounded.
Sergeant John Smith „ A. B. Carmichael Corporal F. Burgess	Bengal Sappers and...... . . . . . . Miners......	 killed. killed.
Bugler Hawthorne .	(52nd foot).	

Soobadar Toola Ram Jemadar Bis Ram Havildar Madhoo	Bengal Sappers and Miners	wounded
" Tilok Singh		mortally wounded
Sepoy Ram Heth		killed

This memorial is placed here as a tribute of respect to these gallant soldiers by General Lord Napier of Magdala Colonel Royal Engineers and Commander-in-Chief in India, 1876."

(*g*) Good.
(*h*) Protected monument.
(*k*) (Mutiny references have not been given as they are hardly within the scope of this volume).

Archer, I, 125.
A. S. I. I, 224.
As. Res. IV, 419.
Auckland, 6, 99, 101.
Baxter, 30.
Carr Stephen, 244.
Catalogue, 40, J. 18.
Cities, 151.
Crane, 148.
C. S. Range, 248—49.
Cooper, 33, 121.
Fanshawe, 6, 17, 172, 207, 220.
Heber II, 305.
Hearn, 3, 21, 38, 130, 205, 267, 201.
Keene, 6, 24.
Orlich II, 4.
Pennell, 147.
Wilson, 43 (photo).

HAMILTON ROAD.

No. 408. (*a*) Hamid Ali Khan's Mosque.
(*b*) On the road.
(*c*) Waqf, Mutawalli Umrao Mirza.
(*d*) III.
(*e*) 1257 A. H. (1841-42 A. D.).
(*f*) On the central arch.

(۱) اعتماد الدوله کز افراط جود — هست در پیش کفش قلزم غدیر
(۲) دیده ور حامد علیخان کز صفا — بیند اسرار ازل را در ضمیر
(۳) ساخت در دهلي همایون مسجدے — [تا] شود طاعتگه برنا و پیر
(۴) غالب ان طوبی نشیمن عندلیب — زد بانداز سخن سنجي صفیر
(۵) شد نظیر کعبه در عالم پدید — سال تعمیرش بود کعبه نظیر

باهتمام مولوي تیغ علي سنه ۱۲۵۷

Translation.

(1) "Itimadu-d-daula, through whose excess of generosity, the Red Sea is as a pond before the palm of his hand."

(2) "The perspicacious Hamid Ali Khan, who on account of his purity, sees the secrets of eternity within his mind,"

(3) "Erected, in Delhi, an auspicious mosque which should become a place of worship for young and old."

(4) "Ghalib, that nightingale who has his nest in *Tuba* (a tree in paradise) sang out after the manner of poets,"

(5) "A second *Kaba* has appeared in the world; the year of its erection is '*Kaba* resembling.'"

"Under the supervision of Maulvi Tegh Ali; the year 1257."

(*g*) Good.

(*h*) Unnecessary.

(*j*) The mosque stands on a raised platform, and is approached from the south by seventeen stone steps. Its court is enclosed on the east by an arcade, and on the west by the mosque proper which consists of two halls; at the south-east corner of the court is a small tank, the *Qullatain* of the Shias.

The poetic inscription on the central arch records that the mosque was built by Itimadu-d-daula Hamid Ali Khan who was the prime minister of Bahadur Shah II. This inscription was composed by Ghalib the famous poet of Delhi of the last century.

LOTHIAN ROAD.

No. 409. (*a*) Dara Shikoh's Library.

(*b*) On the road.

(*c*) Government.

(*d*) II*a*.

(*e*) Time of Shahjahan.

(*f*) None.

(*g*) Fair.

(*h*) Unnecessary.

(*j*) Dara Shikoh was the eldest son of Shahjahan. He was defeated and killed by Aurangzeb in the fratricidal war that had raged for the possession of the throne during the life time of Shahjahan. A short history of the building is inscribed on a marble slab built into one of the two pillars that form a doorway to it. The tablet is inscribed as follows:—

"Government High School" . . . .

Formerly

"The Library of Dara Shikoh, son of Shahjahan . 1637"

"Residence of Ali Mardan Khan Moghal Viceroy of the Punjab . . . . . 1639"

"The Residency of Sir David Ochterlony, Bart. . 1803"

"Government College . . . . . . 1804-1877"

"District School . . . . 1877-1886"

"Municipal Board School . . . . . 1886-1904"

(*k*) *As. Res.*, IV, 420.
Hodges, 119.
Oriental Annual (1838), 70.

ROUND THE CITY.

No. 410 (*a*) City wall.
(*b*) Round the city.
(*c*) Government.
(*d*) II*a*.
(*e*) Shah Jahan's reign.
(*f*) None.
(*g*) Good.
(*h*) Should be declared a Protected Monument.
(*j*) The walls were originally built of stone and mud in 1060 A. H. (1650 A. D.) at a cost of a lac and-a-half of rupees and were finished in four months. They were soon, however, destroyed by heavy rains, and new masonry walls were built in seven years at a cost of four lacs of rupees. The masonry walls were 6,664 yards long, 4 yards wide and 9 yards high with twenty-seven towers about thirty feet high. The city had fourteen gates and fourteen wickets. The martello towers and larger bastions were erected during the first British occupation of Delhi.
(*k*) *Archer*, I, 105.
A. S. I., I, 224, IV, 419.
As. Res., IV, 419.
Auckland, 7.
Bernier, 242.
Carr Stephen, 248.
Cooper, 32, 33, (bastions, etc.).
Fanshawe, 5.
Heber, II, 285.
Historical, II, 227.
Mundy, 173.
Orlich, II, 4.
Oriental Annual, (1835) 70.
Roberts, II, 215.
Wilson, 45.

APPENDIX I.

List of drawings of Delhi (Shahjahanabad) buildings in the Office of the Superintendent, Muhammadan and British Monuments, Northern Circle, Agra.

Serial No.	Office No.	Year.	Title.	On what paper, in ink or pencil.	Scale.
			SHAHJAHANABAD, DELHI.		
1	...	...	Delhi Palace	Paper, ink .	1"=50'.
2	8	...	Painted ceiling Diwan-i-Khas .	"	¼ Full size.
3	...	1891	Excavations in front of Mumtaz Mahal.	Square paper, ink.	8'=1".
4	...	...	Plan of Delhi Palace . . .	Paper, ink .	1"=100'.
5	1911	...	Excavations in Delhi Fort between Diwan-i-Amm and Rang Mahal.	" .	$\frac{1}{16}$"=1'.
6	...	...	Plan of Shah-Burj . . .	Paper, pencil .	8'=1".
7	1	...	Diagram of mosaics at the back of the Throne in Diwan-i-Amm.	" .	...
8	...	...	Part plan of Delhi Fort . .	Blue print .	50'=1".
9	...	...	Part plan of Delhi Fort, Archæological Area.	Square paper, pencil.	"
10	1441	1912-13	Mumtaz Mahal . . .	Tracing cloth .	8'=1".
11	1438	"	Plan of Delhi Fort, Archæological Area.	" .	...
12	...	...	Hayat Bakhsh Gardens . .	Square paper .	6'=1".
13	...	...	Sketches of mosaics Diwan-i-Amm 7 sheets.	Paper pencil .	Full size.
14	...	...	Proposed Copper gilt cupolas, *Chattris* of Rang Mahal.	Paper, coloured	1½"=1'.
15	...	...	Sketch design of *Jali* work in Basement of Rang Mahal.	Paper, ink .	Half Full size.
16	1161	...	Sketch of Throne, Diwan-i-Amm .	Paper, coloured	Full size.
17	...	1911	Plan of Naubat Khana, Delhi Fort, 2 sheets.	Blue print .	8'=1".
18	...	"	Elevation of an Archway Mumtaz Mahal.	Paper, pencil .	2'=1".
19	82	"	Painted ceiling in Diwan-i-Khas .	Printed . .	¼ Full size.
20	...	...	Drawing showing proposed arrangements of shrubs. Gardens, Delhi Fort.	Paper, ink .	1"=199'.
21	1223	1906	Delhi Fort; proposed plaster panelling Diwan-i-Amm East Facade.	" .	½"=1'.
22	...	1910	Part Plan of Shah Burj showing central channel.	Square paper .	2'=1".

List of drawings of Delhi (Shahjahanabad) buildings in the Office of the Superintendent, Muhammadan and British Monuments, Northern Circle, Agra—continued.

Serial No.	Office No.	Year.	Title.	On what paper, in ink or pencil.	Scale.
			SHAHJAHANABAD, DELHI—*continued*.		
23	...	1908	Iron railing Hayat Bakhsh Gardens, Delhi Fort.	Paper, pencil .	...
24	1296	...	Marble railing, Delhi Fort . .	„ .	Full size.
25	1313	...	Finial for Shah Burj pavilion, Delhi. 2 sheets.	„ .	½ and ⅓ full size.
26	...	1905	Plans and measurements, Delhi Fort. 24 sheets.	„ .	...
27	...	1884	Sawan pavilion, Delhi Fort . .	Paper, ink .	4′=1″.
28	370	...	Details of Diwan-i-Khas, Delhi Fort.	Paper, pencil .	...
29	367	...	Diwan-i-Khas Delhi Fort drawings 2 sheets.	Partly painted	⅓ and ¼ full size.
30	362	...	Showing construction of roof of Diwan-i-Khas, Delhi Fort.	Paper, ink .	¾″=1′.
31	...	...	Sketch scales of justice, Delhi Fort	„ .	4″-1′.
32	1296	...	Marble railing in Delhi Fort .	Paper, pencil .	Full size.
33	2009	1908	Sketch design for railing Jami Masjid, Delhi.	Tracing cloth, ink.	2′=1″.
34	1314	...	Ditto ditto . .	Paper, pencil .	1″=1′.
35	2009	...	Sketch design for railing Jami Masjid.	„ .	2′=1″.
36	1316	1909	Head of *Muttaka* posts of railing Jami Masjid.	„ .	Full size.
37	1013	1908	Sketch design for doors Jami Masjid.	„ .	1″=1′.
38	60	...	Fathpuri Masjid and surrounding buildings.	Paper, ink .	12′=1″.
39	...	...	Front elevation plan and details Fathpuri Masjid.	„ .	...
40	...	1883	Kalan Mosque	Printed .	12′=1″.
41	...	...	Sketches for Delhi Durbar Archway Memorial 9 sheets.	Tracing paper, ink and pencil.	...

APPENDIX II.

A list of photographic Negatives of Indian Antiquities in the collection of the Indian Museum.

Serial No.	District.	Place.	Subject.	Serial number of plate in Box.	Size of plate.
			SHAHJAHANABAD, DELHI.		
869	Delhi .	Delhi .	Jami Masjid of Shahjahan; front view from inside.	E1.21	12 x 10
871	" .	" .	Kali Masjid or Kalan Masjid. View of interior.	E1.13	12 x 10
876	" .	" .	Palace of Shahjahan: lattice in bath room.	E2.29	10 x 8
877	" .	" .	Ditto ditto		
			Stone elephant near palace . .	E2.30	"
878	" .	" .	Ditto ditto		
			Statues of riders on stone elephants in verandah of house.	E2.31	"
916	" .	" .	Female Statue in Museum: front view.	E2.32	"
917	" .	" .	Ditto back view . . .	E2.33	"

INDEX.

H

L

M

N

O

P

Q

R